Your Borland® C++
Consultant

Your
Borland® C++
Consultant

Paul Perry

A Division of Prentice Hall Computer Publishing
11711 North College, Carmel, Indiana 46032 USA

96   95   94   93   4   3   2   1

Interpretation of the printing code: the rightmost double-digit number is the year of the book's printing; the rightmost single-digit, the number of the book's printing. For example, a printing code of 93-1 shows that the first printing of the book occurred in 1993.

Composed in AGaramond and MCPdigital by Prentice Hall Computer Publishing

Printed in the United States of America

Trademarks

Publisher
Richard K. Swadley

Associate Publisher
Jordan Gold

Acquisitions Manager
Stacy Hiquet

Acquisitions Editor
Gregory Croy

Development Editor
Phillip Paxton

Senior Editor
Erik Dafforn

Production Editor
Melba Hopper

Copy Editor
Kathy Grida-Carlyle

Editorial Coordinator
Bill Whitmer

Editorial Assistants
Sharon Cox
Molly Carmody

Technical Reviewer
Greg Guntle

Marketing Manager
Greg Wiegand

Cover Designer
Jean Bisesi

**Director of Production
and Manufacturing**
Jeff Valler

Imprint Manager
Kelli Widdifield

Book Designer
Michele Laseau

Production Analyst
Mary Beth Wakefield

**Proofreading/Indexing
Coordinator**
Joelynn Gifford

Graphics Image Specialists
Dennis Sheehan
Sue Vandewalle
Tim Montgomery

Production
Danielle Bird
Julie Brown
Meshell Dinn
Mark Enochs
Heather Kaufman
Bob LaRoche
Linda Seifert
Sandy Shay
Tina Trettin
Michelle Worthington
Lillian Yates

Indexer
Joy Dean Lee

Overview

Contents

Acknowledgments

Thanks to the truly talented people I have had a chance to work with, including Greg Croy at Sams and Bruneau Babet at Borland. These individuals certainly are a pleasure to work with.

Dedication

To Alexander Graham Bell (the U.S. inventor of the telephone), who himself was a master at asking questions.

Author Biography

Paul J. Perry has been programming in the C programming language for over five years. He is the author of *Turbo C++ for Windows Programming for Beginners* (Sams Publishing, 1993) and *Do It Yourself Turbo C++* (Sams Publishing, 1992), as well as several other books. Mr. Perry was a technical support engineer for Borland International, where customers paid $2 per minute for Windows consulting. At Borland he was also in charge of support forums on CompuServe and involved in writing technical information documents. He is now a software engineer at Sony Electronic Publishing Company, where he specializes in Windows multimedia programming.

Who Should Use This Book?

Your Borland C++ Consultant is a different kind of book. It is written for the person who is already familiar with programming Windows using the Borland C++ language development tools and wants to learn how to add features found in commercial applications.

Virtually all the existing books about programming for Windows teach the reader how to create simple programs and introduce Windows programming concepts and principles. *Your Borland C++ Consultant* shows you how to do things the other books don't cover. The bottom line is *this book is full of tricks and techniques of all kinds.*

For example, you will learn how to create a ToolBar, flash iconic programs, make buttons containing bitmap graphics, and remember the size and location of a program's window so the next time it is opened it will appear in the same place. You will learn how to create a status line, how to use custom drag-and-drop features, and how to change the size of fonts in an edit control. There are details on how to create animation sequences, display graphics images inside a listbox, and even how to access the multimedia features of Windows 3.1.

As a Technical Support Engineer for Borland, I have helped programmers get the most out of the Borland C++ and Turbo C++ products. The topics covered in this book are questions asked every day by programmers who pay $2 per minute to speak with me. I think you will find the topics covered in this book interesting.

What You Should Know to Use This Book

You probably know that programming for the Windows environment requires special knowledge. If you are not familiar with Windows programming, this book is not the one to teach you how.

You should have a firm grasp of the C programming language as well as how to program for the Windows environment. You should understand what a window class is used for, what a message loop is, and what a window procedure does.

If these terms are not familiar, you might want to check out my book *Turbo C++ for Windows Programming for Beginners*. It will give you a solid foundation for learning about the topics covered here.

Question and Answer Format

The book is arranged in a question and answer format. The book is divided into chapters by topic, and each chapter contains answers to the most common questions asked every day by programmers nationwide. Each answer contains a sample program with complete details on the implementation.

What You Need to Use This Book

As the title suggests, this book is for programmers using Borland C++. If you have Turbo C++ for Windows, you will be able to take full advantage of this book. The book assumes you are using at least version 3.1 of the compiler.

If you use Microsoft C along with the Software Development Kit (SDK), much of the information about Windows programming is still valid, and you can make good use of it in your own programs. However, the examples have not been tested with the SDK, so there is no guarantee they work with anything other than the Borland compilers. My personal recommendation (no matter how biased it may be) is to switch immediately to the Borland development tools.

Organization of This Book

This book is divided into six chapters, as follows:

■ Chapter 1, "Windows," covers special techniques for adding features to the main window of your program. You will learn how to create a status bar, how to create a SpeedBar, how to change class parameters, how to store the exact location of a window, and how to restore your program to the same size it was the last time the program was exited.

■ Chapter 2, "Dialog Boxes," teaches techniques for adding pizzazz to your program's dialog boxes. You will learn how to use the fancy Borland Windows Custom Controls, how to display graphics inside a dialog box, how to customize the Windows 3.1 common dialogs, and how to create dynamic dialog boxes.

■ Chapter 3, "Multimedia," takes a look at the special multimedia extensions included with Windows 3.1. You will learn about playing sound files within your program, and how to store the wave file as a custom resource type. You will find out how to use the Media Control Interface (MCI) commands to access multimedia hardware. The musical instrument digital interface (MIDI) is examined to find out how to access huge amounts of music with very little hard disk space required. Finally, the hidden joystick interface routines are examined to see how to access a joystick from a Windows program.

■ Chapter 4, "Graphics," covers topics involved with bitmaps, including how to display bitmaps (both those stored as a resource, and those stored as a BMP file), how to create a splash screen, and how to create a gradient fill color.

■ Chapter 5, "Miscellaneous," looks at a variety of tips and techniques including using the drag-and-drop features of Windows 3.1, creating screen savers, using special fonts inside a menu, changing the font used in edit controls, and finding the amount of system resources currently available to a program.

■ Chapter 6, "Even More Help," examines some third party tools that make programming Windows easier. You will learn about systems for creating Help files, custom control libraries, the best books available, and the current magazines and trade journals you might want to access.

About the Example Programs

Each example program in this book was written in straight C code. The assumption is that if you are using a class library (like ObjectWindows), you can easily convert the concepts and techniques over to your code. This allows those who don't understand C++ to have access to all the information presented.

All example programs were written using the STRICT type checking directive. If you don't know about this already, I recommend checking it out. By defining STRICT in your program, you can find type mismatch errors quickly.

The STRICT compile-time checking helps you find programming errors when you compile your application—rather than at runtime. The STRICT definition is a real benefit, especially with code under development, because it helps you catch bugs right away when you compile your code, rather than having to track them down at runtime with a debugger. Also, STRICT will help you more easily migrate your code to the 32-bit Windows NT platform in the future. It helps you locate and deal with type incompatiblities that arise when migrating to 32 bits.

Programs are also written using the WINDOWSX.H header file. This file is in addition to WINDOWS.H and it provides function prototypes, structure declarations, and symbol name identifiers for programming in Windows.

TIP   If you are not familiar with the STRICT definition or with using WINDOWSX.H, check out the on-line documentation that comes with the compiler. The file named C:\BORLANDC\DOC\WIN31.DOC provides complete information for you.

About Each Entry

Each chapter is divided into sections, and each section includes specific headings. The following text gives a short description of what is covered in each heading.

Level

Either Beginner, Intermediate, or Advanced. It specifies the minimum skill level required to make best use of the information included for this section.

Question

The question to which the section is devoted.

Description

A short description about the question.

Answer

The answer to the question posed earlier.

Comments

Other information that is useful when processing the information presented.

See Also

Additional information you can read. Most often, this will point you to certain API functions which are described in the section. You can check your API manuals or the on-line Help system for the additional information.

Example Code

An example program (.C, .H, .RC, and .DEF files as required) that demonstrates the answer to the question.

Notation and Conventions

To get the most out of this book, you need to know something about how it is designed. The chapters contain bold text, italicized text, bulleted lists, numbered lists, figures, program listings, code fragments, and tables of information. All these design features should help you understand the material being presented.

Italic type is used to emphasize an important word or phrase. You should pay close attention to italicized text. It is also used to introduce new technical terms. An italicized term is usually followed by a definition or an explanation.

Bulleted lists have the following characteristics:

- Each item in a bulleted list is preceded by a shadowed box (the bullet). The bullet is a special flag that draws your attention to important material.

- The order of items in a bulleted list is not mandatory. That is, the items represent related points you should understand, but not in any special sequence.

- The text for items in a bulleted list is often longer than the text you see in other kinds of lists. Items in bulleted lists contain explanations, not simple actions.

Numbered lists contain actions you should perform, or lists of items that must be kept in a particular sequence. When you see a numbered list, you should do the following:

1. Start at the beginning of the list. Don't skip ahead to later items in the list; order is important.

2. Make sure that you completely understand each item as you encounter it.

3. Read all the items in the list. Don't skip any of them—each item is important.

Figures are pictures or graphics that can help you understand the text. Each figure has a number in the form *c.n*: *c* is the chapter in which the figure appears, and *n* is the number of the figure in a sequence within the chapter.

Program listings give the C source code for a complete program, or perhaps for a program module. In either case, source code shown in a program listing can, in fact, be compiled. Program Listing IN.1, for example, shows the source code for a complete program. (Most complete programs are much longer than this short sample.)

Listing IN.1. START.C. A Sample Program Listing.

```c
// START.C - Sample C Program Listing
//
// Your Borland C++ Consultant by Paul J. Perry
//

#include <windowsx.h>

int PASCAL WinMain(HINSTANCE hInstance, HINSTANCE
                   hPrevInstance, LPSTR, CommandLine,
                   int nCommandShow)
{

    MessageBox(NULL, "Just A Test", "Your Borland C++
               Consultant", MB_ICONEXCLAMATION |
               MB_OK);

    return 0;
}
```

You should notice a couple of things about Listing IN.1. Program listings, like figures, are numbered (see the header for Listing IN.1). However, the reference numbers for figures and program listings are independent. Each program starts with a comment section that instantly identifies the program and gives a brief description of its purpose.

A *code fragment* also shows C source code, but the code does not make up a complete program (the fragment cannot be compiled). Code fragments are inserted directly in the text and do not have headings, reference numbers, or line numbers. Code fragments contain enough source code to illustrate a point, but they are short (usually only five or six lines). Note that a special monospace type face is used for `keywords`, `program listings`, and `code fragments`.

> **TIP** Tip boxes like this serve to provide useful or insightful tips. You will find things like programming tips, tricks, and shortcuts in a tip box.

NOTE	Note boxes provide convenient notes that help you learn to program for Windows. A note box includes a brief statement to remind you about important facts regarding programming.

WARNING	Warning boxes are used to provide important warnings of problems or possible unwanted side effects that may occur in your code, as well as any cautions that you should know about.

Tables appear when lists and columns of information are suitable. Tables also have their own headings and reference numbers—again, independent of the numbers for figures and program listings. Table IN.1 shows how a table is presented in this book.

Table IN.1. The formatting conventions used in this book.

Format Convention	Use
Italic	An eye-catching type style used to emphasize important words or phrases.
Bulleted lists	A list of items with a bullet flagging each item; the sequence of items is usually not important.
Numbered lists	A list of items with numbers flagging each item; sequence is important.
Program listings	Complete programs that can be compiled.

Format Convention	Use
Code fragments	A small number of source code lines that illustrate a point; code fragments cannot be compiled apart from other code.
Tip Boxes	Boxed text that gives you programming tips, tricks, and shortcuts.
Note Boxes	Notes about programming.
Warning Boxes	Important warnings of problems that may occur.
Tables	Information arranged in columnar format; tables may or may not contain explanations or descriptions.

A Note on Programming

Because I am assuming that the readers of this book already have experience in writing programs, this will serve as a friendly reminder to reinforce something you already know. In order to learn to program, you must program.

You need to remember an important point about learning new programming concepts: it is impossible to learn without writing code, compiling your programs, and observing the way they work (or possibly don't work).

Because practicing Windows programming is essential to learning Windows programming, many example programs are included so you can run them and see how they work. However, I urge you to try different things in your own programs. It is important to experiment to learn how a program really works.

In This Chapter

- How to keep a window displayed above all others.

- How to remember the specific size and location of a window, so it can be displayed in the same location the next time the application is loaded.

- How to change the title bar text of a window.

- How to create a status bar to display additional menu help information.

- How to create three-dimensional effects inside a program.

- How to flash icons.

- How to create a ToolBar.

Windows

 Keeping a Window on Top

How do I keep the main window of my program on top of all other windows on the desktop?

DESCRIPTION

There are some programs that have a main window which will always appear on top of other windows on the desktop, even if the program is not active. An example is the Clock mini-application (see Figure 1.1) which comes with Windows.

This attribute is most often desired with programs that give some real-time information to the user and should, therefore, be displayed at all times, even if the window is not active. There may also be other specialized applications where you might find it useful to have a window always on top, such as in an entertainment program.

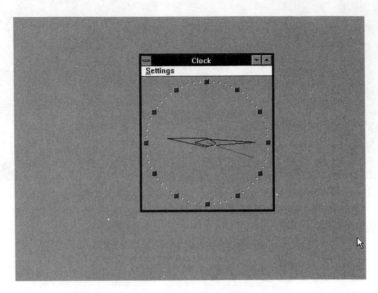

Figure 1.1. *The Windows Clock mini-application.*

ANSWER

Almost every program creates its main window using the `CreateWindow` function. The trick is to use the `CreateWindowEx` function. The functions are similar; however, `CreateWindowEx` takes an extra style parameter. The extended style parameter can be set to one of the definitions in Table 1.1. To create a window that stays on top, use the `WS_EX_TOPMOST` style. You will find some other interesting styles, which will be explored in other areas of this book.

Table 1.1. Extended window style types.

Window style	Description
`WS_EX_ACCEPTFILES`	Specifies that the window created can accept drag-and-drop files.
`WS_EX_DLGMODALFRAME`	Specifies with a double-border window that may optionally be created with a title bar by specifying the `ws_Caption` style flag.

Window style	Description
WS_EX_NOPARENTNOTIFY	Specifies that a child window created with this style will not notify its parent window when the child window is created or destroyed.
WS_EX_TOPMOST	Specifies that the window will be placed as the topmost window on the desktop. No other window can be displayed on top of this window.
WS_EX_TRANSPARENT	Specifies that the window should be transparent. That is, anything underneath the window will be displayed.

COMMENTS

A window created with the CreateWindow function can still be changed to always appear on top. In fact, a program can actually turn its "on top" status on and off again.

It is usually a good idea to allow the user to select whether the window should be displayed on top of all others (the Clock application allows you to do this through the system menu). In your code, it is accomplished using the SetWindowPos function with the HWND_TOPMOST and HWND_NOTOPMOST flags. The following example will make a window always appear on top (it does not change the actual screen location of the window):

```
SetWindowPos(hWnd, HWND_TOPMOST, 0,0,0,0,
SWP_SHOWWINDOW);
```

To turn the HWND_TOPMOST flag off, use the following command:

```
SetWindowPos(hWnd, HWND_NOTOPMOST, 0,0,0,0,
SWP_SHOWWINDOW);
```

A menu option with a checkmark makes a good mechanism for allowing the user to select how the program is to operate.

SEE ALSO

CreateWindowEx API Function
SetWindowPos API Function

EXAMPLE CODE

The example program creates a small overlapped window that will always appear on top of another application, even if the window is not active (see Figure 1.2). The window displays the current time (in 24 hour format). A timer is created while the WM_CREATE message is processed, so the window will be updated constantly with the new time.

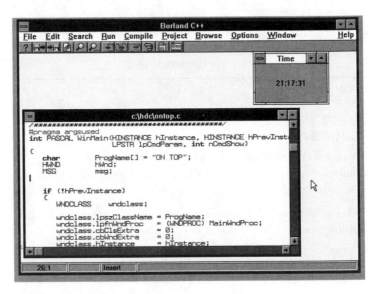

Figure 1.2. *Example program in action.*

Notice that if you minimize the Window, the icon is actually updated. Because the program sets the hIcon element of the wndclass structure to 0, it allows our program to write to the window when it is in its iconic state. The icon is essentially a miniature window. Because the actual area inside the icon is smaller than what would be available when the program is not iconic, the program only displays hours and minutes when it is minimized. Otherwise, it displays hours, minutes, and seconds.

Listing 1.1 contains the source code for the program. Listing 1.2. is the module definition file.

Listing 1.1. ONTOP.C sample program.

```
// ONTOP.C - Example program showing how to keep a
//           program's window displayed at all times.
//
// Your Borland C++ Consultant by Paul J. Perry
//

#define STRICT
#define TIMERID 111

#include <windowsx.h>
#include <stdlib.h>
#include <dos.h>
#include <stdio.h>

// Function Prototypes
LRESULT CALLBACK _export MainWndProc(HWND, UINT,
WPARAM, LPARAM);

/**********************************************/
#pragma argsused
int PASCAL WinMain(HINSTANCE hInstance, HINSTANCE
                   hPrevInstance, LPSTR lpCmdParam,
                   int nCmdShow)
{
    char        ProgName[] = "ON TOP";
    HWND        hWnd;
    MSG         msg;


    if (!hPrevInstance)
    {
        WNDCLASS      wndclass;

        wndclass.lpszClassName = ProgName;
        wndclass.lpfnWndProc   = (WNDPROC) MainWndProc;
        wndclass.cbClsExtra    = 0;
        wndclass.cbWndExtra    = 0;
        wndclass.hInstance     = hInstance;
        wndclass.hIcon         = 0;
        wndclass.hCursor       =LoadCursor(NULL,
                                 IDC_ARROW);
```

continues

Listing 1.1. continued

```c
    wndclass.hbrBackground = GetStockObject(
                             LTGRAY_BRUSH);
    wndclass.lpszMenuName  = NULL;
    wndclass.style         = CS_VREDRAW |
                             CS_HREDRAW;

    if (!RegisterClass(&wndclass))
        exit(1);
}

hWnd = CreateWindowEx(WS_EX_TOPMOST, ProgName,
                      "Time",
                WS_OVERLAPPEDWINDOW,
              CW_USEDEFAULT, CW_USEDEFAULT,
              45, 50, NULL, NULL, hInstance, NULL);

ShowWindow(hWnd, nCmdShow);
UpdateWindow(hWnd);

while (GetMessage(&msg, NULL, 0, 0))
{
    TranslateMessage(&msg);
    DispatchMessage(&msg);
}
return msg.wParam;
}

/**********************************************/
LRESULT CALLBACK _export MainWndProc(HWND hWnd, UINT
                                     message,
                                     WPARAM wParam,
                                     LPARAM lParam)
{
    switch (message)
    {
        case WM_CREATE :
        {
                SetTimer(hWnd, TIMERID, 100, NULL);
            break;
        }

        case WM_TIMER :
        {
            InvalidateRect(hWnd, NULL, TRUE);
            break;
        }

        case WM_PAINT :
```

```
    {
        HDC                 PaintDC;
        RECT                rect;
        PAINTSTRUCT         ps;
        struct dostime_t    t;
        char                buf[25];

        PaintDC = BeginPaint(hWnd, &ps);
        GetClientRect(hWnd, &rect);

        SetBkMode(PaintDC, TRANSPARENT);

        _dos_gettime(&t);

          if (IsIconic(hWnd))      // Only display hrs/
                                   //   min if iconic
            sprintf(buf, "%2d:%02d", t.hour,
                                     t.minute);
          else
            sprintf(buf, "%2d:%02d:%02d", t.hour,
                                          t.minute,
                                          t.second);

        DrawText(PaintDC, buf, -1, &rect,
                    DT_SINGLELINE | DT_CENTER |
                    DT_VCENTER);

        EndPaint(hWnd, &ps);
        return 0;
    }

    case WM_DESTROY :
    {
        PostQuitMessage(0);
        return 0;
    }
  }
  return DefWindowProc (hWnd, message, wParam,
                    lParam);
}
```

Listing 1.2. ONTOP.DEF module definition file.

```
;
; ONTOP.DEF module definition file
```

continues

Listing 1.2. continued

```
;

DESCRIPTION    'OnTop'
NAME           ONTOP
EXETYPE        WINDOWS
STUB           'WINSTUB.EXE'
HEAPSIZE       1024
STACKSIZE      8192
CODE           PRELOAD MOVEABLE DISCARDABLE
DATA           PRELOAD MOVEABLE MULTIPLE
```

 # Remembering a Window's Size and Location

How do I remember the size and location of the main window of my program?

DESCRIPTION

As users work with your program, they usually resize it and reposition it. If a program is able to store its current size and the location of its window, when it is restarted it will reappear in the same location and at the same size as when the user last modified it.

ANSWER

The best way to store configuration information between program sessions is in a disk file. Although we could use the standard fopen disk I/O function, which is defined in the C language, there is a better way.

Windows allows easy accessibility to a special type of configuration file called *profile files*. These profile files make storing configuration information easy. Profile files are usually stored in the WINDOWS subdirectory and have the extension .INI. The files are always ASCII text (so they can be edited manually with a text editor). These files have the following format:

```
; Comments are preceded by a semicolon
[Section]
```

```
Entry=Value
AnotherEntry=AnotherValue
...
EntryX=ValueX
```

The section and entry names are not case-sensitive. You can store both integers and string variables inside the profile file.

There are two types of profile files: *global* and *private*. There is only one global profile file, WIN.INI. It contains information that is used by several applications or by the system as a whole. You are probably familiar with it because most Windows users come into contact with it at one time or another. Most of the time you do not want to store information in the global profile file. Doing so will just slow down the entire system every time a program needs to access the global profile file.

Private profile files are separate files that contain information for one specific application program. A program uses private profile files most frequently.

By using Windows API functions, a program can easily store its current screen locations in a profile string, along with its current state (minimized, maximized, or show normal). There are several functions for accessing profile files (see Table 1.2).

Table 1.2. Profile file functions.

Function Name	Description
GetProfileString	Get string value from global profile file.
GetProfileInt	Get integer value from global profile file.
WriteProfileString	Write string to a profile file.
GetPrivateProfileString	Get string from private profile file.
GetPrivateProfileInt	Get integer from private profile file.
WritePrivateProfileString	Write string to a private profile file.

Notice that there are three functions for reading and writing global profile files, and three functions for reading and writing private profile files. The only difference between the functions is that the ones with `Private` in their name also take a filename as a parameter. The global functions always work on the WIN.INI profile file.

If a program does not specify a full path for a private profile file, Windows searches the WINDOWS directory for the file. If the file does not exist, it is created and then placed in the WINDOWS directory.

Let's take a look at the private profile functions. To get a string from the profile file, use the `GetPrivateProfileString` function. It takes the name of the section, the name of the entry, the default value to use (if no .INI file exists, or if the entry is not in the file), a character buffer (to store the contents in), and the profile filename. To get integer values, use the `GetPrivateProfileInt` function. Instead of returning a string into a buffer, it returns an integer value.

When writing information into a profile file, the information should already be stored in a string.

That means if you are writing an integer, you must use the `wsprintf` formatted string print function to write the integer value into a string. Use the `WritePrivateProfileString` function to write out the information.

COMMENTS

Windows caches profile files to reduce access time. This allows the file to remain in memory until a different profile file is loaded or until an application forces recaching of the file.

To force an .INI file to be recached, make the following call:

```
WritePrivateProfileString(NULL, NULL, NULL,
"FNAME.INI)";
```

where `FNAME.INI` is the name of the application's private profile file.

This call will force the entire profile file in the cache to be invalidated. The next call to either the `GetPrivateProfileString` or `GetPrivateProfileInt` functions will cause the disk file to be recached.

SEE ALSO

GetPrivateProfileInt API Function
GetPrivateProfileString API Function
GetProfileInt API Function
GetProfileString API Function
WritePrivateProfileString API Function
WriteProfileString API Function

EXAMPLE CODE

The example program stores its window coordinates, along with its current state, in a private profile string. This causes its screen location, size, and state to be restored between sessions.

Listing 1.3 contains the C source code; Listing 1.4 contains the module definition file; and Listing 1.5 contains a sample INI file. Note that it is not necessary to have the profile file when the program first runs. If the profile file is not present, default values are selected by Windows at run time.

Listing 1.3. REMEMBER.C example program.

```
// REMEMBER.C - Remember the main window location
//               between sessions
//
// Your Borland C++ Consultant by Paul J. Perry
//

#define STRICT

#include <windowsx.h>
#include <stdlib.h>
#include <stdio.h>

// Function Prototypes
LRESULT CALLBACK _export MainWndProc(HWND, UINT,
                                      WPARAM, LPARAM);

// Global Variables
char ProgName[] = "Remember";
char FileName[] = "REMEMBER.INI";

/**********************************************/
#pragma argsused
int PASCAL WinMain(HINSTANCE hInstance, HINSTANCE
```

continues

Listing 1.3. continued

```
                hPrevInstance, LPSTR lpCmdParam,
                int nCmdShow)
{
    HWND        hWnd;
    MSG         msg;
    UINT        Left, Top, Width, Height, CmdShowState;


    if (!hPrevInstance)
    {
        WNDCLASS    wndclass;

        wndclass.lpszClassName = ProgName;
        wndclass.lpfnWndProc   = (WNDPROC) MainWndProc;
        wndclass.cbClsExtra    = 0;
        wndclass.cbWndExtra    = 0;
        wndclass.hInstance     = hInstance;
        wndclass.hIcon         = LoadIcon(NULL,
                                    IDI_APPLICATION);
        wndclass.hCursor       = LoadCursor(NULL,
                                    IDC_ARROW);
        wndclass.hbrBackground = GetStockObject (
                                    WHITE_BRUSH);

        wndclass.lpszMenuName  = NULL;
        wndclass.style         = CS_VREDRAW ¦
                                    CS_HREDRAW;

        if (!RegisterClass(&wndclass))
            return 0;
    }


    // In [Coordinates] section of REMEMBER.INI
    // Left, Top, Right, Bottom
    Left = GetPrivateProfileInt("Coordinates", "Left",
                            CW_USEDEFAULT,
                            FileName);
    Top = GetPrivateProfileInt("Coordinates", "Top",
                            CW_USEDEFAULT,
                            FileName);
    Width = GetPrivateProfileInt("Coordinates",
                            "Width",
                            CW_USEDEFAULT,
                            FileName);
    Height = GetPrivateProfileInt("Coordinates",
                            "Height",
                            CW_USEDEFAULT,
                            FileName);
```

```
    CmdShowState = GetPrivateProfileInt("Status",
                                        "State",
                                        SW_SHOWNORMAL,
                                        FileName);


    hWnd = CreateWindow(ProgName, ProgName,
                        WS_OVERLAPPEDWINDOW,
                        Left, Top, Width, Height,
                        NULL, NULL, hInstance, NULL);


    ShowWindow(hWnd, CmdShowState);
    UpdateWindow(hWnd);

    while (GetMessage(&msg, NULL, 0, 0))
    {
       TranslateMessage(&msg);
       DispatchMessage(&msg);
    }
    return msg.wParam;
}

/**********************************************/
LRESULT CALLBACK _export MainWndProc(HWND hWnd, UINT
                                     message,
                                     WPARAM wParam,
                                     LPARAM lParam)
{
    switch (message)
    {
       case WM_PAINT :
       {
          HDC        PaintDC;
          RECT       rect;
          PAINTSTRUCT ps;

          PaintDC = BeginPaint(hWnd, &ps);

          GetClientRect(hWnd, &rect);

          DrawText(PaintDC, "Remember window
                   coordinates",-1, &rect,DT_SINGLELINE¦
                   DT_CENTER ¦ DT_VCENTER);
```

continues

Listing 1.3. continued

```
    EndPaint(hWnd, &ps);
    return 0;
}

case WM_DESTROY :
{
    char            buf[15];
    RECT            WindowRect;
    int             ShowState;


    GetWindowRect(hWnd, &WindowRect);

    // Left
    sprintf(buf, "%d", WindowRect.left);
    WritePrivateProfileString("Coordinates",
                              "Left", buf,
                              FileName);

    // Top
    sprintf(buf, "%d", WindowRect.top);
    WritePrivateProfileString("Coordinates",
                              "Top", buf,
                              FileName);

    // extract the actual width and height
    WindowRect.right = WindowRect.right -
                       WindowRect.left;
    WindowRect.bottom = WindowRect.bottom -
                        WindowRect.top;

    // Right (width)
    sprintf(buf, "%d", WindowRect.right);
    WritePrivateProfileString("Coordinates",
                              "Width", buf,
                              FileName);

    // Bottom (height)
    sprintf(buf, "%d", WindowRect.bottom);
    WritePrivateProfileString("Coordinates",
                              "Height", buf,
                              FileName);


    // The show state
    if (IsIconic(hWnd))
        ShowState = SW_SHOWMINIMIZED;
```

```
        else
        if (IsZoomed(hWnd))
            ShowState = SW_SHOWMAXIMIZED;
        else
            ShowState = SW_SHOWNORMAL;

        sprintf(buf, "%u", ShowState);
        WritePrivateProfileString("Status", "State",
                                  buf, FileName);

        PostQuitMessage(0);
        return 0;
      }
    }
    return DefWindowProc (hWnd, message, wParam,
                          lParam);
}
```

Listing 1.4. REMEMBER.DEF module definition file.

```
;
; REMEMBER.DEF module definition file
;

DESCRIPTION     'Remember Window Location'
NAME            REMEMBER
EXETYPE         WINDOWS
STUB            'WINSTUB.EXE'
HEAPSIZE        1024
STACKSIZE       8192
CODE            PRELOAD MOVEABLE DISCARDABLE
DATA            PRELOAD MOVEABLE MULTIPLE
```

Listing 1.5. Sample .INI file.

```
[Coordinates]
Left=15
Top=14
Width=512
Height=331

[Status]
State=1
```

Changing Window Text

How do I change the text associated with the title bar of my Window?

DESCRIPTION

Most Windows programs change the text of the title bar for the main window of the program. Usually, the text changes to add the filename of the work currently being modified by the user; however, programs such as Lotus 1-2-3 for Windows use the title bar as a location to give additional information about menu commands (see Figure 1.3).

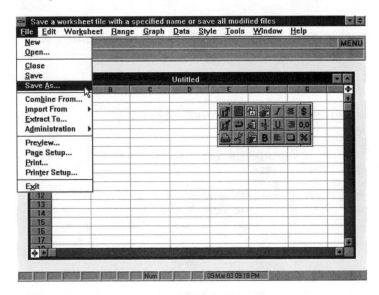

Figure 1.3. *Lotus 1-2-3 for Windows Window text.*

ANSWER

The original text of the title bar is set as the second parameter to the CreateWindow function, as follows:

```
hWnd = CreateWindow("ClassName", "Original Text",
               WS_OVERLAPPEDWINDOW,
               CW_USEDEFAULT, CW_USEDEFAULT,
               CW_USEDEFAULT, CW_USEDEFAULT,
               NULL, NULL, hInstance, NULL);
```

To change the text, Windows provides the `SetWindowText` function. It takes a handle to the window and the string to which the window title is set. A sample call would be as follows:

```
SetWindowText(hWnd, "This is the new title text");
```

The call to `SetWindowText` actually sends a `WM_SETTEXT` to the specified window. This forces the window text to be updated.

COMMENTS

Most often, the window text changes to show that a new file has been loaded. For example, usually Word for Windows has the window text "Microsoft Word." When a new file has loaded, that window title changes to "Microsoft Word—NEWFILE.DOC." This is the standard set by Microsoft.

When a program is minimized, the title text is displayed beneath the icon. A program can still use the `SetTitleText` function to change this text even if the program is displayed as an icon.

SEE ALSO

`CreateWindow` API Function
`CreateWindowEx` API Function
`SetWindowText` API Function

EXAMPLE CODE

The example program changes the title text to correspond to help information relating to the menu item the user is selecting. As the user moves the cursor over different menu items, the title bar changes to show a description of the currently highlighted menu item.

The program knows when the user selects a menu item by trapping the `WM_MENUSELECT` message. It is sent every time the user selects a menu item. When it is sent, the `wParam` contains the ID of the currently highlighted menu item. At the location where the program checks for WM_MENUSELECT, a string resource is loaded that contains the same ID as the menu item currently being selected.

Listing 1.6 contains the C source code; Listing 1.7 contains the header file; Listing 1.8 contains the resource script; and Listing 1.9 contains the module definition file.

Listing 1.6. TITLE.C source code.

```
// TITLE.C - Example program shows how to change
//           title bar of a Window
//
// Your Borland C++ Consultant by Paul J. Perry
//

#define STRICT

#include <windowsx.h>
#include <stdlib.h>
#include <string.h>
#include "title.h"

// Function Prototypes
LRESULT CALLBACK _export MainWndProc(HWND, UINT,
                                     WPARAM, LPARAM);
void WM_CommandHandler(HWND, int, HWND, UINT);

// Global Variables
HINSTANCE ghInstance;
char StartingTitleText[] = "This Will Change!";


/***********************************************/
#pragma argsused
int PASCAL WinMain(HINSTANCE hInstance, HINSTANCE
                   hPrevInstance, LPSTR lpCmdParam,
                   int nCmdShow)
{
    char      ProgName[] = "Title bar example";
    HWND      hWnd;
    MSG       msg;

    ghInstance = hInstance;

    if (!hPrevInstance)
    {
```

```
    WNDCLASS      wndclass;

    wndclass.lpszClassName  = ProgName;
    wndclass.lpfnWndProc    = (WNDPROC) MainWndProc;
    wndclass.cbClsExtra     = 0;
    wndclass.cbWndExtra     = 0;
    wndclass.hInstance      = hInstance;
    wndclass.hIcon          = LoadIcon(NULL,
                              IDI_APPLICATION);
    wndclass.hCursor        = LoadCursor(NULL,
                              IDC_ARROW);
    wndclass.hbrBackground  = GetStockBrush (
                              WHITE_BRUSH);
    wndclass.lpszMenuName   = "MAINMENU";
    wndclass.style          = CS_VREDRAW ¦
                              CS_HREDRAW;

    if (!RegisterClass(&wndclass))
        exit(1);
}

hWnd = CreateWindow(ProgName, StartingTitleText,
                    WS_OVERLAPPEDWINDOW,
                    CW_USEDEFAULT, CW_USEDEFAULT,
                    CW_USEDEFAULT, CW_USEDEFAULT,
                    NULL, NULL, hInstance, NULL);

ShowWindow(hWnd, nCmdShow);
UpdateWindow(hWnd);

while (GetMessage(&msg, NULL, 0, 0))
{
    TranslateMessage(&msg);
    DispatchMessage(&msg);
}
return msg.wParam;
}

/*******************************************/
#pragma argsused
void WM_CommandHandler(HWND hWnd, int id, HWND
hWndCtl, UINT codeNotify)
{
    switch (id)
    {
        case IDM_NEW :
        case IDM_OPEN :
        case IDM_SAVE :
```

continues

Listing 1.6. continued

```
case IDM_SAVEAS :
case IDM_PRINT :
case IDM_CUT :
case IDM_COPY :
case IDM_PASTE :
case IDM_FIND :
case IDM_FINDNEXT :
{
   MessageBox(hWnd, "Function not yet
               implemented", NULL, MB_ICONSTOP ¦
               MB_OK);
   break;
}

case IDM_EXIT :
{
   SendMessage(hWnd, WM_DESTROY, 0, 0L);
   break;
}

case IDM_HELPONHELP :
{
   WinHelp(hWnd, NULL, HELP_HELPONHELP, 0L);
   break;
}

case IDM_ABOUT :
{
   MessageBox(hWnd, "SetTitleText Example",
               "About", MB_ICONQUESTION ¦ MB_OK);
   break;
}

}

   SetWindowText(hWnd, StartingTitleText);
}


/**********************************************/
LRESULT CALLBACK _export MainWndProc(HWND hWnd, UINT
                                     message, WPARAM
                                     wParam, LPARAM
                                     lParam)
{
   switch (message)
```

```
{
    case WM_PAINT :
    {
        HDC           PaintDC;
        RECT          rect;
        PAINTSTRUCT ps;

        PaintDC = BeginPaint(hWnd, &ps);
        GetClientRect(hWnd, &rect);

        DrawText(PaintDC, "Select menu items and
                  watch title bar change", -1, &rect,
                  DT_SINGLELINE | DT_CENTER |
                  DT_VCENTER);

        EndPaint(hWnd, &ps);
        return 0;
    }

    case WM_COMMAND :
    {
        return HANDLE_WM_COMMAND(hWnd, wParam,
                                 lParam,
                                 WM_CommandHandler);
    }

    case WM_MENUSELECT :
    {
        char buff[255];
        int result;

        result = LoadString(ghInstance, wParam, buff,
                            sizeof(buff));

        if (!result)
            strcpy(buff, StartingTitleText);

        SetWindowText(hWnd, buff);
        break;
    }


    case WM_DESTROY :
    {
        PostQuitMessage(0);
        return 0;
    }
```

I

continues

Listing 1.6. continued

```
    }
    return DefWindowProc (hWnd, message, wParam,
                          lParam);
}
```

Listing 1.7. TITLE.H header file.

```
/*
 * TITLE.H Header File
 *
 */

#define IDM_NEW     100
#define IDM_OPEN    110
#define IDM_SAVE    120
#define IDM_SAVEAS  130
#define IDM_PRINT   140
#define IDM_EXIT    150

#define IDM_CUT     200
#define IDM_COPY    210
#define IDM_PASTE   220

#define IDM_FIND       300
#define IDM_FINDNEXT   310

#define IDM_HELPONHELP 400
#define IDM_ABOUT      410
```

Listing 1.8. TITLE.RC header file.

```
/*
 * TITLE.RC Resource Script
 *
 */

#include "title.h"

MAINMENU MENU
BEGIN
     POPUP "&File"
```

```
      BEGIN
            MENUITEM "&New",          IDM_NEW
            MENUITEM "&Open...",      IDM_OPEN
            MENUITEM "&Save...",      IDM_SAVE
            MENUITEM "Save &As...",   IDM_SAVEAS
            MENUITEM SEPARATOR
            MENUITEM "&Print...",     IDM_PRINT
            MENUITEM SEPARATOR
            MENUITEM "E&xit",         IDM_EXIT
      END

      POPUP "&Edit"
      BEGIN
            MENUITEM "Cu&t",    IDM_CUT
            MENUITEM "&Copy",   IDM_COPY
            MENUITEM "&Paste",  IDM_PASTE
      END

      POPUP "&Search"
      BEGIN
            MENUITEM "&Find...", IDM_FIND
            MENUITEM "Find &Next", IDM_FINDNEXT
      END

      POPUP "&Help"
      BEGIN
            MENUITEM "&How to Use Help", IDM_HELPONHELP
            MENUITEM "&About...", IDM_ABOUT
      END

END


STRINGTABLE
BEGIN
        IDM_NEW, "Create a new file"
        IDM_OPEN, "Open a previously created file"
        IDM_SAVE, "Save file"
        IDM_SAVEAS, "Save file with a new name"
        IDM_PRINT, "Print file"
        IDM_EXIT, "Exit program"

        IDM_CUT, "Cut selection and place into
                    clipboard"
        IDM_COPY, "Copy selection into clipboard"
        IDM_PASTE, "Paste clipboard contents into
document"

        IDM_FIND, "Find next occurrence of character"
```

I

continues

Listing 1.8. continued

```
      IDM_FINDNEXT, "Find next occurrence of
                    previously specified character"

      IDM_HELPONHELP, "Display help about using help"
      IDM_ABOUT, "Display information about the
                 program"
END
```

Listing 1.9. TITLE.DEF module definition file.

```
;
; TITLE.DEF module definition file
;

DESCRIPTION     'Changing Window Titles'
NAME            TITLE
EXETYPE         WINDOWS
STUB            'WINSTUB.EXE'
HEAPSIZE        1024
STACKSIZE       8192
CODE            PRELOAD MOVEABLE DISCARDABLE
DATA            PRELOAD MOVEABLE MULTIPLE
```

 Creating a Status Bar

How do I add a status bar to my program?

DESCRIPTION

A status bar appears horizontally at the bottom of a window and contains a line of text with prompt or status information. Sometimes, the status bar also contains key status information, telling the user if the Caps Lock, Num Lock, or Scroll Lock keys are currently active. Many commercial programs contain status bars, including Paradox for Windows, Word for Windows (see Figure 1.4), and Borland C++ for Windows (BCW), to name just a few.

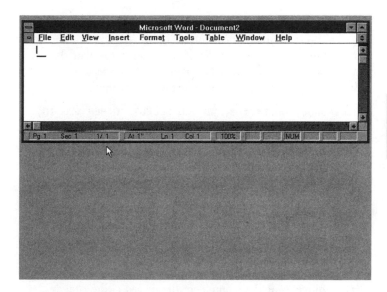

Figure 1.4. *Word for Windows status bar.*

The most common information that appears in the status bar is information about the current menu item. For example, as the user selects the File menu and moves over New, Open, Save, Save As..., and so on, the status bar indicates the purpose of each option.

ANSWER

The best way to create a status bar in your program is to create a child window of the main window. The main job of this child window is to display the status bar information.

The main program must use the MoveWindow function to keep the status bar window displayed at the bottom of the main window at all times. To display menu descriptions in the status window, the program must know what menu item the user is selecting. The WM_MENUSELECT message is sent to the window to which the menu is attached. If we send this message to the status bar window procedure, our program can detect which menu item is currently being selected and use TextOut to display the line of text in the status bar.

COMMENTS

You can also send other types of status information by coming up with a unique way of passing identifiers. You can simulate the call to WM_MENUSELECT by using a SendMessage with the appropriate parameter. For example, you could use a call like this:

```
SendMessage(hWndStatus, WM_MENUSELECT, OTHER_MSG_ID,
            0L);
```

In this case, OTHER_MSG_ID would be an integer value that is defined to relate to a message that has been stored as a string resource.

The best way to store status bar messages is to pull them out of a string resource. This way they are not using valuable space in your program's data segment. An easy way to give identifiers to the string resources is to give them the same identifiers as the menu IDs. Then, when the program receives WM_MENUSELECT, it can load the string resource using the menu identifier passed in the wParam.

Also, it is sometimes nice to let the user hide the status bar. This can be done through menu items, or by options in a dialog box. To hide the status bar window, simply use the ShowWindow function. For example, to hide the status bar, use this command:

```
ShowWindow(hWndStat, SW_HIDE);
```

To make the status bar appear again, use this line:

```
ShowWindow(hWndStat, SW_SHOWNORMAL);
```

Finally, another nice twist is to change the default font used inside the status bar. The Microsoft Windows User Guidelines specify that a program should use a 10-point, sans serif, nonbold font. A program can use CreateFont or CreateFontIndirect to get a handle to the new font, and then use SelectFont (from WINDOWSX.H) or SelectObject to select the font in the display context.

SEE ALSO

CheckMenuItem API Function
CreateFont API Function
CreateFontIndirect API Function
ShowWindow API Function
WM_MENUSELECT Windows Message

EXAMPLE CODE

The sample program creates a status bar at the bottom of the main window (see Figure 1.5). It uses a string resource to store the text of the menu identifiers. It also contains an Option menu item that allows the user to hide the status bar. Listing 1.10 contains the C source code. Listing 1.11 contains the resource script; Listing 1.12 contains the header file; and Listing 1.13 contains the module definition file.

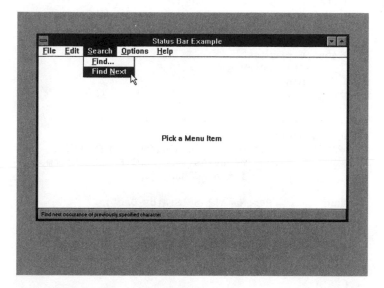

Figure 1.5. *Status bar example program.*

Listing 1.10. The STATUS.C source code.

```
// STATUS.C - Example program that shows how to
//            implement a status bar.
//
// Your Borland C++ Consultant by Paul J. Perry
//

#define STRICT

#include <windowsx.h>
#include <stdlib.h>
```

continues

Listing 1.10. continued

```c
#include "status.h"


// Function Prototypes
LRESULT CALLBACK _export MainWndProc(HWND, UINT,
                                     WPARAM, LPARAM);
LRESULT CALLBACK _export StatusWndProc(HWND, UINT,
                                       WPARAM,LPARAM);
void DrawThreeDim(HDC PaintDC);
void WM_CommandHandler(HWND, int, HWND, UINT);


// Global Variables
int       StatusBarVisible = TRUE;
HWND      hWnd, hWndStat;
HINSTANCE ghInstance;

/*********************************************/
#pragma argsused
int PASCAL WinMain(HINSTANCE hInstance, HINSTANCE
                   hPrevInstance, LPSTR lpCmdParam,
                   int nCmdShow)
{
    char      ProgName[] = "Status Bar";
    MSG       msg;

    ghInstance = hInstance;

    if (!hPrevInstance)
    {
        WNDCLASS      wndclass;

        // Register main window
        wndclass.lpszClassName = ProgName;
        wndclass.lpfnWndProc   = (WNDPROC) MainWndProc;
        wndclass.cbClsExtra    = 0;
        wndclass.cbWndExtra    = 0;
        wndclass.hInstance     = hInstance;
        wndclass.hIcon         = LoadIcon(NULL,
                                   IDI_APPLICATION);
        wndclass.hCursor       = LoadCursor(NULL,
                                   IDC_ARROW);
        wndclass.hbrBackground = GetStockBrush (
                                   WHITE_BRUSH);
        wndclass.lpszMenuName  = "MAINMENU";
        wndclass.style         = CS_VREDRAW |
                                   CS_HREDRAW;
```

```
    if (!RegisterClass(&wndclass))
        exit(1);

    // Register status bar window
    wndclass.lpszClassName = "StatusBar";
    wndclass.lpfnWndProc   = (WNDPROC)
                             StatusWndProc;
    wndclass.cbClsExtra    = 0;
    wndclass.cbWndExtra    = 0;
    wndclass.hInstance     = hInstance;
    wndclass.hIcon         = NULL;
    wndclass.hCursor       = LoadCursor(NULL,
                             IDC_ARROW);
    wndclass.hbrBackground = GetStockBrush (
                             WHITE_BRUSH);
    wndclass.lpszMenuName  = NULL;
    wndclass.style         = NULL;

    if (!RegisterClass(&wndclass))
        exit(1);

}

// Create main window
hWnd = CreateWindow(ProgName,"Status Bar Example",
                    WS_OVERLAPPEDWINDOW,
                    CW_USEDEFAULT, CW_USEDEFAULT,
                    CW_USEDEFAULT, CW_USEDEFAULT,
                    NULL, NULL, hInstance, NULL);

// Create status bar window
//
// It is a child window, with a border, and visible
hWndStat = CreateWindow("StatusBar", NULL,
                    WS_CHILD ¦ WS_BORDER ¦
                    WS_VISIBLE,
                    0, 0, 0, 0, hWnd, NULL,
                    hInstance, NULL);

ShowWindow(hWnd, nCmdShow);
UpdateWindow(hWnd);

// If the status bar is visible, display it now
//   the default is for the status bar to be
     visible, however, that could be changed.
if (StatusBarVisible)
```

continues

Listing 1.10. continued

```
{
    ShowWindow(hWndStat, SW_SHOWNORMAL);
    UpdateWindow(hWndStat);
}

while (GetMessage(&msg, NULL, 0, 0))
{
    TranslateMessage(&msg);
    DispatchMessage(&msg);
}
return msg.wParam;
}

/*******************************************/
#pragma argsused
void WM_CommandHandler(HWND hWnd, int id, HWND
                      hWndCtl, UINT codeNotify)
{
    switch (id)
    {
        case IDM_NEW :
        case IDM_OPEN :
        case IDM_SAVE :
        case IDM_SAVEAS :
        case IDM_PRINT :
        {
            MessageBox(hWnd, "Function not yet
                       implemented", NULL, MB_ICONSTOP
                       | MB_OK);
            break;
        }

        case IDM_EXIT :
        {
            SendMessage(hWnd, WM_DESTROY, 0, 0L);
            break;
        }

        case IDM_CUT :
        case IDM_COPY :
        case IDM_PASTE :
        {
            MessageBox(hWnd, "Function not yet
                       implemented", NULL, MB_ICONSTOP
                       | MB_OK);
            break;
        }
```

```
case IDM_FIND :
case IDM_FINDNEXT :
{
   MessageBox(hWnd, "Function not yet
              implemented", NULL, MB_ICONSTOP
              ¦ MB_OK);
   break;
}

case IDM_STATUS :
{
   BOOL  bChecked;
   HMENU hMenu;

   hMenu = GetMenu(hWnd);
   bChecked = GetMenuState(hMenu, IDM_STATUS,
                           MF_BYCOMMAND);

   if(bChecked & MF_CHECKED)
   {
      CheckMenuItem(hMenu, IDM_STATUS,
                 MF_BYCOMMAND ¦ MF_UNCHECKED);
       StatusBarVisible = FALSE;
      ShowWindow(hWndStat, SW_HIDE);
   }
   else
   {
      CheckMenuItem(hMenu, IDM_STATUS,
                 MF_BYCOMMAND ¦ MF_CHECKED);
       StatusBarVisible = TRUE;
      ShowWindow(hWndStat, SW_SHOWNORMAL);

   }

   break;

}

case IDM_HELPONHELP :
{
   WinHelp(hWnd, NULL, HELP_HELPONHELP, 0L);
   break;
}

case IDM_ABOUT :
{
   MessageBox(hWnd, "Status Line Example",
              "About", MB_ICONQUESTION ¦
              MB_OK);
```

I

continues

Listing 1.10. continued

```
        break;
      }

   }

}


/********************************************/
LRESULT CALLBACK _export MainWndProc(HWND hWnd, UINT
                                message, WPARAM
                                wParam, LPARAM
                                lParam)
{
   switch (message)
   {
      case WM_PAINT :
      {
         HDC         PaintDC;
         RECT        rect;
         PAINTSTRUCT ps;

         PaintDC = BeginPaint(hWnd, &ps);
         GetClientRect(hWnd, &rect);

         DrawText(PaintDC, "Pick a Menu Item",-1,
                  &rect, DT_SINGLELINE ¦
                  DT_CENTER ¦ DT_VCENTER);

         EndPaint(hWnd, &ps);
         return 0;
      }

      case WM_COMMAND :
      {
         return HANDLE_WM_COMMAND(hWnd, wParam,
                                  lParam,
                                  WM_CommandHandler);
      }

      case WM_MENUSELECT :
      {
         // Send the message on to the status bar
         // window only if the user has selected it
         // as visible.
```

```
        if (StatusBarVisible)
          SendMessage(hWndStat, WM_MENUSELECT,
                      wParam, lParam);

      break;
    }

    case WM_SIZE :
    {
        // Change the size and location of status
        // bar window as necessary so it still fits
        // in the correct location if the main
        // window is moved.
        MoveWindow(hWndStat, 0, HIWORD(lParam) -
                   GetSystemMetrics(SM_CYCAPTION),
                   LOWORD(lParam), HIWORD(lParam),
                   TRUE);
        break;

    }

    case WM_DESTROY :
    {
        PostQuitMessage(0);
        return 0;
    }
  }
  return DefWindowProc (hWnd, message, wParam,
                        lParam);
}


/*********************************************/
LRESULT CALLBACK _export StatusWndProc(HWND hWnd, UINT
                                       message, WPARAM
                                       wParam, LPARAM
                                       lParam)
{
  switch (message)
  {

    case WM_PAINT :
    {
        HDC          PaintDC;
        PAINTSTRUCT ps;
```

continues

Listing 1.10. continued

```
        PaintDC = BeginPaint(hWnd, &ps);
        DrawThreeDim(PaintDC);
        EndPaint(hWnd, &ps);

        return 0;
}

case WM_MENUSELECT :
{
    char    buff[255];
    int     len, Y;
    HDC     hDC;
    LOGFONT FontInfo;
    HFONT   hFont, hOldFont;
    DWORD   size;

    // Load text from string table resource.
    //   Notice that the string resource
    //   identifier is given the same identifier
    //   as the menu ID. This is convenient,
    //   because when the program receives
    //   WM_MENUSELECT, the menu ID shows up in
    //   the wParam.
    len = LoadString(ghInstance, wParam, buff,
                     sizeof(buff));

    hDC = GetDC(hWndStat);
    DrawThreeDim(hDC);

    // Set the mapping mode to twentieths of a
    //   point
    SetMapMode(hDC, MM_TWIPS);

    // Create a font.  As per Microsoft Windows
    //   interface guide, we create a 10 point san
    //   serif font.
    FontInfo.lfHeight       = 200;
    // 10 pt.
    FontInfo.lfWidth        = 0;
    // use default width
    FontInfo.lfEscapement   = 0;
    // angle
    FontInfo.lfOrientation  = NULL;
    // not used
```

```
FontInfo.lfWeight          = FW_NORMAL;
                             // not boldface
FontInfo.lfItalic          = 0;
                             // not an italic
                             font
FontInfo.lfUnderline       = 0;
                             // not an italic
                             font
FontInfo.lfStrikeOut       = 0;
                             // not an italic
                             font
FontInfo.lfCharSet         = ANSI_CHARSET;
                             // ANSI character
                             set
FontInfo.lfOutPrecision    = OUT_TT_PRECIS;
                             // Use true type
FontInfo.lfClipPrecision   = CLIP_EMBEDDED;
FontInfo.lfQuality         = PROOF_QUALITY;
FontInfo.lfPitchAndFamily  = FF_SWISS;
                             // Sans-serif
                             font

lstrcpy((LPSTR)FontInfo.lfFaceName[0],
        (LPSTR)"Helv");

// Get a handle to the font
hFont = CreateFontIndirect(&FontInfo);

hOldFont = SelectFont(hDC, hFont);

// Find the vertical location where the text
//    should be displayed.  We go with half
//    the size of the status bar minus half
//    the height of the font. This makes sure
//    it is centered.
size = GetTextExtent(hDC, "Test", 4);
Y = (GetSystemMetrics(SM_CYCAPTION)/2) -
                    (HIWORD(size))/2;

// Set background color to light gray.  This
//    is done to ensure that previous text is
//    cleared from the status bar window
//    before attempting to display next text.
  SetBkColor(hDC, RGB(192, 192, 192));
TextOut(hDC, 100, Y, buff, len);

// Clean up by deleting the font
SelectFont(hDC, hOldFont);
DeleteFont(hFont);
```

continues

Listing 1.10. continued

```
        ReleaseDC(hWndStat, hDC);

        break;
    }


    case WM_DESTROY :
    {
        PostQuitMessage(0);
        return 0;
    }
  }
  return DefWindowProc (hWnd, message, wParam,
                        lParam);

}

/*********************************************/
void DrawThreeDim(HDC PaintDC)
{
    RECT        rect;
    HPEN        hPen;
    HBRUSH      hBrush;

    GetClientRect(hWnd, &rect);

    // Fill background to light gray color
    hBrush = CreateSolidBrush(RGB(192, 192, 192));
    FillRect(PaintDC, &rect, hBrush);
    DeleteBrush(hBrush);

    // Draw three-dimensional effect around top of
        status bar
    MoveTo(PaintDC, rect.left, rect.bottom);

    hPen = GetStockPen(WHITE_PEN);
    SelectPen(PaintDC, hPen);
    LineTo(PaintDC, 0, 0);                      // left side
    LineTo(PaintDC, rect.right, rect.top); // top side

}
```

Listing 1.11. The STATUS.RC resource script.

```
/*
 * STATUS.RC Resource Script
 *
 */

#include "status.h"

MAINMENU MENU
BEGIN
     POPUP "&File"
     BEGIN
          MENUITEM "&New",          IDM_NEW
          MENUITEM "&Open...",      IDM_OPEN
          MENUITEM "&Save...",      IDM_SAVE
          MENUITEM "Save &As...",   IDM_SAVEAS
          MENUITEM SEPARATOR
          MENUITEM "&Print...",     IDM_PRINT
          MENUITEM SEPARATOR
          MENUITEM "E&xit",         IDM_EXIT
     END

     POPUP "&Edit"
     BEGIN
          MENUITEM "Cu&t",    IDM_CUT
          MENUITEM "&Copy",   IDM_COPY
          MENUITEM "&Paste",  IDM_PASTE
     END

     POPUP "&Search"
     BEGIN
          MENUITEM "&Find...", IDM_FIND
          MENUITEM "Find &Next", IDM_FINDNEXT
     END

     POPUP "&Options"
     BEGIN
          MENUITEM "&Status Bar", IDM_STATUS, CHECKED
     END

     POPUP "&Help"
     BEGIN
          MENUITEM "&How to Use Help", IDM_HELPONHELP
          MENUITEM "&About...", IDM_ABOUT
     END

END
```

I

continues

Listing 1.11. continued

```
STRINGTABLE
BEGIN
        IDM_NEW, "Create a new file"
        IDM_OPEN, "Open a previously created file"
        IDM_SAVE, "Save file"
        IDM_SAVEAS, "Save file with a new name"
        IDM_PRINT, "Print file"
        IDM_EXIT, "Exit program"

        IDM_CUT, "Cut selection and place into
                    clipboard"
        IDM_COPY, "Copy selection into clipboard"
        IDM_PASTE, "Paste clipboard contents into
                    document"

        IDM_FIND, "Find next occurrence of character"
        IDM_FINDNEXT, "Find next occurrence of
                    previously specified character"

        IDM_STATUS, "Turn status bar on and off"

        IDM_HELPONHELP, "Display help about using help"
        IDM_ABOUT, "Display information about the
                    program"
END
```

Listing 1.12. The STATUS.H header file.

```
/*
 * STATUS.H Header File
 *
 */

#define IDM_NEW     100
#define IDM_OPEN    110
#define IDM_SAVE    120
#define IDM_SAVEAS  130
#define IDM_PRINT   140
#define IDM_EXIT    150

#define IDM_CUT     200
#define IDM_COPY    210
#define IDM_PASTE   220
```

```
#define IDM_FIND      300
#define IDM_FINDNEXT  310

#define IDM_STATUS    400

#define IDM_HELPONHELP 500
#define IDM_ABOUT     510
```

I

Listing 1.13. The STATUS.DEF module definition file.

```
;
; STATUS.DEF module definition file
;

DESCRIPTION    'Status Bar Example'
NAME           STATUS
EXETYPE        WINDOWS
STUB           'WINSTUB.EXE'
HEAPSIZE       1024
STACKSIZE      8192
CODE           PRELOAD MOVEABLE DISCARDABLE
DATA           PRELOAD MOVEABLE MULTIPLE
```

 Using Three-Dimensional Effects

How can I give my own programs fancy three-dimensional effects?

DESCRIPTION

Programmers see some of the fancy effects in commercial applications and would like to give their own applications the added benefit of fancy-looking output.

ANSWER

The trick is to use shades of gray along with black and white to trick the user into thinking that screen images are three-dimensional.

(Obviously, the screen is only two-dimensional—so we are going to have to play some tricks.) Table 1.3 shows the colors we want to use, along with their corresponding RGB (red, green, and blue) values.

Table 1.3. Color values used to create three-dimensional effects.

Color	RGB Value
Light gray	RGB(192, 192, 192)
Dark gray	RGB(128, 128, 128)
White	RGB(0, 0, 0)
Black	RGB(255, 255, 255)

The effect is actually very simple. First, we set the background color of a window to light gray. This is accomplished by setting the hbrBackground element in the WNDCLASS structure to a stock brush. It can be done like this:

```
wndclass.hbrBackground = GetStockBrush(LTGRAY_BRUSH);
```

Once the background color is set, if our program draws a line in white and then draws another line right next to it in black, it gives the user the impression that the line is a bump (it appears three-dimensional).

To draw text with a three-dimensional appearance, first offset the text location one pixel down and to the right and display the text in black. Then, display it in white at the specified location. It gives the text a nice appearance of being three-dimensional.

COMMENTS

The program listing incorporates some functions you might want to use in your own programs. First, there is TextOut3D which displays text using three-dimensional effects. Next, there is LineTo3D which displays a line that appears like a bump. Finally, there is Rectangle3D which draws a three-dimensional-like rectangle.

All the functions take parameters similar to their non-three-dimensional counterparts. For example, `TextOut3D` takes a handle to the display context, the *x* and *y* location of where to display the text, the string, and the length of the string. For the most part, these three-dimensional functions can be called the same way as their non-three-dimensional friends.

SEE ALSO

`CreateObject` API Function
`CreatePen` Macro Found in WINDOWSX.H
`SelectObject` API Function
`SelectPen` Macro Found in WINDOWSX.H
`SetBkMode` API Function
`SetTextColor` API Function

EXAMPLE CODE

There are only two source code listings to this one. First, THREED.C is the C source code in Listing 1.14 (see Figure 1.6). Then, Listing 1.15 is the module definition file.

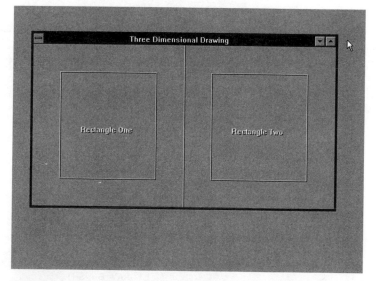

Figure 1.6. *Sample window from THREED example program.*

Listing 1.14. THREED.C source code.

```
// THREED.C -Z Demonstration of three-dimensional
//           drawing effects.
//
// Your Borland C++ Consultant by Paul J. Perry
//

#define STRICT

#include <windowsx.h>
#include <stdlib.h>

// Function Prototypes
LRESULT CALLBACK _export MainWndProc(HWND, UINT,
                                     WPARAM, LPARAM);
BOOL TextOut3D(HDC, int, int, LPCSTR, int);
void LineTo3D(HDC, int, int);
void Rectangle3D(HDC, int, int, int, int);


/**********************************************/
#pragma argsused
int PASCAL WinMain(HINSTANCE hInstance, HINSTANCE
                   hPrevInstance, LPSTR lpCmdParam,
                   int nCmdShow)
{
    char        ProgName[] = "Three Dimensional
                             Drawing";
    HWND        hWnd;
    MSG         msg;


    if (!hPrevInstance)
    {
        WNDCLASS    wndclass;

        wndclass.lpszClassName = ProgName;
        wndclass.lpfnWndProc   = (WNDPROC) MainWndProc;
        wndclass.cbClsExtra    = 0;
        wndclass.cbWndExtra    = 0;
        wndclass.hInstance     = hInstance;
        wndclass.hIcon         = LoadIcon(NULL,
                                   IDI_APPLICATION);
        wndclass.hCursor       = LoadCursor(NULL,
                                   IDC_ARROW);
        wndclass.hbrBackground = GetStockBrush(
                                   LTGRAY_BRUSH);
        wndclass.lpszMenuName  = NULL;
        wndclass.style         = CS_VREDRAW |
```

```
                            CS_HREDRAW;

    if (!RegisterClass(&wndclass))
        exit(1);
}

hWnd = CreateWindow(ProgName, ProgName,
                    WS_OVERLAPPEDWINDOW,
                    CW_USEDEFAULT, CW_USEDEFAULT,
                    CW_USEDEFAULT, CW_USEDEFAULT,
                    NULL, NULL, hInstance, NULL);

ShowWindow(hWnd, nCmdShow);
UpdateWindow(hWnd);

while (GetMessage(&msg, NULL, 0, 0))
{
    TranslateMessage(&msg);
    DispatchMessage(&msg);
}
return msg.wParam;
}

/**********************************************/
BOOL TextOut3D(HDC hDC, int XStart, int YStart,
               LPCSTR lpszString, int cbString)
{
    BOOL result;
    int PrevBKMode;
    COLORREF PrevColor;

    PrevBKMode = SetBkMode(hDC, TRANSPARENT);
    PrevColor = SetTextColor(hDC, RGB(0, 0, 0));

    result = TextOut(hDC, XStart+1, YStart+1,
                     lpszString, cbString);

    SetTextColor(hDC, RGB(255, 255, 255));

    result = TextOut(hDC, XStart, YStart, lpszString,
                     cbString);

    // Reset original display context values
    SetBkMode(hDC, PrevBKMode);
    SetTextColor(hDC, PrevColor);

    return result;

}
```

continues

Listing 1.14. continued

```
/*********************************************/
void LineTo3D(HDC hDC, int xEnd, int yEnd)
{
    DWORD StartPoint;
    HPEN hPen;

    hPen = SelectPen(hDC, GetStockPen(BLACK_PEN));

    // Find out where we are starting
    StartPoint = GetCurrentPosition(hDC);


    MoveTo(hDC, LOWORD(StartPoint)+1,
                    HIWORD(StartPoint+1));
    LineTo(hDC, xEnd+1, yEnd+1);

    MoveTo(hDC, LOWORD(StartPoint),
                    HIWORD(StartPoint));

    SelectPen(hDC, GetStockPen(WHITE_PEN));

    LineTo(hDC, xEnd, yEnd);

    // Select original pen back into display context
    SelectPen(hDC, hPen);

}


/*********************************************/
void Rectangle3D(HDC hDC, int LeftRect, int TopRect,
                int RightRect, int BottomRect)
{
    HBRUSH hBrush;
    HPEN   hPen;

    hBrush = SelectBrush(hDC,
                    GetStockBrush(HOLLOW_BRUSH));

    hPen = SelectPen(hDC, GetStockPen(BLACK_PEN));

    Rectangle(hDC, LeftRect+1, TopRect+1, RightRect+1,
            BottomRect+1);

    SelectPen(hDC, GetStockPen(WHITE_PEN));
```

```
      Rectangle(hDC, LeftRect, TopRect, RightRect,
               BottomRect);

      // Get original values back again
      SelectBrush(hDC, hBrush);
      SelectPen(hDC, hPen);

}


/*********************************************/
LRESULT CALLBACK _export MainWndProc(HWND hWnd, UINT
                                     message,
                                     WPARAM wParam,
                                     LPARAM lParam)
{
    switch (message)
    {
       case WM_PAINT :
       {
          HDC          PaintDC;
          RECT         rect;
          PAINTSTRUCT  ps;
          char         str1[] = "Rectangle One";
          char         str2[] = "Rectangle Two";

          PaintDC = BeginPaint(hWnd, &ps);
          GetClientRect(hWnd, &rect);

          // Text 3D output
          TextOut3D(PaintDC, rect.right/4 -
                    (LOWORD(GetTextExtent(PaintDC,
                     str1, sizeof(str1)))/2),
                     rect.bottom/2, str1,
                     sizeof(str1)- 1);


          TextOut3D(PaintDC, ((rect.right/4)*3) -
                    (LOWORD(GetTextExtent(PaintDC, str2,
                     sizeof(str2)))/2), rect.bottom/2,
                     str2, sizeof(str2)- 1);

          // Create a 3D rectangle
          Rectangle3D(PaintDC, rect.left+50,
                      rect.top+50,
                      rect.right/2-50, rect.bottom-50);
```

continues

Listing 1.14. continued

```
        Rectangle3D(PaintDC, rect.right/2+50,
                        rect.top+50,
                        rect.right-50, rect.bottom-50);

        MoveTo(PaintDC, rect.right/2, rect.top);
        LineTo3D(PaintDC, rect.right/2, rect.bottom);

        EndPaint(hWnd, &ps);
        return 0;
    }

    case WM_DESTROY :
    {
        PostQuitMessage(0);
        return 0;
    }
}
return DefWindowProc (hWnd, message, wParam,
                    lParam);
}
```

Listing 1.15. THREED.DEF module definition file.

```
;
; THREED.DEF module definition file
;

DESCRIPTION     'Three-Dimensional Effects'
NAME            THREED
EXETYPE         WINDOWS
STUB            'WINSTUB.EXE'
HEAPSIZE        1024
STACKSIZE       8192
CODE            PRELOAD MOVEABLE DISCARDABLE
DATA            PRELOAD MOVEABLE MULTIPLE
```

Flashing Icons

How do I draw attention to my program by making the icon for my application flash?

DESCRIPTION

Many programmers would like to have the icon that is associated with the main window of their program flash, thereby alerting the user that something has occurred in the program. A common use is in an e-mail application that flashes the program's icon when new mail messages have arrived and have not been read.

ANSWER

There is a little known API function called *FlashWindow*. Usually, when this function is called, it causes the title bar of a window to momentarily flash. However, if the window is minimized, it causes the icon to flash.

Using this knowledge in combination with a Windows timer, let's write a program to create the illusion of a flashing icon. A program can check when it is minimized by trapping the WM_SIZE message. If the wParam is equal to SIZE_MINIMIZED, we know that the window is about to be minimized, and we can create a timer.

The timer is set, sending a WM_TIMER message to the main window procedure every 500 milliseconds (half a second). The code that processes the WM_TIMER message calls the FlashWindow function. The program also checks the WM_QUERYOPEN message. This tells the program that the window is about to be restored. At this time, we kill the timer using the KillTimer function.

COMMENTS

To use your own custom icon, you must first include the icon in your resource script. Your resource script (.RC file) should contain a line that looks like this:

```
MYICON ICON "filename.ico"
```

You must then specify the name of the icon during window class initialization. The hIcon member of the wndclass structure would be initialized similar to this:

```
wndclass.hIcon = LoadIcon(hInstance, "MYICON");
```

This forces all windows based on the specified window class to use the specified icon when they are minimized.

SEE ALSO

FlashWindow API Function
SetTimer API Function
KillTimer API Function

EXAMPLE CODE

The example program shows how to create a minimized icon that flashes. Listing 1.16 is the C source code, and Listing 1.17 is the module definition file.

Listing 1.16. FLASHER.C source code.

```
// FLASHER.C - Example program to flash icon
//
// Your Borland C++ Consultant by Paul J. Perry
//

#define STRICT

#include <windowsx.h>
#include <stdlib.h>

#define TIMERID 100

// Function Prototypes
LRESULT CALLBACK _export MainWndProc(HWND hWnd, UINT
                                     message, WPARAM
                                     wParam, LPARAM
                                     lParam);

/*********************************************/
#pragma argsused
int PASCAL WinMain(HINSTANCE hInstance, HINSTANCE
                   hPrevInstance, LPSTR lpCmdParam,
                   int nCmdShow)
{
    char       ProgName[] = "Flashing Icon";
    HWND       hWnd;
    MSG        msg;


    if (!hPrevInstance)
    {
        WNDCLASS    wndclass;
```

```
        wndclass.lpszClassName = ProgName;
        wndclass.lpfnWndProc   = (WNDPROC) MainWndProc;
        wndclass.cbClsExtra    = 0;
        wndclass.cbWndExtra    = 0;
        wndclass.hInstance     = hInstance;
        wndclass.hIcon         = LoadIcon(NULL,
                                 IDI_APPLICATION);
        wndclass.hCursor       = LoadCursor(NULL,
                                 IDC_ARROW);
        wndclass.hbrBackground = GetStockObject
                                 (WHITE_BRUSH);
        wndclass.lpszMenuName  = NULL;
        wndclass.style         = CS_VREDRAW |
                                 CS_HREDRAW;

        if (!RegisterClass(&wndclass))
            exit(1);
    }

    hWnd = CreateWindow(ProgName, ProgName,
                        WS_OVERLAPPEDWINDOW,
                        CW_USEDEFAULT, CW_USEDEFAULT,
                        CW_USEDEFAULT, CW_USEDEFAULT,
                        NULL, NULL, hInstance, NULL);

    // Show it initially as an icon
    ShowWindow(hWnd, SW_SHOWMINIMIZED);
    UpdateWindow(hWnd);

    while (GetMessage(&msg, NULL, 0, 0))
    {
        TranslateMessage(&msg);
        DispatchMessage(&msg);
    }
    return msg.wParam;
}

/*********************************************/
LRESULT CALLBACK _export MainWndProc(HWND hWnd, UINT
                                     message,
                                     WPARAM wParam,
                                     LPARAM lParam)
{
    switch (message)
    {
      case WM_QUERYOPEN :
      {
          KillTimer(hWnd, TIMERID);
          return TRUE;
```

continues

Listing 1.16. continued

```
    }

    case WM_SIZE :
    {
       if (wParam == SIZE_MINIMIZED)
           SetTimer(hWnd, TIMERID, 500, NULL);
       return 0;

    }

    case WM_PAINT :
    {
       HDC          PaintDC;
       RECT         rect;
       PAINTSTRUCT  ps;

       PaintDC = BeginPaint(hWnd, &ps);
       GetClientRect(hWnd, &rect);

       DrawText(PaintDC, "Minimize for Flashing
               Icon", -1, &rect, DT_SINGLELINE |
               DT_CENTER | DT_VCENTER);

       EndPaint(hWnd, &ps);
       return 0;
    }

    case WM_TIMER :
    {
       if (IsIconic(hWnd))
           FlashWindow(hWnd, TRUE);
       return 0;
    }

    case WM_DESTROY :
    {
       PostQuitMessage(0);
       return 0;
    }
    }
    return DefWindowProc (hWnd, message, wParam,
                       lParam);
}
```

Listing 1.17. FLASHER.DEF module definition file.

```
;
; FLASHER.DEF module definition file
;

DESCRIPTION    'Flashing Icon Example'
NAME           FLASHER
EXETYPE        WINDOWS
STUB           'WINSTUB.EXE'
HEAPSIZE       1024
STACKSIZE      8192
CODE           PRELOAD MOVEABLE DISCARDABLE
DATA           PRELOAD MOVEABLE MULTIPLE
```

How to Create a ToolBar

How do I create a ToolBar, SpeedBar, ActionBar, or SmartIcon for my program?

DESCRIPTION

Although there are many names for them, a ToolBar is a row of buttons that are always visible within a program's main window. They enable a user to select program actions easily (see Figure 1.7). Microsoft calls them ToolBars; Borland calls them SpeedBars; DataStorm Technologies (Procomm) calls them ActionBars; and Lotus calls them SmartIcons.

Whatever you call them, ToolBars (the term used in this book) can make using your program much easier. The idea is to group commonly accessed functions at one distinct place that can be selected with a click of the mouse.

ANSWER

A ToolBar is going to be created as a separate window. You can then create the image of each ToolBar button and store it in an icon file (.ICO extension). Create each icon with a white, upper-left side, and a dark gray, lower-right side. This gives each icon its three-dimensional appearance.

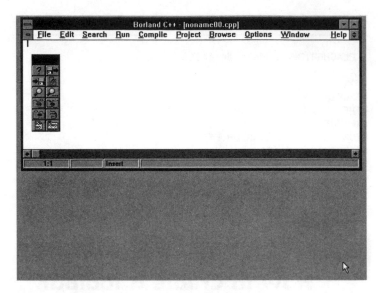

Figure 1.7. *Borland C++ for Windows SpeedBar.*

In response to the WM_PAINT message, the icons are displayed inside the DrawIcon function. Because we are drawing the images ourselves, we must also process mouse messages. We check for WM_LBUTTONDOWN to see which tool the user has clicked with the mouse button. We then repaint the upper-left side dark gray and the lower-right side white (the opposite of how they were created). This gives the impression that the buttons are being pressed. Within the WM_LBUTTONUP message, the original icon is redisplayed, and a global variable is set (letting the rest of the program know which tool is currently selected).

COMMENTS

To give the user even more control, you can allow your ToolBar to be displayed on the top (see Figure 1.8), on the left (see Figure 1.9), or as a floating ToolBar (see Figure 1.10). The Options menu item lets the user select how the ToolBar is displayed. This is useful to the viewer and fits in with Windows' overall concept of letting the user choose one of several ways to access a command.

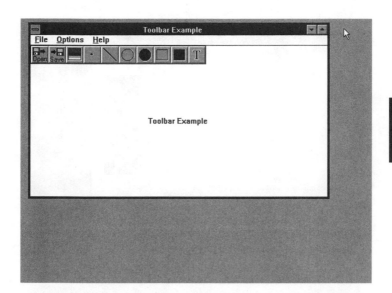

Figure 1.8. *The sample ToolBar displayed at the top of the window.*

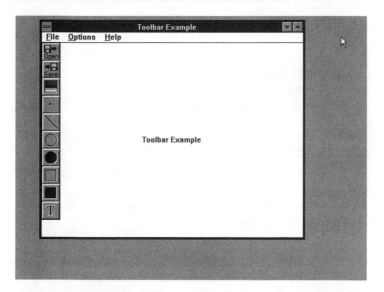

Figure 1.9. *The sample ToolBar displayed on the left side of the window.*

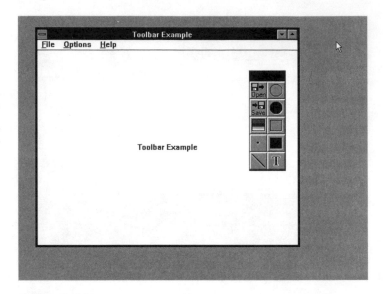

Figure 1.10. *The floating ToolBar.*

SEE ALSO

DrawIcon API Function
WM_LBUTTONDOWN Windows Message
WM_LBUTTONUP Windows Message

EXAMPLE CODE

The sample program creates a ToolBar that could be used within a paint program. To keep the size of the code to a minimum, the program does not actually draw or save files. It just has the main functionality for the ToolBar built into it.

In fact, you could use the example as a shell for your own application. All you would need to do would be to create your own icons, and then specify them in the resource script at the appropriate positions.

The program gives the user the option of displaying the ToolBar in one of three locations: on the top of the window, on the left of the window, or as a floating window. Although the common dialog

I

boxes are used for the File Open, File Save, and Choose Color dialogs, the results are not used.

This code sample was supposed to be short and to the point; however, the example grew. Drawing the ToolBar at one of three different locations takes the most code. Listing 1.18 is the C source code. Listing 1.19 is the resource script. Listing 1.20 is the header file, and Listing 1.21 is the module definition file. When you compile the program, you will also need the following eleven icon files (as referenced in the resource script):

TOOLBAR.ICO	OPEN.ICO
SAVE.ICO	CCOLOR.ICO
POINT.ICO	LINE.ICO
CIRCLE.ICO	FILLCIR.ICO
RECT.ICO	FILLRECT.ICO
TEXT.ICO	

Listing 1.18. TOOLBAR.C source code.

```
// TOOLBAR.C - Example of implementing a ToolBar.
//
// Your Borland C++ Consultant by Paul J. Perry
//

#define STRICT

#include <windowsx.h>
#include <commdlg.h>
#include <stdlib.h>
#include <string.h>
#include <stdio.h>
#include "toolbar.h"


// Function Prototypes
LRESULT CALLBACK _export MainWndProc(HWND, UINT,
                                     WPARAM, LPARAM);
LRESULT CALLBACK _export TBWndProc(HWND, UINT, WPARAM,
                                   LPARAM);
void WM_CommandHandler(HWND, int, HWND, UINT);
void UnCheckPrevious(HMENU);

// Global Variables
HINSTANCE ghInstance;
```

continues

Listing 1.18. continued

```
HWND       hTBWnd, hMainWnd;
int        TBLeft, TBTop, TBWidth, TBHeight;
UINT       HelpMsg;
int        ToolNumber;
char       FileName[256];
int        TBStatus   = TB_FLOAT;
DWORD      TBStyle    = WS_CHILD | WS_BORDER |
                        WS_VISIBLE | WS_CAPTION;
int        CurrentTool = TOOL_POINT;
int        CurrentColor = RGB(0, 0, 0);
BOOL       NeedsUpdate = FALSE;

/*********************************************/
#pragma argsused
int PASCAL WinMain(HINSTANCE hInstance, HINSTANCE
                   hPrevInstance, LPSTR lpCmdParam,
                   int nCmdShow)
{
    char       ProgName[] = "Toolbar Example";
    MSG        msg;

    ghInstance = hInstance;

    if (!hPrevInstance)
    {
        WNDCLASS    wndclass;

        // Register class for main window
        wndclass.lpszClassName = ProgName;
        wndclass.lpfnWndProc   = (WNDPROC) MainWndProc;
        wndclass.cbClsExtra    = 0;
        wndclass.cbWndExtra    = 0;
        wndclass.hInstance     = hInstance;
        wndclass.hIcon         = LoadIcon(hInstance,
                                     "MAINICON");
        wndclass.hCursor       = LoadCursor(NULL,
                                     IDC_CROSS);
        wndclass.hbrBackground = GetStockObject (
                                     WHITE_BRUSH);
        wndclass.lpszMenuName  = "MAINMENU";
        wndclass.style         = CS_VREDRAW |
                                 CS_HREDRAW;

        if (!RegisterClass(&wndclass))
            exit(1);

        // Register toolbar window class
```

```
wndclass.lpszClassName = "ToolBar";
wndclass.lpfnWndProc   = (WNDPROC) TBWndProc;
wndclass.cbClsExtra    = 0;
wndclass.cbWndExtra    = 0;
wndclass.hInstance     = hInstance;
wndclass.hIcon         = NULL;
wndclass.hCursor       = LoadCursor(NULL,
                           IDC_ARROW);
wndclass.hbrBackground = GetStockBrush (
                           BLACK_BRUSH);
wndclass.lpszMenuName  = NULL;
wndclass.style         = NULL;

if (!RegisterClass(&wndclass))
exit(1);

// Register message for "Help" button inside
    Choose Color dialog
HelpMsg = RegisterWindowMessage(HELPMSGSTRING);

}

// Create main window programs
hMainWnd = CreateWindow(ProgName,"Toolbar Example",
                WS_OVERLAPPEDWINDOW,
                CW_USEDEFAULT, CW_USEDEFAULT,
                CW_USEDEFAULT, CW_USEDEFAULT,
                NULL, NULL, hInstance, NULL);

ShowWindow(hMainWnd, nCmdShow);
UpdateWindow(hMainWnd);


// Create toolbar window
hTBWnd = CreateWindow("ToolBar", NULL, TBStyle,
                TBLeft, TBTop, TBWidth,
                TBHeight, hMainWnd, NULL,
                hInstance, NULL);

ShowWindow(hTBWnd, nCmdShow);
UpdateWindow(hTBWnd);


while (GetMessage(&msg, NULL, 0, 0))
{
   TranslateMessage(&msg);
   DispatchMessage(&msg);
}
```

continues

Listing 1.18. continued

```
    return msg.wParam;
}

/*******************************************/
#pragma argsused
void WM_CommandHandler(HWND hWnd, int id, HWND
                       hWndCtl, UINT codeNotify)
{
    switch (id)
    {
        case IDM_OPEN :
        {
            OPENFILENAME OpenFileName;
            char Filters[] = "Windows Metafiles
                             (*.WMF)\0*.WMF\0";

            memset(&OpenFileName, 0,
                   sizeof(OPENFILENAME));

            OpenFileName.lpstrTitle   = "File Open";
            OpenFileName.hwndOwner     = hMainWnd;
            OpenFileName.lpstrFilter   = (LPSTR)Filters;
            OpenFileName.nFilterIndex = 1;
            OpenFileName.lpstrFile     = (LPSTR)FileName;
            OpenFileName.nMaxFile      = sizeof(FileName);
            OpenFileName.Flags         = OFN_FILEMUSTEXIST
                                         ¦ \
                                         OFN_HIDEREADONLY
                                         ¦ \
                                         OFN_PATHMUSTEXIST;
            OpenFileName.lpstrDefExt   = "*";
            OpenFileName.lStructSize   = sizeof(
                                         OPENFILENAME);

            GetOpenFileName(&OpenFileName);

            break;
        }

        case IDM_SAVE :
        {
            OPENFILENAME SaveFileName;
            char Filters[] = "Windows Metafiles
                             (*.WMF)\0*.WMF\0";

            memset(&SaveFileName, 0,
                   sizeof(OPENFILENAME));
```

```
        SaveFileName.lpstrTitle     = "File Save";
        SaveFileName.hwndOwner       = hMainWnd;
        SaveFileName.lpstrFilter     = (LPSTR)Filters;
        SaveFileName.nFilterIndex    = 1;
        SaveFileName.lpstrFile       = (LPSTR)FileName;
        SaveFileName.nMaxFile        = sizeof(FileName);
        SaveFileName.Flags           = OFN_FILEMUSTEXIST
                                       ¦ \
                                       OFN_HIDEREADONLY
                                       ¦ \
                                       OFN_PATHMUSTEXIST;
        SaveFileName.lpstrDefExt     = "*";
        SaveFileName.lStructSize     = sizeof(
                                       OPENFILENAME);

        GetSaveFileName(&SaveFileName);

        break;
    }

    case IDM_EXIT :
    {
        SendMessage(hMainWnd, WM_CLOSE, 0, 0L);
        break;
    }

    case IDM_COLOR :
    {
        CHOOSECOLOR cc;
        COLORREF    CustomColors[16];

        memset(&cc, 0, sizeof(CHOOSECOLOR));

        cc.lStructSize   = sizeof(CHOOSECOLOR);
        cc.hwndOwner     = hMainWnd;
        cc.rgbResult     = CurrentColor;
        cc.lpCustColors  = CustomColors;
        cc.Flags         = CC_RGBINIT ¦ CC_SHOWHELP;

        ChooseColor(&cc);

        CurrentColor = cc.rgbResult;

        break;
    }

    case IDM_FLOAT :
    {
```

continues

Listing 1.18. continued

```
RECT rect;
HMENU hMenu;

SetWindowLong(hTBWnd, GWL_STYLE,
            WS_CHILD | WS_BORDER |
            WS_VISIBLE | WS_CAPTION);
GetClientRect(hMainWnd, &rect);

TBLeft = rect.right -
        GetSystemMetrics(SM_CXICON)*2 - 10;
TBTop = GetSystemMetrics(SM_CYBORDER) +
        GetSystemMetrics(SM_CYCAPTION) +
        GetSystemMetrics(SM_CYFRAME) +
        GetSystemMetrics(SM_CYMENU);

TBWidth = GetSystemMetrics(SM_CXICON) * 2 +
        2;
TBHeight = (GetSystemMetrics(SM_CYICON) *
            NUMBEROFTOOLS / 2) +
            GetSystemMetrics(SM_CYCAPTION)+2;

MoveWindow(hTBWnd, TBLeft, TBTop, TBWidth,
        TBHeight, TRUE);

hMenu = GetMenu(hMainWnd);
UnCheckPrevious(hMenu);
CheckMenuItem(hMenu, IDM_FLOAT, MF_BYCOMMAND
            | MF_CHECKED);

TBStatus = TB_FLOAT;
break;
}

case IDM_ONTOP :
{
    HMENU hMenu;

    SetWindowLong(hTBWnd, GWL_STYLE, WS_CHILD |
                WS_BORDER | WS_VISIBLE);

    TBLeft = 0;
    TBTop = 0;
    TBWidth = GetSystemMetrics(SM_CXICON) *
            NUMBEROFTOOLS+2;
    TBHeight = GetSystemMetrics(SM_CYICON)+2;
```

```
            MoveWindow(hTBWnd, TBLeft, TBTop, TBWidth,
                    TBHeight, TRUE);

            hMenu = GetMenu(hMainWnd);
            UnCheckPrevious(hMenu);
            CheckMenuItem(hMenu, IDM_ONTOP, MF_BYCOMMAND
                        ¦ MF_CHECKED);

            TBStatus = TB_TOP;
            break;
        }

        case IDM_ONLEFT :
        {
            HMENU hMenu;

            SetWindowLong(hTBWnd, GWL_STYLE, WS_CHILD ¦
                        WS_BORDER ¦ WS_VISIBLE);

            TBLeft = 0;
            TBTop = 0;
            TBHeight  = GetSystemMetrics(SM_CXICON) *
                        NUMBEROFTOOLS+2;
            TBWidth = GetSystemMetrics(SM_CYICON)+2;

            MoveWindow(hTBWnd, TBLeft, TBTop, TBWidth,
                    TBHeight, TRUE);

            hMenu = GetMenu(hMainWnd);
            UnCheckPrevious(hMenu);
            CheckMenuItem(hMenu, IDM_ONLEFT, MF_BYCOMMAND
                        ¦ MF_CHECKED);

            TBStatus = TB_LEFT;
            break;
        }

        case IDM_ABOUT :
        {
            MessageBox(hMainWnd, "Toolbar Example ",
                    "About", MB_ICONEXCLAMATION ¦
                    MB_OK);
            break;
        }

    }

}
```

continues

Listing 1.18. continued

```
/*********************************************/
void UnCheckPrevious(HMENU hMenu)
{
    switch (TBStatus)
    {
      case TB_TOP :
      {
         CheckMenuItem(hMenu, IDM_ONTOP, MF_BYCOMMAND
                     ¦ MF_UNCHECKED);
         break;
      }

      case TB_FLOAT :
      {
         CheckMenuItem(hMenu, IDM_FLOAT, MF_BYCOMMAND
                     ¦ MF_UNCHECKED);
         break;
      }


      case TB_LEFT :
      {
         CheckMenuItem(hMenu, IDM_ONLEFT, MF_BYCOMMAND
                     ¦ MF_UNCHECKED);
         break;
      }

    }
}


/*********************************************/
LRESULT CALLBACK _export MainWndProc(HWND hWnd, UINT
                                     message,
                                     WPARAM wParam,
                                     LPARAM lParam)
{
    switch (message)
    {
      case WM_CREATE :
      {
         switch(TBStatus)
         {
            case TB_FLOAT :
            {
               RECT rect;
```

```
          GetClientRect(hWnd, &rect);

          TBLeft = rect.right -
                   GetSystemMetrics(
                   SM_CXICON)*2 - 10;
          TBTop = GetSystemMetrics(SM_CYBORDER) +
                  GetSystemMetrics(SM_CYCAPTION) +
                  GetSystemMetrics(SM_CYFRAME) +
                  GetSystemMetrics(SM_CYMENU);

          TBWidth  = GetSystemMetrics(
                     SM_CXICON)*2+2;
          TBHeight = (GetSystemMetrics(SM_CYICON)
                     * NUMBEROFTOOLS / 2) +
                  GetSystemMetrics(SM_CYCAPTION)+2;
          break;
       }

       case TB_TOP :
       {
          TBLeft = 0;
          TBTop = 0;
          TBWidth  = GetSystemMetrics(SM_CXICON)
                     * NUMBEROFTOOLS + 2;
          TBHeight = GetSystemMetrics(
                     SM_CYICON)+2;
          break;
       }

       case TB_LEFT :
       {
          TBLeft = 0;
          TBTop = 0;
          TBHeight  = GetSystemMetrics(SM_CXICON)
                      * NUMBEROFTOOLS+2;
          TBWidth =   GetSystemMetrics(
                      SM_CYICON)+2;
          break;
       }
     }
  }

case WM_PAINT :
{
   HDC         PaintDC;
   RECT        rect;
   PAINTSTRUCT ps;
```

continues

Listing 1.18. continued

```
        PaintDC = BeginPaint(hMainWnd, &ps);

    GetClientRect(hMainWnd, &rect);

        DrawText(PaintDC, "Toolbar Example",
                 -1, &rect, DT_SINGLELINE | DT_CENTER
                 | DT_VCENTER);

        EndPaint(hMainWnd, &ps);
        return 0;
    }

    case WM_SIZE :
    {
        if (TBStatus == TB_FLOAT)
            MoveWindow(hTBWnd, LOWORD(lParam) -
                       TBWidth - 10, TBTop, TBWidth,
                       TBHeight, TRUE);
        else
            MoveWindow(hTBWnd, TBLeft, TBTop, TBWidth,
TBHeight, TRUE);

        return 0;

    }


    case WM_COMMAND :
    {
        return HANDLE_WM_COMMAND(hWnd, wParam,
                                 lParam,
                                 WM_CommandHandler);
    }

    case WM_DESTROY :
    {
        PostQuitMessage(0);
        return 0;
    }
    }

    // Was "Help" button pressed inside choose color
       dialog?
    if (message == HelpMsg)
    {
        MessageBox(hMainWnd, "Select a Color to Use For
                   Painting",
```

```
                    "Choose Color Dialog Box Help",
                    MB_OK ¦ MB_ICONINFORMATION);
        return 0;
    }

    return DefWindowProc (hWnd, message, wParam,
                          lParam);
}


/*********************************************/
#pragma argsused
LRESULT CALLBACK _export TBWndProc(HWND hWnd, UINT
                                   message,
                                   WPARAM wParam,
                                   LPARAM lParam)
{
    switch (message)
    {
        case WM_PAINT :
        {
            PAINTSTRUCT ps;

            HDC    PaintDC;
            int    x;
            HICON  hIcon;

            PaintDC = BeginPaint(hWnd, &ps);

            switch(TBStatus)
            {
                case TB_FLOAT :
                {
                    // Paint left side
                    for (x=0; x<NUMBEROFTOOLS/2; x++)
                    {
                        hIcon = LoadIcon(ghInstance,
                                MAKEINTRESOURCE(x+1));
                        DrawIcon(PaintDC, 0,
                                GetSystemMetrics(SM_CXICON)
                                * x, hIcon);

                    }
                    // Paint right side
                    for (x=0; x<NUMBEROFTOOLS/2; x++)
                    {
                        hIcon = LoadIcon(ghInstance,
                                MAKEINTRESOURCE(x+6));
```

continues

Listing 1.18. continued

```
                DrawIcon(PaintDC,
                        GetSystemMetrics(SM_CYICON),
                        GetSystemMetrics(SM_CXICON)
                        * x, hIcon);

            }

            break;
        }

        case TB_LEFT :
        {
            for (x=0; x<NUMBEROFTOOLS; x++)
            {
                hIcon = LoadIcon(ghInstance,
                        MAKEINTRESOURCE(x+1));
                DrawIcon(PaintDC, 0,
                        GetSystemMetrics(SM_CXICON)
                        * x, hIcon);
            }
            break;
        }

        case TB_TOP :
        {
            for (x=0; x<NUMBEROFTOOLS; x++)
            {
                hIcon = LoadIcon(ghInstance,
                        MAKEINTRESOURCE(x+1));
                DrawIcon(PaintDC,
                        GetSystemMetrics(SM_CXICON)
                        * x, 0, hIcon);
            }
            break;
        }
    }

    EndPaint(hWnd, &ps);
    return 0;
}

case WM_LBUTTONDOWN :
{
    int    xPos, yPos;
    HPEN   hWhitePen, hDarkGrayPen;
    HDC    hDC;
```

I

```
// We force mouse messages to come to us.
//    The reason for this is in case the user
//    presses the mouse button over a tool,
//    we display it as pressed, then the user
//    drags the mouse outside of the window.
//    It never would get the button up error
//    message, and would not be repainted
//    correctly.
SetCapture(hTBWnd);

xPos = LOWORD(lParam);      // horizontal
                           // position of
                           // cursor
yPos = HIWORD(lParam);      // vertical
                           // position of
                           // cursor
ToolNumber = 0;

hDC = GetDC(hWnd);
hWhitePen = CreatePen(PS_SOLID, 2, RGB(255,
                    255, 255));
hDarkGrayPen = CreatePen(PS_SOLID, 2,
                    RGB(128, 128, 128));
// Select dark gray pen initially
SelectPen(hDC, hDarkGrayPen);

switch(TBStatus)
{
   case TB_TOP :
   {
      // Figure out which tool was pressed
      while (xPos>0)
      {
         xPos = xPos - GetSystemMetrics(
                 SM_CXICON);
         ToolNumber++;
      }
      // Move to upper Right Corner of tool
      MoveTo(hDC, GetSystemMetrics(
       SM_CXICON)*ToolNumber-1, 1);
      // Draw top line of tool
      LineTo(hDC, (GetSystemMetrics(
       SM_CXICON)*ToolNumber) -
             GetSystemMetrics(SM_CXICON), 1);
      // Draw left side of tool
      LineTo(hDC, (GetSystemMetrics(
       SM_CXICON)*ToolNumber) -
             GetSystemMetrics(SM_CXICON),
```

continues

Listing 1.18. continued

```
                GetSystemMetrics(SM_CYICON)-1);
        // Select white pen
        SelectPen(hDC, hWhitePen);
        // Draw bottom side of tool
        LineTo(hDC,
         GetSystemMetrics(SM_CXICON)*ToolNumber,
                GetSystemMetrics(SM_CYICON)-1);
        // Draw right side of tool in white
        LineTo(hDC,
         GetSystemMetrics(SM_CXICON)*ToolNumber,
         1);

        break;
    }

    case TB_LEFT :
    {
        while (yPos>0)
        {
           yPos = yPos -
         GetSystemMetrics(SM_CYICON);
           ToolNumber++;
        }
        // Move to upper right corner of tool
        MoveTo(hDC,
         GetSystemMetrics(SM_CXICON),
          GetSystemMetrics(SM_CYICON)*(ToolNumber-
                                  1)+1);
        // Draw top line
        LineTo(hDC, 1,
         GetSystemMetrics(SM_CYICON)*(ToolNumber-
                                 1));
        // Draw left line
        LineTo(hDC, 1,
          GetSystemMetrics(SM_CYICON)*ToolNumber-
          1);

        // Draw bottom line
        SelectPen(hDC, hWhitePen);
        LineTo(hDC,
         GetSystemMetrics(SM_CXICON)-1,
         GetSystemMetrics(SM_CYICON)*ToolNumber-
          1);
        // Draw right line
        LineTo(hDC,
         GetSystemMetrics(SM_CXICON)-1,
         GetSystemMetrics(SM_CYICON)*(ToolNumber-
                                  1));
```

```
      break;
}

case TB_FLOAT :
{
   // First decide which button was
      pressed
   if (xPos < GetSystemMetrics(SM_CXICON))
   {
      while (yPos>0)
      {
         yPos = yPos -
                 GetSystemMetrics(
                 SM_CYICON);
         ToolNumber++;
      }
   }
   else
   {
      ToolNumber = 5;
      while (yPos>0)
      {
         yPos = yPos -
                 GetSystemMetrics(
                 SM_CYICON);
         ToolNumber++;
      }
   }

   // Now, make the button appear pressed
   //

   // For tools 1 through 5
   if (ToolNumber<=5)
   {
      // Move to upper right corner of
         tool
      MoveTo(hDC,
       GetSystemMetrics(SM_CXICON),
       GetSystemMetrics(SM_CYICON)*(ToolNumber-
                                 1)+1);
      // Draw top line
      LineTo(hDC, 1,
      GetSystemMetrics(SM_CYICON)*(ToolNumber-
                                1));
      // Draw left line
      LineTo(hDC, 1,
      GetSystemMetrics(SM_CYICON)*ToolNumber-
         1);
```

continues

Listing 1.18. continued

```
// Draw bottom line
SelectPen(hDC, hWhitePen);
LineTo(hDC,
 GetSystemMetrics(SM_CXICON)-1,
GetSystemMetrics(SM_CYICON)*ToolNumber-
    1);
// Draw right line
LineTo(hDC,
 GetSystemMetrics(SM_CXICON)-1,
GetSystemMetrics(SM_CYICON)*(ToolNumber-
                            1));


}
else                    // For tools 6
                           through 10
{

   // Move to upper right corner of
       tool
   MoveTo(hDC,
         GetSystemMetrics(SM_CXICON)*2,
           GetSystemMetrics(SM_CYICON)*
              (ToolNumber-5-1)+1);
   // Draw top line
   LineTo(hDC,
         GetSystemMetrics(SM_CXICON),
   GetSystemMetrics(SM_CYICON)*(ToolNumber-
                            1-5)+1);
   // Draw left line
   LineTo(hDC,
    GetSystemMetrics(SM_CXICON),
   (GetSystemMetrics(SM_CYICON)*(ToolNumber-
                            5)-1));

   // Draw bottom line
   SelectPen(hDC, hWhitePen);
   LineTo(hDC,
         GetSystemMetrics(
           SM_CXICON)*2-1,
   (GetSystemMetrics(SM_CYICON)*(ToolNumber-
                            5)-1));

   // Draw right line
   LineTo(hDC,
         GetSystemMetrics(
           SM_CXICON)*2-1,
   GetSystemMetrics(SM_CYICON)*(ToolNumber-
                            5-1));
```

I

```
            }

        }

    }
    // Clean up
    SelectPen(hDC, GetStockPen(WHITE_PEN));
    DeletePen(hWhitePen);
    DeletePen(hDarkGrayPen);
    ReleaseDC(hWnd, hDC);

    return 0;

}

case WM_LBUTTONUP :
{
    HBRUSH hWhiteBrush, hDarkBrush;
    HDC    hDC;
    HICON  hIcon;

    ReleaseCapture();

    hDC = GetDC(hWnd);
    hIcon = LoadIcon(ghInstance,
                     MAKEINTRESOURCE(ToolNumber));


    switch(TBStatus)
    {
        case TB_TOP :
        {
            DrawIcon(hDC,
              GetSystemMetrics(SM_CXICON)*(ToolNumber-
                                                1),
                     0, hIcon);
            break;
        }

        case TB_LEFT :
        {
            DrawIcon(hDC, 0,
                     GetSystemMetrics(SM_CXICON)*
                     (ToolNumber-1), hIcon);
            break;
        }
```

continues

Listing 1.18. continued

```
case TB_FLOAT :
{
   if (ToolNumber<=5)   // Left side of
                           floating
                           toolbar
      DrawIcon(hDC, 0,
      GetSystemMetrics(SM_CYICON)*(ToolNumber-
                             1),
                           hIcon);
      else                 // Right side of
                           floating
                           toolbar
      DrawIcon(hDC,
              GetSystemMetrics(SM_CXICON),
      GetSystemMetrics(SM_CYICON)*(ToolNumber-
                          1-5),
              hIcon);
      break;
   }
}

ReleaseDC(hWnd, hDC);


// If user clicked over first toolbar items,
//   process them next.
switch (ToolNumber)
{
   case TOOL_OPEN :
   {
      SendMessage(hMainWnd, WM_COMMAND,
               IDM_OPEN, 0L);
      break;
   }

   case TOOL_SAVE :
   {
      SendMessage(hMainWnd, WM_COMMAND,
               IDM_SAVE, 0L);
      break;
   }

   case TOOL_COLOR :
   {
      SendMessage(hMainWnd, WM_COMMAND,
               IDM_COLOR, 0L);
      break;
```

```
        }
    }

    return 0;

}

case WM_NCPAINT :
{
    RECT    rects, rectc;  // Wnd rect in screen &
                                   client coordinates
    HDC     hDC;
    HBRUSH  hBrush;

    // When the toolbar is a floating toolbar, we
        must paint the caption ourselves.
        Otherwise, we need to paint the
        background color ourselves.
    GetWindowRect(hWnd, &rects);
    hDC = GetWindowDC(hWnd);

    rectc.left = 0;
    rectc.top = 0;
    rectc.right = rects.right - rects.left;
    rectc.bottom = rects.bottom - rects.top;


    hBrush = GetStockBrush(BLACK_BRUSH);
    FillRect(hDC, &rectc, hBrush);

    if(TBStatus == TB_FLOAT)
    {
        // Get the size of the toolbar
        rectc.bottom = GetSystemMetrics(
                    SM_CYCAPTION);

        // Get a handle to the color of the active
            border
        hBrush = CreateSolidBrush(
                GetSysColor(COLOR_ACTIVECAPTION));

        // Display caption bar
        FillRect(hDC, &rectc, hBrush);

        // Cleanup
        DeleteBrush(hBrush);
    }
```

continues

Listing 1.18. continued

```
        ReleaseDC(hWnd, hDC);
        InvalidateRect(
                       hTBWnd, NULL, TRUE);
                       // Repaint Window

        return 0;
    }

    case WM_DESTROY :
    {
        PostQuitMessage(0);
        return 0;
    }
}
    return DefWindowProc (hWnd, message, wParam,
lParam);

}
```

Listing 1.19. TOOLBAR.RC resource script.

```
/*
 * TOOLBAR.RC resource script
 *
 */

#include "toolbar.h"

MAINICON ICON "toolbar.ico"

1  ICON "open.ico"
2  ICON "save.ico"
3  ICON "color.ico"
4  ICON "point.ico"
5  ICON "line.ico"
6  ICON "circle.ico"
7  ICON "fillcir.ico"
8  ICON "rect.ico"
9  ICON "fillrec.ico"
10 ICON "text.ico"


MAINMENU MENU
```

```
BEGIN
     POPUP "&File"
     BEGIN
          MENUITEM "Open...", IDM_OPEN
          MENUITEM "&Save As...", IDM_SAVE
          MENUITEM SEPARATOR
          MENUITEM "E&xit", IDM_EXIT
     END

     POPUP "&Options"
     BEGIN
          MENUITEM "Current &Color", IDM_COLOR
          MENUITEM SEPARATOR
          MENUITEM "&Floating Toolbar", IDM_FLOAT,
            CHECKED
          MENUITEM "Toolbar at &Top", IDM_ONTOP
          MENUITEM "Toolbar on &Left", IDM_ONLEFT
     END

     POPUP "&Help"
     BEGIN
          MENUITEM "&About", IDM_ABOUT
     END

END
```

Listing 1.20. TOOLBAR.H header file.

```
/*
 * TOOLBAR.H header file
 *
 */

#define NUMBEROFTOOLS 10

#define IDM_OPEN 100
#define IDM_SAVE 110
#define IDM_EXIT 120

#define IDM_COLOR  200
#define IDM_FLOAT  210
#define IDM_ONTOP  220
#define IDM_ONLEFT 230
```

continues

Listing 1.20. continued

```c
#define IDM_ABOUT 300

/*
 * The following defines are used only inside the .C
 *    source code module.
 *
 */

#define TOOL_OPEN         1
#define TOOL_SAVE         2
#define TOOL_COLOR        3
#define TOOL_POINT        4
#define TOOL_LINE         5
#define TOOL_RECT         6
#define TOOL_FILLEDRECT   7
#define TOOL_CIRCLE       8
#define TOOL_FILLEDCIRCLE 9
#define TOOL_TEXT        10

#define TB_LEFT  0
#define TB_TOP   1
#define TB_FLOAT 2
```

Listing 1.21. TOOLBAR.DEF module definition file.

```
;
; TOOLBAR.DEF module definition file
;

DESCRIPTION    'Toolbar Example'
NAME           TOOLBAR
EXETYPE        WINDOWS
STUB           'WINSTUB.EXE'
HEAPSIZE       1024
STACKSIZE      8192
CODE           PRELOAD MOVEABLE DISCARDABLE
DATA           PRELOAD MOVEABLE MULTIPLE
```

I

In This Chapter

■ How to make programs have the "look of chiseled steel," which is part of the Borland Windows Custom Controls (BWCC).

■ What is required to display bitmap graphical images inside a dialog box.

■ How to customize the common dialogs that come as part of Windows 3.1.

■ How to create an application with a dialog box as the main window.

■ How to center a dialog box inside the main window of a program.

■ How to create short animation sequences inside a dialog box.

■ How to add context-sensitive help to a dialog box.

Dialog Boxes

Using the Borland Windows Custom Controls

How do I use the cool-looking Borland Windows Custom Controls (BWCC)?

DESCRIPTION

The Borland Windows Custom Controls are the hot-looking dialog boxes Borland uses in all its Windows applications. They contain what is referred to as the "look of chiseled steel." The same look is used in Quattro Pro for Windows, Paradox for Windows, Borland C++ (BCW), and Resource Workshop (see Figure 2.1). Lately, the look has been popping up in other third party applications too, such as Fastback for Windows.

Best of all, with the purchase of Borland C++ or Turbo C++ for Windows, Borland provides the programmer with everything needed to create and use dialog boxes based on BWCC.

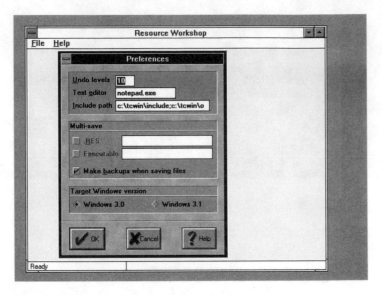

Figure 2.1. *Borland Windows Custom Controls used in Resource Workshop.*

ANSWER

Besides the checkered gray background look of the Borland Windows Custom Controls, BWCC also provides a new style of checkboxes, radio buttons, static bitmaps, and buttons. In addition to containing text, the Borland buttons can also contain graphical images.

Using BWCC is easy. When you are designing your bitmap in Resource Workshop, the first thing you want to do is double-click the dialog box and display the Window Style dialog (see Figure 2.2). Give the dialog box the class name of BORDLG (either uppercase or lowercase) and press Enter. This will instantly give your dialog the gray background look.

To use the controls available with BWCC, choose the tools from the far right side of the dialog box editor tools palette (see Figure 2.3). The controls you can select include the new checkboxes, new radio buttons, shade boxes, bumps, dips, and Borland buttons.

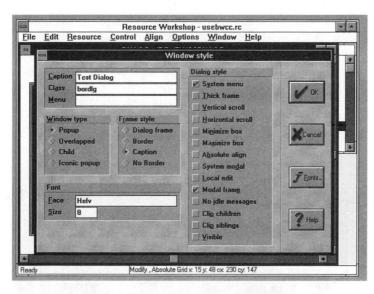

Figure 2.2. *Window-style dialog box in Resource Workshop.*

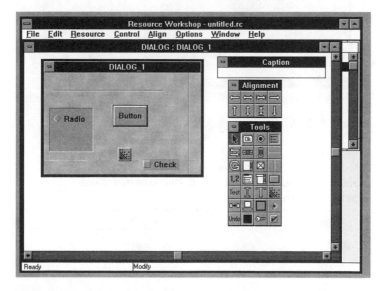

Figure 2.3. *Tools palette in Resource Workshop.*

There are eight predefined Borland buttons with predefined images, such as OK, Cancel, and Help. To use one of these predefined buttons, double-click on the button and display the Borland button-style dialog box (see Figure 2.4). For the control id edit box, enter one of the identifiers found in Table 2.1. When you press Enter, the button will have the specified image inside it. BWCC takes care of all processing and displaying of the images inside the button automatically.

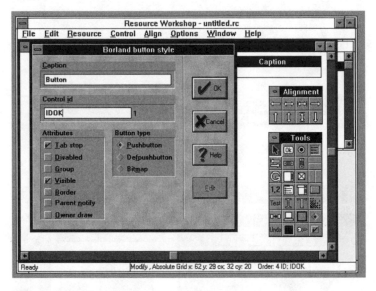

Figure 2.4. *Borland button style dialog box.*

Table 2.1. Identifiers used for predefined Borland bitmaps.

Identifier	Description
IDOK	OK button
IDCANCEL	Cancel button
IDABORT	Abort button
IDRETRY	Retry button
IDIGNORE	Ignore button

Identifier	Description
IDYES	Yes button
IDNO	No button
IDHELP	Help button

II

Custom bitmaps can also be used inside a button. If you choose to use this feature, you will need a minimum of two bitmap images. One is the bitmap in the pressed state, and the other is the bitmap in the unpressed state. You can create them using the Resource Workshop bitmap editor. Make sure you make the images the same size so the buttons come out looking correct. The default buttons that come with BWCC are 32 pixels wide by 20 pixels high.

Now, here is where things get a little tricky. You need to name your bitmap images using a special convention. Start by giving the button an integer identifier less than 1000. After that, you need to give each bitmap an integer identifier. The first bitmap, which is the one for the button in the unpressed state, should be given an identifier of the button ID plus 1000. The bitmap that is pressed should be given an identifier of the button identifier plus 3000. Finally, you can also create a bitmap image for the button when it is in the focused state. If you choose to do this, you need to give it an identifier of 5000 plus your button identifier value. These values are for VGA only. Table 2.2 shows the values for EGA and VGA systems and their associated values.

Table 2.2. Bitmap naming convention.

Bitmap Identifier	Description
ID + 1000	Unpressed bitmap image for VGA
ID + 3000	Pressed bitmap image for EGA
ID + 5000	Focused bitmap image for VGA
ID + 2000	Unpressed bitmap image for EGA
ID + 4000	Pressed bitmap image for VGA
ID + 6000	Focused bitmap image for EGA

How about an example? Suppose we give the button an identifier of 25. Then, we need to give the bitmap with the unpressed image an identifier of 1025. The bitmap with the pressed button image is given a value of 3025. The bitmap with the focused bitmap image is given a value of 5025. These are for a VGA system. For EGA you would use the bitmap identifiers 2025, 4025, and 6025.

> **WARNING** If your application has the chance of being run on an EGA system, make sure you include images for EGA systems. If you don't and the program is run on an EGA system, the buttons will appear white with nothing displayed on them. This usually confuses the user, and does not look very good on the side of the developer.

Static bitmap images can be included in your dialog boxes even more easily than buttons containing multiple images. Basically, a static bitmap image is a Borland button with the button type set to bitmap. You still need to give the static bitmap an identifier less than 1000 and then give the bitmap an identifier of 1000 plus the button identifier.

All the functionality for BWCC is inside a dynamic link library. To run your program correctly, you need to link with the BWCC.LIB import library. You probably will need to include the BWCC.H header file within your source code also.

COMMENTS

You must make sure that you ship BWCC.DLL with your application. If you don't ship BWCC.DLL with your application, your dialog boxes won't be displayed.

> **NOTE** If your program uses the MessageBox routine to flash display a short message, the white background may appear strange to the user. Therefore, BWCC provides another routine, BWCCMessageBox, which mimics the regular

MessageBox routine, except it provides the gray background look. If you use the BWCC dialog boxes, you will also want to use the BWCCMessageBox routine to make your application's appearance consistent.

SEE ALSO

C:\BORLANDC\DOC\BWCCAPI.RW Document File

II

EXAMPLE CODE

The example program shows the new checkboxes, the radio buttons, an example of a bitmap, and all the predefined buttons available with BWCC (see Figure 2.5). You need the following files to compile the program: USEBWCC.C (in Listing 2.1), USEBWCC.RC (in Listing 2.2), USEBWCC.DEF (in Listing 2.3), BWCC.LIB (in C:\BORLANDC\LIB), PRESSED.BMP, UNPRESS.BMP, and USEBWCC.BMP.

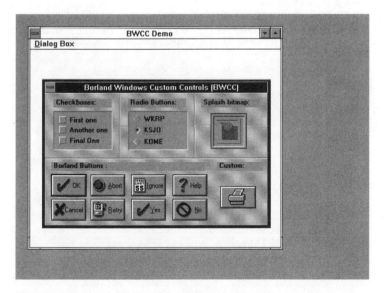

Figure 2.5. *Example program using the Borland Windows Custom Controls.*

Listing 2.1. USEBWCC.C source code.

```
// USEBWCC.C - Example showing how to use the
//             Borland Windows Custom Controls
//             (BWCC).
//
// Your Borland C++ Consultant by Paul J. Perry
//

#define STRICT

#include <windowsx.h>
#include <bwcc.h>
#include <stdlib.h>

// Global Variables
HINSTANCE ghInstance;

// Function Prototypes
LRESULT CALLBACK _export MainWndProc(HWND, UINT,
                          WPARAM, LPARAM);
BOOL CALLBACK _export MainDlgProc(HWND, UINT, WPARAM,
                      LPARAM);
void WM_Command_Dlg_Handler(HWND, int, HWND, UINT);

/*********************************************/
#pragma argsused
int PASCAL WinMain(HINSTANCE hInstance, HINSTANCE
           hPrevInstance,
                LPSTR lpCmdParam, int nCmdShow)
{
    char        ProgName[] = "BWCC Demo";
    HWND        hWnd;
    MSG         msg;


    if (!hPrevInstance)
    {
        WNDCLASS    wndclass;

        wndclass.lpszClassName = ProgName;
        wndclass.lpfnWndProc   = (WNDPROC) MainWndProc;
        wndclass.cbClsExtra    = 0;
        wndclass.cbWndExtra    = 0;
        wndclass.hInstance     = hInstance;
        wndclass.hIcon         = LoadIcon(NULL,
                                 IDI_APPLICATION);
        wndclass.hCursor       = LoadCursor(NULL,
                                 IDC_ARROW);
```

```
      wndclass.hbrBackground = GetStockObject(
                               WHITE_BRUSH);
      wndclass.lpszMenuName  = "MAINMENU";
      wndclass.style         = CS_VREDRAW |
                               CS_HREDRAW;

      if (!RegisterClass(&wndclass))
          exit(1);
   }

   ghInstance = hInstance;

   hWnd = CreateWindow(ProgName, ProgName,
                       WS_OVERLAPPEDWINDOW,
                       CW_USEDEFAULT, CW_USEDEFAULT,
                       CW_USEDEFAULT, CW_USEDEFAULT,
                       NULL, NULL, hInstance, NULL);

   ShowWindow(hWnd, nCmdShow);
   UpdateWindow(hWnd);

   while (GetMessage(&msg, NULL, 0, 0))
   {
      TranslateMessage(&msg);
      DispatchMessage(&msg);
   }
   return msg.wParam;
}

/********************************************/
BOOL CALLBACK _export MainDlgProc(HWND hDlg, UINT
                       message, WPARAM wParam, LPARAM
                       lParam)
{
   switch(message)
   {
      case WM_INITDIALOG :
      {
         return TRUE;
      }

      case WM_COMMAND :
      {
         return (BOOL)HANDLE_WM_COMMAND(hDlg, wParam,
                      lParam, WM_Command_Dlg_Handler);
      }

   }
```

continues

Listing 2.1. continued

```c
    return FALSE;

}


/*********************************************/
#pragma argsused
void WM_Command_Dlg_Handler(HWND hDlg, int id,
                            HWND hwndCtl, UINT
                            codeNotify)
{
   switch(id)
   {
      case IDOK :
      case IDCANCEL :
      {
         EndDialog(hDlg, 0);
         break;
      }

   }
}

/*********************************************/
LRESULT CALLBACK _export MainWndProc(HWND hWnd, UINT
                          message, WPARAM wParam,
                          LPARAM lParam)
{
   switch (message)
   {
      case WM_PAINT :
      {
         HDC        PaintDC;
         RECT       rect;
         PAINTSTRUCT ps;

         PaintDC = BeginPaint(hWnd, &ps);
         GetClientRect(hWnd, &rect);

         DrawText(PaintDC, "Select the Dialog",
                  -1, &rect, DT_SINGLELINE | DT_CENTER
                  | DT_VCENTER);

         EndPaint(hWnd, &ps);
         return 0;
```

```
        }

        case WM_COMMAND :
        {
            // Usually we would use a message cracker to
            //    sort out which menu item was selected.
            //    However, because there is only one menu
            //    item, we won't worry about message
            //    crackers.
            DLGPROC DlgProc;

            DlgProc = (DLGPROC)MakeProcInstance(
                        (FARPROC)MainDlgProc,
                        ghInstance);
            DialogBox(ghInstance, "IDD_BWCCDIALOG", hWnd,
DlgProc);
            FreeProcInstance((FARPROC)DlgProc);
            return 0;
        }

        case WM_DESTROY :
        {
            PostQuitMessage(0);
            return 0;
        }
    }
    return DefWindowProc (hWnd, message, wParam,
                          lParam);
}
```

Listing 2.2. USEBWCC.RC resource script.

```
/*
 * USEBWCC.RC resource script
 *
 */

// Static button image
1099 BITMAP "usebwcc.bmp"

// Custom bitmap button
1088 BITMAP "unpress.bmp"
3088 BITMAP "pressed.bmp"
```

continues

Listing 2.2. continued

```
IDD_BWCCDIALOG DIALOG 15, 48, 230, 147
STYLE DS_MODALFRAME | WS_POPUP | WS_CAPTION |
WS_SYSMENU
CLASS "bordlg"
CAPTION "Borland Windows Custom Controls (BWCC)"
FONT 8, "Helv"
BEGIN
    CONTROL "First one", 1000, "BorCheck",
BS_AUTOCHECKBOX | WS_CHILD | WS_VISIBLE | WS_TABSTOP,
15, 25, 53, 10
    CONTROL "Another one", 1001, "BorCheck",
BS_AUTOCHECKBOX | WS_CHILD | WS_VISIBLE | WS_TABSTOP,
15, 36, 52, 10
    CONTROL "Final One", 1002, "BorCheck",
BS_AUTOCHECKBOX | WS_CHILD | WS_VISIBLE | WS_TABSTOP,
15, 48, 48, 10
    CONTROL "WKRP", 1004, "BorRadio",
BS_AUTORADIOBUTTON | WS_CHILD | WS_VISIBLE |
WS_TABSTOP, 92, 24, 39, 10
    CONTROL "KSJO", 1005, "BorRadio", 9 | WS_CHILD |
WS_VISIBLE, 92, 36, 32, 10
    CONTROL "KOME", 1006, "BorRadio", 9 | WS_CHILD |
WS_VISIBLE, 92, 49, 32, 10
    CONTROL "Button", IDOK, "BorBtn", BS_PUSHBUTTON |
WS_CHILD | WS_VISIBLE | WS_TABSTOP, 6, 90, 32, 20
    CONTROL "", IDCANCEL, "BorBtn", BS_PUSHBUTTON |
WS_CHILD | WS_VISIBLE | WS_TABSTOP, 6, 117, 32, 20
    CONTROL "Button", IDABORT, "BorBtn",
BS_PUSHBUTTON | WS_CHILD | WS_VISIBLE | WS_TABSTOP,
47, 90, 32, 20
    CONTROL "Button", IDRETRY, "BorBtn",
BS_PUSHBUTTON | WS_CHILD | WS_VISIBLE | WS_TABSTOP,
47, 117, 32, 20
    CONTROL "Button", IDIGNORE, "BorBtn",
BS_PUSHBUTTON | WS_CHILD | WS_VISIBLE | WS_TABSTOP,
89, 90, 32, 20
    CONTROL "Button", IDYES, "BorBtn", BS_PUSHBUTTON
| WS_CHILD | WS_VISIBLE | WS_TABSTOP, 89, 117, 32, 20
    CONTROL "", IDHELP, "BorBtn", BS_PUSHBUTTON |
WS_CHILD | WS_VISIBLE | WS_TABSTOP, 132, 90, 32, 20
    CONTROL "Button", IDNO, "BorBtn", BS_PUSHBUTTON |
WS_CHILD | WS_VISIBLE | WS_TABSTOP, 132, 117, 32, 20
    CONTROL "Button", 88, "BorBtn", BS_PUSHBUTTON |
WS_CHILD | WS_VISIBLE | WS_TABSTOP, 181, 103, 38, 28
    LTEXT " Borland Buttons :", -1, 7, 76, 160, 10,
WS_CHILD | WS_VISIBLE | WS_GROUP
```

```
      LTEXT " Custom:", -1, 178, 76, 46, 10, WS_CHILD ¦
WS_VISIBLE ¦ WS_GROUP
      LTEXT " Splash bitmap:", -1, 162, 6, 60, 10,
WS_CHILD ¦ WS_VISIBLE ¦ WS_GROUP
      LTEXT " Radio Buttons:", -1, 86, 6, 60, 10,
WS_CHILD ¦ WS_VISIBLE ¦ WS_GROUP
      LTEXT " Checkboxes:", -1, 9, 6, 60, 10, WS_CHILD
¦ WS_VISIBLE ¦ WS_GROUP
      CONTROL "", 1009, "BorShade", 32769 ¦ WS_CHILD ¦
WS_VISIBLE, 9, 20, 61, 43
      CONTROL "", 1009, "BorShade", 32769 ¦ WS_CHILD ¦
WS_VISIBLE, 87, 20, 61, 43
      CONTROL "Button", 99, "BorBtn", BBS_BITMAP ¦
WS_CHILD ¦ WS_VISIBLE, 172, 23, 38, 42
      CONTROL "", 999, "BorShade", 2 ¦ WS_CHILD ¦
WS_VISIBLE, -1, 72, 231, 1
      CONTROL "", 1008, "BorShade", 3 ¦ WS_CHILD ¦
WS_VISIBLE, 77, 1, 1, 71
      CONTROL "", 1008, "BorShade", 3 ¦ WS_CHILD ¦
WS_VISIBLE, 154, 1, 1, 71
END


MAINMENU MENU
BEGIN
      POPUP "&Dialog Box"
      BEGIN
            MENUITEM "&BWCC", 1
      END

END
```

Listing 2.3. USEBWCC.DEF module definition file.

```
;
; USEBWCC.DEF module definition file
;

DESCRIPTION    'BWCC Demo'
NAME           USEBWCC
EXETYPE        WINDOWS
STUB           'WINSTUB.EXE'
HEAPSIZE       1024
STACKSIZE      8192
CODE           PRELOAD MOVEABLE DISCARDABLE
DATA           PRELOAD MOVEABLE MULTIPLE
```

Displaying Bitmaps Inside a Dialog Box

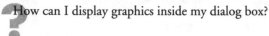

How can I display graphics inside my dialog box?

DESCRIPTION

Although you can easily use an icon to display a graphical image inside a dialog box, the 32 pixel by 32 pixel size of an icon is somewhat limited. It would be nice to include larger images that were created with the bitmap editor inside Resource Workshop.

ANSWER

A dialog box receives `WM_PAINT` messages, just like any other window. Therefore, you can trap the `WM_PAINT` message and display anything you like.

Probably the easiest way to include a bitmap image inside your application is to use the Borland Windows Custom Controls (see the earlier part of this chapter). However, if you don't want to rely on and ship BWCC.DLL with your application, displaying your own bitmap is relatively easy.

When designing your dialog box, use a group box to specify the placement of the bitmap inside the dialog box. To make it easier to create your dialog box, make the group box about the same size as the bitmap. Before you save the dialog box, make sure you give the group box the invisible attribute.

Inside your dialog box procedure, trap the `WM_PAINT` message. Use `BeginPaint` to get a handle to the display context. Once you have the handle to the display context, you can find the location of the group box inside the dialog box by using the `GetDlgItem` function. Then, you can get the `GetWindowRect` function in conjunction with `GetClientRect` to get the coordinates of the group box.

Now that you have the upper-left corner of the group box, you can use the `BitBlt` function to display the bitmap image inside the dialog box (see Chapter 4, "Graphics," for information on displaying graphics). Finally, remember to use `EndPaint` before you return control to Windows.

COMMENTS

Fortunately, Borland included a static bitmap control within BWCC. Although regular dialog boxes allow you to trap WM_PAINT messages, the Borland windows custom controls never pass WM_PAINT on to your application. Borland wanted to set a consistent standard for the way the background looks inside a BWCC dialog box. In other words, if you try to use this technique with the Borland Windows Custom Controls, it will not work.

SEE ALSO

BitBlt API Function
CreateCompatibleDC API Function
GetClientRect API Function
GetDlgItem API Function
SelectObject API Function
SelectBitmap Macro Found in WINDOWSX.H

II

EXAMPLE CODE

The sample program displays two controls inside the dialog box (see Figure 2.6). One is a bitmap image, and the other is an OK button. You can use the logic in your own program by cutting and pasting the DisplayBitmapControl and DisplayBitmap functions. If you have both of these functions in your code, you can display the bitmap with the following code:

```
hBitmap = LoadBitmap(ghInstance, "DIALOGBMP");
DisplayBitmapControl(PaintDC, hDlg, hBitmap,
                     IDD_BITMAP);
DeleteBitmap(hBitmap);
```

This code simply gets a handle to the bitmap, passes that handle on to the DisplayBitmapControl function, and then deletes the handle to the bitmap. It is important to free system resources by deleting bitmaps, or your program will cause memory problems with the rest of the system.

The function DisplayBitmapControl finds the location of the static control inside the dialog box and then calls the DisplayBitmap function to display the bitmap. DisplayBitmap uses a five-step process for displaying a bitmap:

1. The routine needs to create a compatible display context.

2. It then selects the bitmap into the compatible DC.

3. The `BitBlt` (bit-block-transfer) API function is used to copy the image from the compatible DC to the screen DC.

4. Now that the image has been displayed, we need to select the old image back into the compatible DC.

5. Now we must delete the compatible DC and then delete the bitmap (more about these steps in Chapter 4, "Graphics").

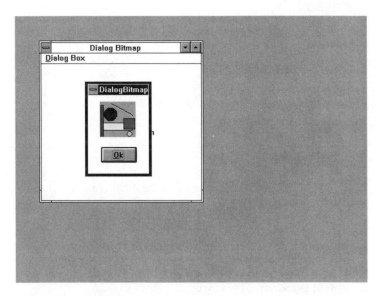

Figure 2.6. *DLGBMP.EXE example program.*

Listing 2.4 contains the source code; Listing 2.5 contains the resource script; and Listing 2.6 contains the module definition file. To compile the program, you also will need the file DLGBMP.BMP.

Listing 2.4. DLGBMP.C source code.

```
// DLGBMP.C - Display a bitmap inside a regular
//            Windows dialog box.
//
```

```
// Your Borland C++ Consultant by Paul J. Perry
//

#define STRICT
// Usually the following two lines
//   would go in a header file
#define IDM_DIALOG 100
#define IDD_BITMAP 101

#include <windowsx.h>
#include <stdlib.h>

// Function Prototypes
LRESULT CALLBACK _export MainWndProc(HWND, UINT,
                         WPARAM, LPARAM);
BOOL CALLBACK _export MainDlgProc(HWND, UINT, WPARAM,
                       LPARAM);
void WM_Command_Dlg_Handler(HWND, int, HWND, UINT);
BOOL DisplayBitmapControl(HDC, HWND, HBITMAP, int);
BOOL DisplayBitmap(HDC, HBITMAP, int, int, DWORD);


// Global Variables
HINSTANCE ghInstance;

/*********************************************/
#pragma argsused
int PASCAL WinMain(HINSTANCE hInstance, HINSTANCE
           hPrevInstance, LPSTR lpCmdParam,
           int nCmdShow)
{
   char       ProgName[] = "Dialog Bitmap";
   HWND       hWnd;
   MSG        msg;


   if (!hPrevInstance)
   {
      WNDCLASS    wndclass;

      wndclass.lpszClassName = ProgName;
      wndclass.lpfnWndProc   = (WNDPROC) MainWndProc;
      wndclass.cbClsExtra    = 0;
      wndclass.cbWndExtra    = 0;
      wndclass.hInstance     = hInstance;
      wndclass.hIcon         = LoadIcon(NULL,
                               IDI_APPLICATION);
      wndclass.hCursor       = LoadCursor(NULL,
                               IDC_ARROW);
```

II

continues

Listing 2.4. continued

```
    wndclass.hbrBackground = GetStockObject(
                             WHITE_BRUSH);
    wndclass.lpszMenuName = "MAINMENU";
    wndclass.style        = CS_VREDRAW ¦
                            CS_HREDRAW;

    if (!RegisterClass(&wndclass))
        exit(1);
}

ghInstance = hInstance;

hWnd = CreateWindow(ProgName, ProgName,
                    WS_OVERLAPPEDWINDOW,
                    CW_USEDEFAULT, CW_USEDEFAULT,
                    CW_USEDEFAULT, CW_USEDEFAULT,
                    NULL, NULL, hInstance, NULL);

ShowWindow(hWnd, nCmdShow);
UpdateWindow(hWnd);

while (GetMessage(&msg, NULL, 0, 0))
{
    TranslateMessage(&msg);
    DispatchMessage(&msg);
}
return msg.wParam;
}

/*********************************************/
#pragma argsused
void WM_Command_Dlg_Handler(HWND hDlg, int id,
                            HWND hwndCtl, UINT
                            codeNotify)
{
    switch(id)
    {
        case IDOK :
        case IDCANCEL :
        {
            EndDialog(hDlg, 0);
            break;
        }

    }
}
```

```
/*********************************************/
BOOL CALLBACK _export MainDlgProc(HWND hDlg, UINT
                        message, WPARAM wParam, LPARAM
                        lParam)
{
    switch(message)
    {
        case WM_INITDIALOG :
        {
            return TRUE;
        }

        case WM_PAINT :
        {
            HDC          PaintDC;
            PAINTSTRUCT ps;
            HBITMAP      hBitmap;

            PaintDC = BeginPaint(hDlg, &ps);

            hBitmap = LoadBitmap(ghInstance,
                                "DIALOGBMP");
            DisplayBitmapControl(PaintDC, hDlg, hBitmap,
                                IDD_BITMAP);
            DeleteBitmap(hBitmap);

            EndPaint(hDlg, &ps);

            return TRUE;

        }

        case WM_COMMAND :
        {
            return (BOOL)HANDLE_WM_COMMAND(hDlg, wParam,
                                        lParam,
                                    WM_Command_Dlg_Handler);
        }

    }

    return FALSE;

}

/*********************************************/
BOOL DisplayBitmapControl(HDC hDC, HWND hDlg,
```

continues

Listing 2.4. continued

```
                              HBITMAP hBitmap, int
                              idControl)
{
   HWND     hBmpCtl;
   RECT     rect, rect2;
   POINT    pt;
   int      result;

   // Find the location of the control on the screen
   hBmpCtl = GetDlgItem(hDlg, idControl);
   GetWindowRect(hBmpCtl, &rect);

   GetClientRect(hDlg, &rect2);

   pt.x = rect.left;
   pt.y = rect.top;
   // Convert the location of control from screen
   //   coordinates to coordinates within the dialog
   //   box
   ScreenToClient(hDlg, &pt);

   // Go display that bitmap
   result = DisplayBitmap(hDC, hBitmap, pt.x, pt.y,
                          SRCCOPY);

   return result;

}

/**********************************************/
BOOL DisplayBitmap(HDC hDC, HBITMAP hBitmap,
                   int X, int Y, DWORD RopCode)
{
/*
 * Steps to displaying a bitmap:
 *
 * 1. Create a compatible display context.
 * 2. Select bitmap into compatible display context.
 * 3. Do a bit-block-transfer (BitBlt) command.
 * 4. Clean-up afterwards.
 *
 */

   HDC      hCompatDC;
   HBITMAP  hOldBitmap;
   BITMAP   BM;
   BOOL     result;
```

```
    // Create compatible display context
    hCompatDC = CreateCompatibleDC(hDC);

    // Select bitmap into compatible display context
    hOldBitmap = SelectBitmap(hCompatDC, hBitmap);

    // Get dimensions of bitmap
    GetObject(hBitmap, sizeof(BM), &BM);

    // Blast those bits to the screen
    result = BitBlt(hDC, X, Y, BM.bmWidth, BM.bmHeight,
                    hCompatDC, 0, 0, RopCode);

    // De-select the bitmap
    SelectBitmap(hCompatDC, hOldBitmap);

    // Clean up after we are done
    DeleteDC(hCompatDC);

    return result;

}


/*********************************************/
LRESULT CALLBACK _export MainWndProc(HWND hWnd, UINT
                        message, WPARAM wParam,
                        LPARAM lParam)
{
   switch (message)
   {
     case WM_PAINT :
     {
        HDC         PaintDC;
        RECT        rect;
        PAINTSTRUCT ps;

        PaintDC = BeginPaint(hWnd, &ps);
        GetClientRect(hWnd, &rect);

        DrawText(PaintDC, "Choose Menu Item",
                 -1, &rect, DT_SINGLELINE | DT_CENTER
                 | DT_VCENTER);

        EndPaint(hWnd, &ps);
        return 0;
     }
```

II

continues

Listing 2.4. continued

```
    case WM_COMMAND :
    {
        // Usually we would use a message cracker to
        //    sort out which menu item was selected.
        //    However, because there is only one menu
        //    item, we won't worry about message
        //    crackers.
        DLGPROC DlgProc;

        DlgProc = (DLGPROC)MakeProcInstance(
                  (FARPROC)MainDlgProc,
                   ghInstance);
        DialogBox(ghInstance, "IDD_DIALOG", hWnd,
                  DlgProc);
        FreeProcInstance((FARPROC)DlgProc);
        return 0;
    }


    case WM_DESTROY :
    {
        PostQuitMessage(0);
        return 0;
    }
    }
    return DefWindowProc (hWnd, message, wParam,
        lParam);
}
```

Listing 2.5. DLGBMP.RC resource script.

```
/*
 * DLGBMP.RC resource script
 *
 */


IDD_DIALOG DIALOG 32, 33, 55, 71
STYLE DS_MODALFRAME ¦ WS_POPUP ¦ WS_CAPTION ¦
WS_SYSMENU
CAPTION "DialogBitmap"
BEGIN
```

```
    CONTROL "", 101, "button", BS_GROUPBOX ¦ WS_CHILD
¦ NOT WS_VISIBLE, 11, 6, 32, 32
    PUSHBUTTON "&Ok", IDOK, 12, 47, 32, 14, WS_CHILD
¦ WS_VISIBLE ¦ WS_TABSTOP
END


DIALOGBMP BITMAP "dlgbmp.bmp"

MAINMENU MENU
BEGIN
    POPUP "&Dialog Box"
    BEGIN
        MENUITEM "&Bitmap in a Dialog", 100
    END

END
```

Listing 2.6. DLGBMP.DEF module definition file.

```
;
; DLGBMP.DEF module definition file
;

DESCRIPTION     'Dialog Bitmap'
NAME            DLGBMP
EXETYPE         WINDOWS
STUB            'WINSTUB.EXE'
HEAPSIZE        1024
STACKSIZE       8192
CODE            PRELOAD MOVEABLE DISCARDABLE
DATA            PRELOAD MOVEABLE MULTIPLE
```

Customizing the Common Dialog Boxes

How do I customize the common dialog boxes that come with Windows 3.1?

DESCRIPTION

Windows 3.1 includes seven dialog boxes that are collectively known as the common dialogs. The dialogs include File Open/Save, Choose Color, Select Font, Find/Replace, and Print. They are all located in a Windows DLL with the name COMMDLG.DLL. For the most part, all your program needs to do in order to use the common dialogs is fill out a related data structure and make a function call (see Table 2.3).

Table 2.3. Common dialog boxes, associated data structure, and function calls.

Type	Data structure	API function call
Select Color	CHOOSECOLOR	ChooseColor
Select Font	CHOOSEFONT	ChooseFont
File Open	OPENFILENAME	GetOpenFileName
File Save As	OPENFILENAME	GetSaveFileName
Print	PRINTDLG	PrintDlg
Find	FINDREPLACE	FindText
Replace	FINDREPLACE	ReplaceText

Many programmers want to use the common dialogs, but they don't want their programs to take on a "generic" appearance. By customizing the common dialog boxes, your program can still look unique, but you can take advantage of the functionality of the common dialog boxes.

ANSWER

There are basically two ways to customize the common dialogs. The first is to create a special hook function. The second is to create a new dialog box template. Sometimes these two methods are used in combination.

When a program specifies a new hook function, it lets your program (the hook function) look at all the dialog box messages before they are passed on to the routines inside the common dialog boxes.

Therefore, the hook function could trap the message that specifies the background color of the dialog box and change the background color to bright red (or whatever).

When your program specifies a new dialog box template, you actually create the template of the dialog box inside Resource Workshop, and it replaces the one usually used by the common dialogs. Therefore, you can completely rearrange the layout of the dialog box.

By using a combination of the two customization methods, you could add a new control to the dialog box and then catch its message inside the hook function. Microsoft obviously put some thought into designing the common dialog library.

The structure for each common dialog box function contains a `Flags` element that specifies whether the application supplies a hook function or a new template name. Then, there is an element for `lpfnHook` which is a pointer to the hook function, which is returned by `MakeProcInstance`. The hook function is declared like this:

```
UINT CALLBACK _export OpenFileHook(HWND hDlg, UINT msg,
                      WPARAM wParam, LPARAM lParam)
```

If the hook function processes a message, it should return `FALSE`. If the hook function is to ignore the message, it should return a `FALSE` value.

To use a custom template, you need to set the name of the `lpTemplateName` element to the name, as declared in the resource. The easiest way to create your own dialog box templates is to open COMMDLG.DLL in Resource Workshop and modify the dialog box you need. Then, save the modified template as a .DLG file. You can then #include the .DLG file inside your own resource script. As mentioned, if you add any new controls to the dialog box when using your own template, you will also need to create a hook function to process those controls.

One of the last things you might want to do with the common dialogs is to enable the Help buttons. If this is done, a special message is sent to the window procedure of your main program. Your program needs to first register the message with Windows, and then check for that message in its window procedure.

II

To register the message, use the `RegisterWindowMessage` API function, as follows:

```
UINT        ColorHelpMsg;

ColorHelpMsg = RegisterWindowMessage(HELPMSGSTRING);
```

Then, to check for the unique message, use the following code:

```
if (message == HelpMsg)
{
    MessageBox(NULL, "Enter a Valid Selection",
            "*** HELP ***",
            MB_OK ¦ MB_ICONQUESTION);
}
```

The sample shows calling `MessageBox`. In a full-blown application, you would want to use the `WinHelp` function to bring up the Windows Help system.

COMMENTS

Remember that all of the common dialog box functions are modal dialog boxes except for two. The Find Text and Find/Replace dialog boxes are both modeless. This means that messages for these dialog boxes all come through the main window procedure of your program.

SEE ALSO

`ChooseColor` API Function
`CHOOSECOLOR` Data Structure
`ChooseFont` API Function
`CHOOSEFONT` Data Structure
`FINDREPLACE` Data Structure
`FindText` API Function
`GetOpenFileName` API Function
`GetSaveFileName` API Function
`OPENFILENAME` Data Structure
`PrintDlg` API Function
`PRINTDLG` Data Structure
`RegisterWindowMessage` API Function
`ReplaceText` API Function

EXAMPLE CODE

The example program shows the common dialog boxes with no
customizations under one menu item and then with customization
on the other menu item. The customizations (see Figure 2.7)
include specifying a new background color, adding a Help button,
and rearranging the layout inside the custom dialog box.

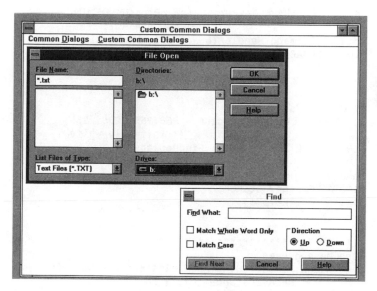

Figure 2.7. *The Custom Common Dialogs example.*

Listing 2.7 is the C source code for the CUCOMDLG.C source
code. Listing 2.8 is the resource script. Listing 2.9 is the module
definition file. Listing 2.10 is the header file.

Listing 2.7. CUCOMDLG.C source code.

```
// CUCOMDLG.C - How to customize the common dialogs
//              that are part of Windows 3.1.
//
// Your Borland C++ Consultant by Paul J. Perry
//

#define STRICT

#include <windowsx.h>
```

continues

Listing 2.7. continued

```
#include <stdlib.h>
#include <string.h>
#include <commdlg.h>
#include "cucomdlg.h"

// Function Prototypes
LRESULT CALLBACK _export MainWndProc(HWND, UINT,
                        WPARAM, LPARAM);
void WM_Command_Handler(HWND, int, HWND, UINT);
UINT CALLBACK _export OpenFileHook(HWND, UINT, WPARAM,
                        LPARAM);


// Global Variables
COLORREF    CurrentBkColor = RGB(255, 255, 255);
                        // Initially white
FINDREPLACE FindReplace, FindReplace2;
HWND        hMainWnd, hFindDlg, hFindCustDlg;
char        Buffer[255];
HINSTANCE   ghInstance;
UINT        HelpMsg;


/*********************************************/
#pragma argsused
int PASCAL WinMain(HINSTANCE hInstance, HINSTANCE
           hPrevInstance, LPSTR lpCmdParam,
           int nCmdShow)
{
    char        ProgName[] = "Custom Common Dialogs";
    HWND        hWnd;
    MSG         msg;

    if (!hPrevInstance)
    {
        WNDCLASS    wndclass;

        wndclass.lpszClassName = ProgName;
        wndclass.lpfnWndProc   = (WNDPROC) MainWndProc;
        wndclass.cbClsExtra    = 0;
        wndclass.cbWndExtra    = 0;
        wndclass.hInstance     = hInstance;
        wndclass.hIcon         = LoadIcon(NULL,
                            IDI_APPLICATION);
        wndclass.hCursor       = LoadCursor(NULL,
                            IDC_ARROW);
        wndclass.hbrBackground = GetStockObject(
                            WHITE_BRUSH);
```

```
      wndclass.lpszMenuName  = "MAINMENU";
      wndclass.style         = CS_VREDRAW |
                               CS_HREDRAW;

      if (!RegisterClass(&wndclass))
         exit(1);
   }

   ghInstance = hInstance;

   // To process the help button in the custom
   //   dialogs, we must register the message first.
   HelpMsg = RegisterWindowMessage(HELPMSGSTRING);

   hWnd = CreateWindow(ProgName, ProgName,
                       WS_OVERLAPPEDWINDOW,
                       CW_USEDEFAULT, CW_USEDEFAULT,
                       CW_USEDEFAULT, CW_USEDEFAULT,
                       NULL, NULL, hInstance, NULL);

   hMainWnd = hWnd;
   ShowWindow(hWnd, nCmdShow);
   UpdateWindow(hWnd);

   while (GetMessage(&msg, NULL, 0, 0))
   {
      TranslateMessage(&msg);
      DispatchMessage(&msg);
   }
   return msg.wParam;
}


/*********************************************/
#pragma argsused
void WM_Command_Handler(HWND hWnd, int id, HWND
                        hWndCtl, UINT codeNotify)
{
   switch (id)
   {
      case IDM_FILEOPEN :
      {
         OPENFILENAME OpenFileName;
         char Filters[] = "Text Files
                         (*.TXT)\0*.TXT\0"
                         "ASCII Files
                         (*.ASC)\0*.ASC\0";
         char FileName[255] = "\0";
```

continues

Listing 2.7. continued

```
    memset(&OpenFileName, 0,
        sizeof(OPENFILENAME));

    OpenFileName.lpstrTitle    = "File Open";
    OpenFileName.hwndOwner      = hMainWnd;
    OpenFileName.lpstrFilter    = (LPSTR)Filters;
    OpenFileName.nFilterIndex   = 1;
    OpenFileName.lpstrFile      = (LPSTR)FileName;
    OpenFileName.nMaxFile       = sizeof(FileName);
    OpenFileName.Flags          = OFN_FILEMUSTEXIST
                                    | \
                                  OFN_HIDEREADONLY
                                    | \
                                  OFN_PATHMUSTEXIST;
    OpenFileName.lpstrDefExt    = "*";
    OpenFileName.lStructSize    = sizeof(
                                    OPENFILENAME);

    GetOpenFileName(&OpenFileName);

    break;
}

case IDM_FILESAVE :
{
    OPENFILENAME SaveFileName;
    char Filters[] = "Text Files
                        (*.TXT)\0*.TXT\0"
                      "ASCII Files
                        (*.ASC)\0*.ASC\0";
    char FileName[255] = "\0";

    memset(&SaveFileName, 0,
      sizeof(OPENFILENAME));

    SaveFileName.lpstrTitle    = "File Save";
    SaveFileName.hwndOwner      = hMainWnd;
    SaveFileName.lpstrFilter    = (LPSTR)Filters;
    SaveFileName.nFilterIndex   = 1;
    SaveFileName.lpstrFile      = (LPSTR)FileName;
    SaveFileName.nMaxFile       = sizeof(FileName);
    SaveFileName.Flags          = OFN_FILEMUSTEXIST
                                    | \
                                  OFN_HIDEREADONLY
                                    | \
                                  OFN_PATHMUSTEXIST;
    SaveFileName.lpstrDefExt    = "*";
```

```
    SaveFileName.lStructSize  = sizeof(
                                OPENFILENAME);

    GetSaveFileName(&SaveFileName);


    break;
}

case IDM_CHOOSECOLOR :
{
    CHOOSECOLOR cc;
    COLORREF    CustomColors[16];

    memset(&cc, 0, sizeof(CHOOSECOLOR));

    cc.lStructSize   = sizeof(CHOOSECOLOR);
    cc.hwndOwner     = hMainWnd;
    cc.rgbResult     = CurrentBkColor;
    cc.lpCustColors  = CustomColors;
    cc.Flags         = CC_RGBINIT;

    ChooseColor(&cc);

    CurrentBkColor = cc.rgbResult;

    // Repaint window
    InvalidateRect(hWnd, NULL, TRUE);

    break;
}

case IDM_FIND :
{
    memset(&FindReplace, 0, sizeof(FINDREPLACE));

    FindReplace.lStructSize    = sizeof(
                                 FINDREPLACE);
    FindReplace.hwndOwner      = hMainWnd;
    FindReplace.lpstrFindWhat  = Buffer;
    FindReplace.wFindWhatLen   = sizeof(Buffer);

    hFindDlg = FindText(&FindReplace);

    break;

}

case IDM_FILEOPEN_CUSTOM :
```

continues

Listing 2.7. continued

```
{
    OPENFILENAME OpenFileName;
    FARPROC      lpfnHook;
    char Filters[] = "Text Files
                    (*.TXT)\0*.TXT\0"
                    "ASCII Files
                    (*.ASC)\0*.ASC\0";
    char FileName[255] = "\0";

    memset(&OpenFileName, 0,
            sizeof(OPENFILENAME));

    OpenFileName.lpstrTitle   = "File Open";
    OpenFileName.hwndOwner    = hMainWnd;
    OpenFileName.lpstrFilter  = (LPSTR)Filters;
    OpenFileName.nFilterIndex = 1;
    OpenFileName.lpstrFile    = (LPSTR)FileName;
    OpenFileName.nMaxFile     = sizeof(FileName);

    // We must specify the hook function next,
    //   to enable the customization.  We also add
    //   the style flag of OFN_ENABLEHOOK below.
    lpfnHook = MakeProcInstance (
                (FARPROC)OpenFileHook,
                ghInstance);
    OpenFileName.lpfnHook     =
            (UINT(CALLBACK*)(HWND, UINT, WPARAM,
                            LPARAM))lpfnHook;

    OpenFileName.Flags        = OFN_FILEMUSTEXIST
                              | \
                              OFN_HIDEREADONLY
                              | \
                              OFN_PATHMUSTEXIST
                              | \
                              OFN_ENABLEHOOK
                              | \
                              OFN_SHOWHELP;
    OpenFileName.lpstrDefExt  = "*";
    OpenFileName.lStructSize  = sizeof(
                            OPENFILENAME);

    GetOpenFileName(&OpenFileName);

    // Clean up after ourselves
    FreeProcInstance(lpfnHook);
```

```
    break;
}

case IDM_FILESAVE_CUSTOM :
{
    OPENFILENAME SaveFileName;
    FARPROC      lpfnHook;

    char Filters[] = "Text Files
                      (*.TXT)\0*.TXT\0"
                      "ASCII Files
                      (*.ASC)\0*.ASC\0";
    char FileName[255] = "\0";

    memset(&SaveFileName, 0,
           sizeof(OPENFILENAME));

    SaveFileName.lpstrTitle  = "File Save";
    SaveFileName.hwndOwner   = hMainWnd;
    SaveFileName.lpstrFilter = (LPSTR)Filters;
    SaveFileName.nFilterIndex = 1;
    SaveFileName.lpstrFile   = (LPSTR)FileName;
    SaveFileName.nMaxFile    = sizeof(FileName);

    // Again, we specify a custom hook function
    //   for the dialog.  We are going to use the
    //   same hook function as used by the custom
    //   File Open dialog box.
    lpfnHook = MakeProcInstance (
               (FARPROC)OpenFileHook,
               ghInstance);
    SaveFileName.lpfnHook    =
               (UINT(CALLBACK*)(HWND, UINT, WPARAM,
               LPARAM))lpfnHook;
    SaveFileName.Flags       = OFN_FILEMUSTEXIST
                                 ¦ \
                               OFN_HIDEREADONLY
                                 ¦ \
                               OFN_PATHMUSTEXIST
                                 ¦ \
                               OFN_ENABLEHOOK
                                 ¦ \
                               OFN_SHOWHELP;
    SaveFileName.lpstrDefExt = "*";
    SaveFileName.lStructSize = sizeof(
                               OPENFILENAME);

    GetSaveFileName(&SaveFileName);
```

continues

Listing 2.7. continued

```
    // Clean up after ourselves
    FreeProcInstance(lpfnHook);

    break;
}

case IDM_CHOOSECOLOR_CUSTOM :
{
    CHOOSECOLOR ccc;
    COLORREF    CustomColors[16];

    memset(&ccc, 0, sizeof(CHOOSECOLOR));

    ccc.lStructSize    = sizeof(CHOOSECOLOR);
    ccc.hwndOwner      = hMainWnd;
    ccc.hInstance      = (HWND)ghInstance;
    ccc.rgbResult      = CurrentBkColor;
    ccc.lpCustColors   = CustomColors;
    ccc.lpTemplateName = "CHOOSECOLORCUST";
    ccc.Flags          = CC_RGBINIT ¦ \
                         CC_SHOWHELP ¦ \
                         CC_ENABLETEMPLATE;

    ChooseColor(&ccc);

    CurrentBkColor = ccc.rgbResult;

    // Repaint window
    InvalidateRect(hWnd, NULL, TRUE);

    break;
}

case IDM_FIND_CUSTOM :
{

    memset(&FindReplace2, 0,
           sizeof(FINDREPLACE));

    FindReplace2.lStructSize    = sizeof(
                                  FINDREPLACE);
    FindReplace2.hInstance      = ghInstance;
    FindReplace2.hwndOwner      = hMainWnd;
    FindReplace2.lpstrFindWhat  = Buffer;
    FindReplace2.lpTemplateName = "FINDCUST";
    FindReplace2.Flags          = FR_ENABLE-
                                  TEMPLATE ¦ \
```

```
                                        FR_SHOWHELP;
            FindReplace2.wFindWhatLen   = sizeof(Buffer);

            hFindCustDlg = FindText(&FindReplace2);

            break;
         }

      }

}


/**********************************************/
#pragma argsused
UINT CALLBACK _export OpenFileHook(HWND hDlg, UINT
                      msg, WPARAM wParam, LPARAM
                      lParam)
{
   if (msg == WM_CTLCOLOR)
   {
      switch (HIWORD(lParam))
      {
         case CTLCOLOR_DLG :
         case CTLCOLOR_STATIC :
         {
            // Setbackground color
            SetBkColor((HDC)wParam, RGB(192, 192,
                                        192));
            // Change background brush
            return (UINT)GetStockBrush(LTGRAY_BRUSH);
         }
      }
   }

   return 0;
}


/**********************************************/
LRESULT CALLBACK _export MainWndProc(HWND hWnd, UINT
                      message, WPARAM wParam,
                      LPARAM lParam)
{
   switch (message)
   {
      case WM_COMMAND :
      {
```

continues

Listing 2.7. continued

```
      return HANDLE_WM_COMMAND(hWnd, wParam,
              lParam, WM_Command_Handler);
   }

   case WM_PAINT :
   {
      HDC          PaintDC;
      RECT         rect;
      PAINTSTRUCT  ps;
      HBRUSH       hBrush;

      PaintDC = BeginPaint(hMainWnd, &ps);
      GetClientRect(hMainWnd, &rect);

      hBrush = CreateSolidBrush(CurrentBkColor);
      FillRect(PaintDC, &rect, hBrush);

      SetBkMode(PaintDC, TRANSPARENT);

      DrawText(PaintDC, "Custom Common Dialog Box
              Examples",
              -1, &rect, DT_SINGLELINE | DT_CENTER
              | DT_VCENTER);

      DeleteBrush(hBrush);

      EndPaint(hMainWnd, &ps);
      return 0;
   }


   case WM_DESTROY :
   {
      PostQuitMessage(0);
      return 0;
   }

}
// Check for Help button being pressed in
//   Custom Color or Custom Find Dialog Box.
if (message == HelpMsg)
{
   MessageBox(NULL, "Enter a Valid Selection",
           "*** HELP ***",
           MB_OK | MB_ICONQUESTION);
}
```

```
        return DefWindowProc (hWnd, message, wParam,
                              lParam);
}
```

Listing 2.8. CUCOMDLG. RC resource script.

```
/*
 * CUCOMDLG.RC resource script
 *
 */

#include "commdlg.h"
#include "cucomdlg.h"

MAINMENU MENU
BEGIN
     POPUP "Common &Dialogs"
     BEGIN
          MENUITEM "File &Open...", IDM_FILEOPEN
          MENUITEM "File Save &As...", IDM_FILESAVE
          MENUITEM "Choose &Color...", IDM_CHOOSECOLOR
          MENUITEM "&Find...", IDM_FIND
     END

     POPUP "&Custom Common Dialogs"
     BEGIN
          MENUITEM "File &Open...",
                    IDM_FILEOPEN_CUSTOM
          MENUITEM "File Save &As...",
                    IDM_FILESAVE_CUSTOM
          MENUITEM "&Choose Color...",
                    IDM_CHOOSECOLOR_CUSTOM
          MENUITEM "&Find...", IDM_FIND_CUSTOM
     END

END


FINDCUST DIALOG LOADONCALL MOVEABLE DISCARDABLE 24,
43, 177, 78
STYLE DS_MODALFRAME ¦ WS_POPUP ¦ WS_CAPTION ¦
WS_SYSMENU
CAPTION "Find"
FONT 8, "Helv"
```

continues

Listing 2.8. continued

```
BEGIN
    CONTROL "Fi&nd What:", -1, "STATIC", SS_LEFT |
WS_CHILD | WS_VISIBLE, 4, 8, 42, 8
    CONTROL "", 1152, "EDIT", ES_LEFT |
ES_AUTOHSCROLL | WS_CHILD | WS_VISIBLE | WS_BORDER |
WS_GROUP | WS_TABSTOP, 47, 7, 128, 12
    CONTROL "Match &Whole Word Only", 1040, "BUTTON",
BS_AUTOCHECKBOX | WS_CHILD | WS_VISIBLE | WS_GROUP |
WS_TABSTOP, 4, 26, 100, 12
    CONTROL "Match &Case", 1041, "BUTTON",
BS_AUTOCHECKBOX | WS_CHILD | WS_VISIBLE | WS_TABSTOP,
4, 42, 64, 12
    CONTROL "Direction", 1072, "BUTTON", BS_GROUPBOX
| WS_CHILD | WS_VISIBLE, 107, 26, 68, 28
    CONTROL "&Up", 1056, "BUTTON", BS_AUTORADIOBUTTON
| WS_CHILD | WS_VISIBLE | WS_GROUP | WS_TABSTOP, 111,
38, 20, 12
    CONTROL "&Down", 1057, "BUTTON",
BS_AUTORADIOBUTTON | WS_CHILD | WS_VISIBLE |
WS_TABSTOP, 138, 38, 30, 12
    CONTROL "&Find Next", 1, "BUTTON",
BS_DEFPUSHBUTTON | WS_CHILD | WS_VISIBLE | WS_GROUP |
WS_TABSTOP, 4, 62, 50, 14
    CONTROL "Cancel", 2, "BUTTON", BS_PUSHBUTTON |
WS_CHILD | WS_VISIBLE | WS_GROUP | WS_TABSTOP, 63, 62,
50, 14
    CONTROL "&Help", 1038, "BUTTON", BS_PUSHBUTTON |
WS_CHILD | WS_VISIBLE | WS_GROUP | WS_TABSTOP, 122,
62, 50, 14
END


CHOOSECOLORCUST DIALOG 2, 0, 148, 122
STYLE DS_MODALFRAME | WS_POPUP | WS_CAPTION |
WS_SYSMENU
CAPTION "Choose Color"
FONT 8, "Helv"
BEGIN
    LTEXT "&Basic Colors:", -1, 4, 4, 140, 9
    CONTROL "", 720, "STATIC", SS_SIMPLE | WS_CHILD |
WS_VISIBLE | WS_GROUP | WS_TABSTOP, 4, 14, 140, 86
    CONTROL "OK", 1, "BUTTON", BS_DEFPUSHBUTTON |
```

```
WS_CHILD | WS_VISIBLE | WS_GROUP | WS_TABSTOP, 4, 106,
44, 14
    CONTROL "Cancel", 2, "BUTTON", BS_PUSHBUTTON |
WS_CHILD | WS_VISIBLE | WS_GROUP | WS_TABSTOP, 52,
106, 44, 14
    CONTROL "&Help", 1038, "BUTTON", BS_PUSHBUTTON |
WS_CHILD | WS_VISIBLE | WS_GROUP | WS_TABSTOP, 100,
106, 44, 14
    LTEXT "&Custom Colors:", -1, 8, 137, 140, 9
    CONTROL "", 721, "STATIC", SS_SIMPLE | WS_CHILD |
WS_VISIBLE | WS_GROUP, 177, 123, 140, 28
    CONTROL "&Define Custom Colors...", 719,
"BUTTON", BS_PUSHBUTTON | WS_CHILD | WS_VISIBLE |
WS_GROUP, 4, 150, 140, 14
    CONTROL "", 710, "STATIC", SS_BLACKFRAME |
WS_CHILD | WS_VISIBLE, 152, 4, 118, 116
    CONTROL "", 702, "STATIC", SS_SIMPLE | WS_CHILD |
WS_VISIBLE, 280, 4, 8, 116
    CONTROL "", 709, "STATIC", SS_BLACKFRAME |
WS_CHILD | WS_VISIBLE, 152, 124, 40, 26
    CONTROL "&o", 713, "BUTTON", BS_PUSHBUTTON |
WS_CHILD | WS_VISIBLE | WS_GROUP, 300, 200, 4, 14
    RTEXT "Color|", -1, 152, 151, 20, 9
    LTEXT "S&olid", -1, 172, 151, 20, 9
    RTEXT "&Hue:", 723, 194, 126, 20, 9
    CONTROL "", 703, "EDIT", ES_LEFT | WS_CHILD |
WS_VISIBLE | WS_BORDER | WS_GROUP, 216, 124, 18, 12
    RTEXT "&Sat:", 724, 194, 140, 20, 9
    CONTROL "", 704, "EDIT", ES_LEFT | WS_CHILD |
WS_VISIBLE | WS_BORDER | WS_GROUP, 216, 138, 18, 12
    RTEXT "&Lum:", 725, 194, 154, 20, 9
    CONTROL "", 705, "EDIT", ES_LEFT | WS_CHILD |
WS_VISIBLE | WS_BORDER | WS_GROUP, 216, 152, 18, 12
    RTEXT "&Red:", 726, 243, 126, 24, 9
    CONTROL "", 706, "EDIT", ES_LEFT | WS_CHILD |
WS_VISIBLE | WS_BORDER | WS_GROUP, 269, 124, 18, 12
    RTEXT "&Green:", 727, 243, 140, 24, 9
    CONTROL "", 707, "EDIT", ES_LEFT | WS_CHILD |
WS_VISIBLE | WS_BORDER | WS_GROUP, 269, 138, 18, 12
    RTEXT "Bl&ue:", 728, 243, 154, 24, 9
    CONTROL "", 708, "EDIT", ES_LEFT | WS_CHILD |
WS_VISIBLE | WS_BORDER | WS_GROUP, 269, 152, 18, 12
    CONTROL "&Add to Custom Colors", 712, "BUTTON",
BS_PUSHBUTTON | WS_CHILD | WS_VISIBLE | WS_GROUP, 152,
166, 142, 14
END
```

II

Listing 2.9. CUCOMDLG.DEF module definition file.

```
;
; CUCOMDLG.DEF module definition file
;

DESCRIPTION      'Custom Common Dialog Boxes'
NAME             CUCOMDLG
EXETYPE          WINDOWS
STUB             'WINSTUB.EXE'
HEAPSIZE         1024
STACKSIZE        8192
CODE             PRELOAD MOVEABLE DISCARDABLE
DATA             PRELOAD MOVEABLE MULTIPLE
```

Listing 2.10. CUCOMDLG.H header file.

```
/*
 * CUCOMDLG.H header file
 *
 */

#define IDM_FILEOPEN             100
#define IDM_FILESAVE             105
#define IDM_CHOOSECOLOR          110
#define IDM_FIND                 115

#define IDM_FILEOPEN_CUSTOM      200
#define IDM_FILESAVE_CUSTOM      205
#define IDM_CHOOSECOLOR_CUSTOM   210
#define IDM_FIND_CUSTOM          215
```

Using a Dialog Box as the Main Window of a Program

How do I create an application with a dialog box as the main window?

DESCRIPTION

Most dialog boxes are activated once the user has selected a menu item. At times, it would be nice to have a dialog box as the main window of the program. This is usually the case for smaller utility-type programs.

ANSWER

Most Windows programs use the WinMain entry point as the location to register a Window class, create the window, display the window, and then go into a message loop that dispatches messages to the window's message procedure.

However, there is no law that says what to do within the WinMain function. A program can just as easily display a dialog box. To display a dialog box, all that is necessary is to create a procedure instance with MakeProcInstance, display the dialog box with DialogBox, and then free the procedure instance with FreeProcInstance.

When the dialog box takes focus, control is passed to the dialog box procedure. The program has to do a couple of special things inside the dialog box procedure. First, unless our program does something special, the dialog box will always be displayed in the upper-left corner of the screen. So, our program catches the WM_INITDIALOG message and calculates the center of the desktop. It then moves the dialog box to the center of the screen.

The other trick is that all dialog boxes share a common window class. Therefore, if a dialog box has a minimize button, it needs to simulate the icon that would normally be displayed when the program is iconized. Therefore, the program can catch the WM_PAINT message and check whether the program is minimized. If it is, then the program needs to paint its icon itself. The code looks like this:

```
PaintDC = BeginPaint(hDlg, &ps);

DefWindowProc (hDlg, WM_ICONERASEBKGND,
               (WPARAM)PaintDC, 0L);

hIcon = LoadIcon(ghInstance, "MAINICON");
DrawIcon(PaintDC, 0, 0, hIcon);
EndPaint(hDlg, &ps);
```

```
return TRUE;
```

Now, there is nothing mysterious about the `BeginPaint` and `EndPaint` sequence. This sequence is required in any code that traps the `WM_PAINT` message. What is different is the call to `DefWindowProc` for the message `WM_ICONERASEBKGND`. This call passes just the single message on to the default window procedure. Its purpose is to draw a small border around the minimized icon. The program then uses `DrawIcon` to display its own icon within the minimized window.

If a program like this has a menu, the `WM_COMMAND` message is passed through to the dialog box procedure. You specify a menu when you design the dialog box. Double-click on the dialog box, and the Window Style dialog box will be displayed (see Figure 2.8). The edit control has a space for `Menu` which allows you to type in the menu name identifier.

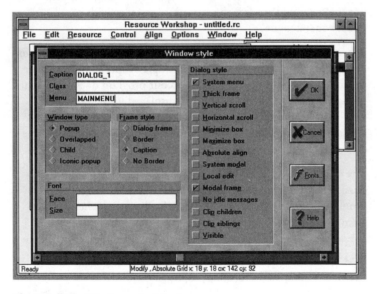

Figure 2.8. *Window style dialog box.*

To process the dialog box controls, the messages are passed through the `WM_COMMAND` message for the dialog box. If your dialog box has a menu, these messages are also passed through the `WM_COMMAND` message. Therefore, make sure the identifiers between dialog box items and menu items are unique.

COMMENTS

If you remove the minimize button from your dialog box, you don't have to worry about painting the icon, because your program will never be displayed as an icon.

> **NOTE** Be careful when designing the dialog box. If it is designed with a Modal frame (DS_MODALFRAME) and a minimize button (WS_MINIMIZEBOX), the dialog box will look all right at first appearance. However, when the user goes to minimize the dialog box, the upper-right corner gets painted incorrectly. It does not cause any major error; however, it looks sloppy.
>
> This strange behavior occurs because the two windows styles were never meant to be used together. Microsoft is aware of the situation, and their official word on it is that the two styles should not be used together. This behavior is a glitch in Windows itself, and not with the compiler.

SEE ALSO

DialogBox API Function
DrawIcon API Function
FreeProcInstance API Function
MakeProcInstance API Function
SetWindowPos API Function

EXAMPLE CODE

The example program shows how to create an application that has a dialog box as the main window (see Figure 2.9). It also has a main menu, and allows you to minimize the program to an icon. The program needs four files: DLGWIN.C (Listing 2.11), DLGWIN.H (Listing 2.12), DLGWIN.RC (Listing 2.13), and DLGWIN.DEF (Listing 2.14).

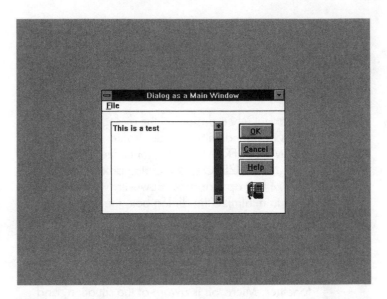

Figure 2.9. *Dialog window sample application.*

Listing 2.11. DLGWIN.C source code for dialog window example.

```
// DLGWIN.C - Dialog as a Main Window Example
//
// Your Borland C++ Consultant by Paul J. Perry
//

#define STRICT

#include <windowsx.h>
#include <stdlib.h>
#include "dlgwin.h"

// Function Prototypes
BOOL CALLBACK _export MainDlgProc(HWND, UINT, UINT,
                        LONG);
void WM_Command_Dlg_Handler(HWND, int, HWND, UINT);

// Global Variables
HINSTANCE  ghInstance;
```

```
/*********************************************/
#pragma argsused
int PASCAL WinMain(HINSTANCE hInstance, HINSTANCE
                   hPrevInstance, LPSTR lpCmdParam,
                   int nCmdShow)
{
   DLGPROC  lpfnDialog;

   ghInstance = hInstance;

   lpfnDialog = (DLGPROC)MakeProcInstance(
                (FARPROC)MainDlgProc, hInstance);
   DialogBox(hInstance, "MAINDIALOG",
             NULL, (DLGPROC)lpfnDialog);
   FreeProcInstance((FARPROC)lpfnDialog);

   return 0;

}


/*********************************************/
#pragma argsused
void WM_Command_Dlg_Handler(HWND hDlg, int id,
                            HWND hwndCtl, UINT
                            codeNotify)
{
   switch(id)
   {
      case IDM_ABOUT :
      {
         MessageBox(hDlg, "Dialog as a Main
                    Window\n\n"
                    "by Paul J. Perry",
                    "About...",
                    MB_OK | MB_ICONINFORMATION);
         break;
      }

      case IDD_HELP :
      {
         MessageBox(hDlg, "Enter a Note", "*** HELP
                    ***", MB_OK | MB_ICONINFORMATION);
         break;
      }

      case IDM_EXIT :    //  Menu Item
      case IDOK :        //  OK Button
```

continues

Listing 2.11. continued

```
    case IDCANCEL :    //  Cancel Button
    {
       EndDialog(hDlg, 0);
       break;
    }

  }
}


/************************************************/
BOOL CALLBACK _export MainDlgProc(HWND hDlg, UINT
                                  message,
                                  UINT wParam, LONG
                                  lParam)
{
   switch(message)
   {
      case WM_INITDIALOG :
      {
         // If we don't specify a new location to
         //   display the dialog box, it will always
         //   appear in the upper-left corner.
         //   Instead, this program centers the dialog
         //   box on the desktop.
         RECT rc, rcDTop;
         int NewX, NewY, CenterX, CenterY;
         HWND hDTopWnd;

         hDTopWnd = GetDesktopWindow();

         // desktop rectangle size
         GetWindowRect(hDTopWnd, &rcDTop);

         // dialog box rectangle size
         GetWindowRect(hDlg, &rc);

         // Do some calculations
         CenterX = (rcDTop.left + rcDTop.right)/2;
         CenterY = (rcDTop.top + rcDTop.bottom)/2;
```

```
        NewX = CenterX - ((rc.right - rc.left)/2);
        NewY = CenterY - ((rc.bottom - rc.top)/2);

        // Give it a new location
        SetWindowPos(hDlg, NULL, NewX, NewY, 0, 0,
                     SWP_NOSIZE | SWP_NOACTIVATE);

        return TRUE;
    }

    case WM_PAINT :
    {
        PAINTSTRUCT ps;
        HDC         PaintDC;
        HICON       hIcon;

        if (!IsIconic(hDlg))
            return FALSE;

        // We need to paint the minimized icon
        //   ourselves
        PaintDC = BeginPaint(hDlg, &ps);

        DefWindowProc (hDlg, WM_ICONERASEBKGND,
                      (WPARAM)PaintDC, 0L);


        hIcon = LoadIcon(ghInstance, "MAINICON");

        DrawIcon(PaintDC, 0, 0, hIcon);

        EndPaint(hDlg, &ps);
        return TRUE;
    }

    case WM_COMMAND :
    {
        return (BOOL)HANDLE_WM_COMMAND(hDlg, wParam,
               lParam,  WM_Command_Dlg_Handler);
    }

    }
    return FALSE;
}
```

II

Listing 2.12. DLGWIN.H header file.

```
/*
 * DLGWIN.H header file
 *
 */

// dialog box identifiers
#define IDD_HELP   666
#define IDD_EDIT   777

// menu identifiers
#define IDM_ABOUT 888
#define IDM_EXIT   999
```

Listing 2.13. DLGWIN.RC resource script.

```
/*
 * DLGWIN.RC resource script
 *
 */

#include "dlgwin.h"

MAINICON ICON "dlgwin.ico"

MAINDIALOG DIALOG 10, 19, 165, 92
STYLE WS_OVERLAPPED ¦ WS_VISIBLE ¦ WS_CAPTION ¦
WS_SYSMENU ¦ WS_MINIMIZEBOX
CAPTION "Dialog as a Main Window"
MENU MAINMENU
BEGIN
    CONTROL "", 106, "EDIT", ES_LEFT ¦ ES_MULTILINE ¦
ES_AUTOVSCROLL ¦ WS_CHILD ¦ WS_VISIBLE ¦ WS_BORDER ¦
WS_VSCROLL ¦ WS_TABSTOP, 8, 9, 102, 74
    DEFPUSHBUTTON "&OK", IDOK, 124, 11, 31, 14,
WS_CHILD ¦ WS_VISIBLE ¦ WS_TABSTOP
    PUSHBUTTON "&Cancel", IDCANCEL, 124, 27, 31, 14,
WS_CHILD ¦ WS_VISIBLE ¦ WS_TABSTOP
    PUSHBUTTON "&Help", IDD_HELP, 124, 43, 31, 14,
WS_CHILD ¦ WS_VISIBLE ¦ WS_TABSTOP
    ICON "MAINICON", -1, 131, 63, 16, 16, WS_CHILD ¦
WS_VISIBLE
```

```
END

MAINMENU MENU
BEGIN
     POPUP "&File"
     BEGIN
          MENUITEM "&About", IDM_ABOUT
          MENUITEM SEPARATOR
          MENUITEM "E&xit", IDM_EXIT
     END

END
```

II

Listing 2.14. DLGWIN.DEF module definition file.

```
;
; DLGWIN.DEF module definition file
;

DESCRIPTION     'Dialog as a Main Windows'
NAME            DLGWIN
EXETYPE         WINDOWS
STUB            'WINSTUB.EXE'
HEAPSIZE        1024
STACKSIZE       8192
CODE            PRELOAD MOVEABLE DISCARDABLE
DATA            PRELOAD MOVEABLE MULTIPLE
```

Centering Dialog Boxes

How can a dialog box be centered within another window?

DESCRIPTION

At times it would be nice to have more control over the placement of dialog boxes. When a program normally displays a dialog box, Windows decides on a default location to display the dialog box. However, by trapping a single message, the program can move the dialog box to a unique location and override Windows' default placement of the icon.

ANSWER

The WM_INITDIALOG message is sent after the dialog box has been created, but before it has been displayed. By trapping the WM_INITDIALOG message, a program can use the SetWindowPos function to move the dialog box to a new screen location.

A program can choose a new default location, such as the upper-left or lower-right corner of the screen, or calculate a new location. When the program needs to center the dialog box, it finds the coordinates of its parent window, as well as its own, and then calculates the new coordinates for the dialog box and calls the SetWindowPos function.

COMMENTS

If a program tries to center the dialog box on the screen, it should use the GetDesktopWindow function to find the coordinates of the screen. The program can then calculate the center based on these dimensions. Never hard-code dimensions (such as 640×480) as the size of the screen into your program. When the program is run on a system with super VGA (which can be 600×800 or 1024×768 or maybe even 1280×960 resolution), the dialog box will no longer be centered on the screen.

SEE ALSO

SetWindowPos API Function
WM_INITDIALOG Windows Message

EXAMPLE CODE

The example program lets the user choose where to display a fictitious Page Layout dialog box. The user can select a menu item to display the dialog box in the default location, in the upper-left corner of the screen, or in the center of the main window.

Listing 2.14 contains the CTRDLG.C source code; Listing 2.15 contains the CTRDLG.H header file; Listing 2.16 contains the CTRDLG.RC resource script; and Listing 2.17 contains the CTRDLG.DEF module definition file.

Listing 2.15. CTRDLG.C source code.

```c
// CTRDLG.C - Show how to center dialog box on screen
//
//
// Your Borland C++ Consultant by Paul J. Perry
//

#define STRICT

#include <windowsx.h>
#include <stdlib.h>
#include "ctrdlg.h"

// Function Prototypes
LRESULT CALLBACK _export MainWndProc(HWND, UINT,
                         WPARAM, LPARAM);
BOOL CALLBACK _export RegularDlgProc(HWND, UINT,
                         WPARAM, LPARAM);
BOOL CALLBACK _export CenteredDlgProc(HWND, UINT,
                         WPARAM, LPARAM);
BOOL CALLBACK _export LeftTopDlgProc(HWND, UINT,
                         WPARAM, LPARAM);
void WM_CommandHandler(HWND, int, HWND, UINT);
void WM_Command_Dlg_Handler(HWND, int, HWND, UINT);
BOOL CenterDialog(HWND hWndParent, HWND hDlg);


// Global Variables
HINSTANCE ghInstance;
HWND      hMainWnd;

/***********************************************/
#pragma argsused
int PASCAL WinMain(HINSTANCE hInstance, HINSTANCE
                   hPrevInstance, LPSTR lpCmdParam,
                   int nCmdShow)
{
    char      ProgName[] = "CTRDLG";
    HWND      hWnd;
    MSG       msg;


    if (!hPrevInstance)
    {
        WNDCLASS    wndclass;
```

continues

Listing 2.15. continued

```
    wndclass.lpszClassName = ProgName;
    wndclass.lpfnWndProc   = (WNDPROC) MainWndProc;
    wndclass.cbClsExtra    = 0;
    wndclass.cbWndExtra    = 0;
    wndclass.hInstance     = hInstance;
    wndclass.hIcon         = LoadIcon(NULL,
                               IDI_APPLICATION);
    wndclass.hCursor       = LoadCursor(NULL,
                               IDC_ARROW);
    wndclass.hbrBackground = GetStockObject(
                               WHITE_BRUSH);
    wndclass.lpszMenuName  = "MAINMENU";
    wndclass.style         = CS_VREDRAW ¦
                               CS_HREDRAW;

    if (!RegisterClass(&wndclass))
        exit(1);
}

ghInstance = hInstance;

hWnd = CreateWindow(ProgName, ProgName,
                    WS_OVERLAPPEDWINDOW,
                    CW_USEDEFAULT, CW_USEDEFAULT,
                    CW_USEDEFAULT, CW_USEDEFAULT,
                    NULL, NULL, hInstance, NULL);

hMainWnd = hWnd;

ShowWindow(hWnd, SW_SHOWMAXIMIZED);
UpdateWindow(hWnd);

while (GetMessage(&msg, NULL, 0, 0))
{
    TranslateMessage(&msg);
    DispatchMessage(&msg);
}

return msg.wParam;
}

/*********************************************/
#pragma argsused
void WM_Command_Dlg_Handler(HWND hDlg, int id,
                            HWND hwndCtl, UINT
                            codeNotify)
{
```

```
      // This is a universal handler for dialog box
      //    control elements.  It is used for all the
      //    dialog boxes in this example.
      switch(id)
      {
         case IDOK :
         case IDCANCEL :
         {
            EndDialog(hDlg, 0);
            break;
         }
      }
   }

/*******************************************/
BOOL CALLBACK _export RegularDlgProc(HWND hDlg, UINT
                       message, WPARAM wParam,
                       LPARAM lParam)
{
   switch(message)
   {
      case WM_INITDIALOG :
      {
         return TRUE;
      }

      case WM_COMMAND :
      {
         return (BOOL)HANDLE_WM_COMMAND(hDlg, wParam,
               lParam, WM_Command_Dlg_Handler);
      }
   }

   return FALSE;
}

/*******************************************/
BOOL CALLBACK _export CenteredDlgProc(HWND hDlg, UINT
                       message, WPARAM wParam, LPARAM
                       lParam)
{
   switch(message)
   {
      case WM_INITDIALOG :
      {
         CenterDialog(hMainWnd, hDlg);
         return TRUE;
      }
```

continues

Listing 2.15. continued

```
      case WM_COMMAND :
      {
          return (BOOL)HANDLE_WM_COMMAND(hDlg, wParam,
                  lParam, WM_Command_Dlg_Handler);
      }

  }

  return FALSE;
}

/********************************************/
BOOL CALLBACK _export LeftTopDlgProc(HWND hDlg, UINT
                    message, WPARAM wParam, LPARAM
                    lParam)
{
    switch(message)
    {
      case WM_INITDIALOG :
      {
          RECT rect;

          GetClientRect(hDlg, &rect);

          // The first two zeros refer to upper-left
          //    corner of the screen.  The second two
          //    zeros tell the routine not to change the
          //    size of the dialog.
          SetWindowPos(hDlg, NULL, 0, 0, 0, 0,
                      SWP_NOSIZE ¦ SWP_NOACTIVATE);

          return TRUE;
      }

      case WM_COMMAND :
      {
          return (BOOL)HANDLE_WM_COMMAND(hDlg, wParam,
                  lParam, WM_Command_Dlg_Handler);
      }

    }
```

```
      return FALSE;
}

/*******************************************/
BOOL CenterDialog(HWND hWndParent, HWND hDlg)
{
   RECT rc, rcParent;
   int NewX, NewY, CenterX, CenterY;

   // main window rectangle size
   GetWindowRect(hWndParent, &rcParent);

   // dialog box rectangle size
   GetWindowRect(hDlg, &rc);

   CenterX = (rcParent.left + rcParent.right)/2;
   CenterY = (rcParent.top + rcParent.bottom)/2;

   NewX = CenterX - ((rc.right - rc.left)/2);
   NewY = CenterY - ((rc.bottom - rc.top)/2);

   // Give it a new location
   return SetWindowPos(hDlg, NULL, NewX, NewY, 0, 0,
                    SWP_NOSIZE | SWP_NOACTIVATE);
}

/*******************************************/
#pragma argsused
void WM_CommandHandler(HWND hWnd, int id, HWND
                     hWndCtl, UINT codeNotify)
{
   DLGPROC DlgProc;

   switch (id)
   {
      case IDM_EXIT :
      {
         SendMessage(hWnd, WM_CLOSE, 0, 0L);
         break;
      }

      case IDM_NOTCENTERED :
      {
```

continues

Listing 2.15. continued

```c
            DlgProc = (DLGPROC)MakeProcInstance(
                    (FARPROC)RegularDlgProc,
                    ghInstance);
            DialogBox(ghInstance, "PAGELAYOUTDIALOG",
                    hWnd, DlgProc);
            FreeProcInstance((FARPROC)DlgProc);
            break;
        }


        case IDM_CENTERED :
        {
            DlgProc = (DLGPROC)MakeProcInstance(
                    (FARPROC)CenteredDlgProc,
                    ghInstance);
            DialogBox(ghInstance, "PAGELAYOUTDIALOG",
                    hWnd, DlgProc);
            FreeProcInstance((FARPROC)DlgProc);
            break;
        }

        case IDM_LEFTOP :
        {
            DlgProc = (DLGPROC)MakeProcInstance(
                    (FARPROC)LeftTopDlgProc,
                    ghInstance);
            DialogBox(ghInstance, "PAGELAYOUTDIALOG",
                    hWnd, DlgProc);
            FreeProcInstance((FARPROC)DlgProc);
            break;
        }

    }

}

/*********************************************/
LRESULT CALLBACK _export MainWndProc(HWND hWnd, UINT
                    message, WPARAM wParam, LPARAM
                    lParam)
{
    switch (message)
    {
```

```
case WM_PAINT :
{
    HDC          PaintDC;
    RECT         rect;
    PAINTSTRUCT  ps;

    PaintDC = BeginPaint(hWnd, &ps);
    GetClientRect(hWnd, &rect);

    // The double ampersand is used because, if
    //   it is encountered, the DrawText routine
    //   changes the next character (in this case
    //   a space) to be displayed underlined.
    //   This occurs because DrawText actually
    //   calls the same routine that Windows uses
    //   to display menus and text inside a dialog
    //   box.
    DrawText(PaintDC, "Moving && Centering
            Dialogs", -1, &rect, DT_SINGLELINE |
            DT_CENTER | DT_VCENTER);

    EndPaint(hWnd, &ps);
    return 0;
}

case WM_COMMAND :
{
    return HANDLE_WM_COMMAND(hWnd, wParam,
                             lParam,
                             WM_CommandHandler);
}


case WM_DESTROY :
{
    PostQuitMessage(0);
    return 0;
}

}

return DefWindowProc (hWnd, message, wParam,
                      lParam);
}
```

Listing 2.16. CTRDLG.H header file.

```
/*
 * CTRDLG.H header file
 *
 */

#define IDM_EXIT        111
#define IDM_NOTCENTERED 222
#define IDM_CENTERED    333
#define IDM_LEFTOP      444
```

Listing 2.17. CTRDLG.RC resource script.

```
/*
 * CTRDLG.RC resource script
 *
 */

#include "ctrdlg.h"

PAGELAYOUTDIALOG DIALOG 26, 30, 180, 110
STYLE DS_MODALFRAME ¦ WS_POPUP ¦ WS_CAPTION ¦
WS_SYSMENU
CAPTION "Page Layout"
FONT 8, "Helv"
BEGIN
     LTEXT "&Start Page Numbers At:", -1, 5, 7, 88, 12
     CONTROL "", 3, "EDIT", ES_LEFT ¦ ES_AUTOHSCROLL ¦
WS_CHILD ¦ WS_VISIBLE ¦ WS_BORDER ¦ WS_TABSTOP, 95, 5,
30, 12
     LTEXT "Margins:", -1, 5, 33, 40, 12
     LTEXT "&Left:", -1, 12, 48, 20, 12
     CONTROL "", 4, "EDIT", ES_LEFT ¦ ES_AUTOHSCROLL ¦
WS_CHILD ¦ WS_VISIBLE ¦ WS_BORDER ¦ WS_TABSTOP, 35,
46, 40, 12
     LTEXT "&Right:", -1, 85, 48, 30, 12
     CONTROL "", 5, "EDIT", ES_LEFT ¦ ES_AUTOHSCROLL ¦
WS_CHILD ¦ WS_VISIBLE ¦ WS_BORDER ¦ WS_TABSTOP, 117,
46, 40, 12
     LTEXT "&Top:", -1, 12, 65, 20, 12
     CONTROL "", 6, "EDIT", ES_LEFT ¦ ES_AUTOHSCROLL ¦
```

```
WS_CHILD | WS_VISIBLE | WS_BORDER | WS_TABSTOP, 35,
63, 40, 12
    LTEXT "&Bottom:", -1, 85, 65, 30, 12
    CONTROL "", 7, "EDIT", ES_LEFT | ES_AUTOHSCROLL |
WS_CHILD | WS_VISIBLE | WS_BORDER | WS_TABSTOP, 117,
63, 40, 12
    LTEXT "Measurements:", -1, 5, 84, 63, 12
    CONTROL "&inch", 8, "BUTTON", BS_AUTORADIOBUTTON
| WS_CHILD | WS_VISIBLE | WS_TABSTOP, 12, 94, 27, 12
    CONTROL "&cm", 9, "BUTTON", BS_AUTORADIOBUTTON |
WS_CHILD | WS_VISIBLE, 44, 94, 26, 12
    CONTROL "OK", 1, "BUTTON", BS_DEFPUSHBUTTON |
WS_CHILD | WS_VISIBLE | WS_GROUP | WS_TABSTOP, 135, 5,
40, 14
    CONTROL "Cancel", 2, "BUTTON", BS_PUSHBUTTON |
WS_CHILD | WS_VISIBLE | WS_GROUP | WS_TABSTOP, 135,
23, 40, 14
    LTEXT "Options:", -1, 86, 84, 63, 12, WS_CHILD |
WS_VISIBLE | WS_GROUP
    CONTROL "Print page status", 10, "BUTTON",
BS_AUTOCHECKBOX | WS_CHILD | WS_VISIBLE | WS_TABSTOP,
96, 94, 71, 12
END


MAINMENU MENU
BEGIN
    POPUP "&File"
    BEGIN
        MENUITEM "E&xit", IDM_EXIT
    END

    POPUP "&Dialogs"
    BEGIN
        MENUITEM "Default &Placement",
IDM_NOTCENTERED
        MENUITEM "&Centered", IDM_CENTERED
        MENUITEM "&Top Left", IDM_LEFTOP
    END

END
```

Listing 2.18 CTRDLG.DEF module definition file.

```
;
; CTRDLG.DEF module definition file
;

DESCRIPTION       'Center/Move Dialogs'
NAME              CTRDLG
EXETYPE           WINDOWS
STUB              'WINSTUB.EXE'
HEAPSIZE          1024
STACKSIZE         8192
CODE              PRELOAD MOVEABLE DISCARDABLE
DATA              PRELOAD MOVEABLE MULTIPLE
```

 # Creating Short Animation Sequences

 How can I create a short animation sequence inside my dialog box?

DESCRIPTION

Although most Windows programs are not known for their excellent animation, there are situations in which animation is used to add special effects to About dialog boxes, or to let the user know the progress of a certain activity.

ANSWER

Animation is the process of putting something into action. Any type of animation in Windows requires the use of a timer. This will allow the program to receive messages on a fairly regular basis. At each timer message, the image can be changed, thereby causing the image to appear animated.

A programmer can create the image of animation by using a series of bitmap images. The first bitmap is the starting position of the image. The final bitmap is how the image appears at its final position. The series of bitmaps in-between are steps of the animation. Then, each time the program receives a `WM_TIMER` message, it displays the next bitmap in the sequence of images.

COMMENTS

The hardest part about using bitmaps to create animation effects is creating the bitmap images. It helps if you are a good artist, or if you have a friend who is an artist.

Also, it is important to make the animation look smooth. Any graphical effects in a Windows program that are not smooth are going to stand out like a sore thumb. The programmer/artist can help smooth animation by using a transparent color (selected by Resource Workshop) within the bitmap. This removes a lot of the flickering that can occur when displaying animated images.

SEE ALSO

`SetTimer` API Function
`KillTimer` API Function

EXAMPLE CODE

The example program uses the image of a book with flipping pages to demonstrate animation. To make the example easier to understand, the image is actually stored as an icon (it is easier just to call `DrawIcon`, rather than use `BitBlt`). There are four images (see Figure 2.10) that comprise the animation in the program.

There are eight files to this program. Listing 2.19 contains the ANIMDLG.C source code; Listing 2.20 contains the ANIMDLG.H header file; Listing 2.21 contains the ANIMDLG.RC resource script; and Listing 2.22 contains the ANIMDLG.DEF module definition file. To compile the program, you also need the four icon files: BOOK1.ICO, BOOK2.ICO, BOOK3.ICO, and BOOK4.ICO.

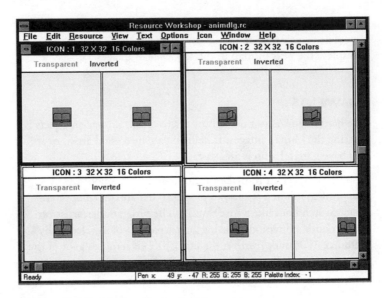

Figure 2.10. *The four flipping book images.*

Listing 2.19. ANIMDLG.C source code.

```
// ANIMDLG.C - Example of animation inside a dialog
//             box.
//
// Your Borland C++ Consultant by Paul J. Perry
//

#define STRICT
#define TIMERID        11
#define NUMBEROFICONS  4

#include <windowsx.h>
#include <stdlib.h>
#include <stdio.h>
#include "animdlg.h"


// Function Prototypes
LRESULT CALLBACK _export MainWndProc(HWND, UINT,
                                      WPARAM, LPARAM);
BOOL CALLBACK _export MainDlgProc(HWND, UINT, WPARAM,
                                   LPARAM);
void WM_CommandHandler(HWND, int, HWND, UINT);
```

```
void WM_Command_Dlg_Handler(HWND, int, HWND, UINT);


// Global Variables
HINSTANCE  ghInstance;

/********************************************/
#pragma argsused
int PASCAL WinMain(HINSTANCE hInstance, HINSTANCE
            hPrevInstance,
                   LPSTR lpCmdParam, int nCmdShow)
{
    char         ProgName[] = "Dialog Animation";
    HWND         hWnd;
    MSG          msg;


    if (!hPrevInstance)
    {
        WNDCLASS    wndclass;

        wndclass.lpszClassName = ProgName;
        wndclass.lpfnWndProc   = (WNDPROC) MainWndProc;
        wndclass.cbClsExtra    = 0;
        wndclass.cbWndExtra    = 0;
        wndclass.hInstance     = hInstance;
        wndclass.hIcon         = LoadIcon(NULL,
                                    IDI_APPLICATION);
        wndclass.hCursor       = LoadCursor(NULL,
                                    IDC_ARROW);
        wndclass.hbrBackground = GetStockObject(
                                    WHITE_BRUSH);
        wndclass.lpszMenuName  = "MAINMENU";
        wndclass.style         = CS_VREDRAW |
                                    CS_HREDRAW;

        if (!RegisterClass(&wndclass))
            exit(1);
    }

    ghInstance = hInstance;

    hWnd = CreateWindow(ProgName, ProgName,
                    WS_OVERLAPPEDWINDOW,
                    CW_USEDEFAULT, CW_USEDEFAULT,
                    CW_USEDEFAULT, CW_USEDEFAULT,
                    NULL, NULL, hInstance, NULL);

    ShowWindow(hWnd, nCmdShow);
```

II

continues

Listing 2.19. continued

```
  UpdateWindow(hWnd);

  while (GetMessage(&msg, NULL, 0, 0))
  {
     TranslateMessage(&msg);
     DispatchMessage(&msg);
  }
  return msg.wParam;
}

/**********************************************/
#pragma argsused
void WM_Command_Dlg_Handler(HWND hDlg, int id,
                            HWND hwndCtl, UINT
                            codeNotify)
{
   switch(id)
   {
      case IDOK :
      case IDCANCEL :
      {
         EndDialog(hDlg, 0);
         break;
      }
   }
}


/**********************************************/
BOOL CALLBACK _export MainDlgProc(HWND hDlg, UINT
                     message, WPARAM wParam,
                     LPARAM lParam)
{
   static int IconNumber = 1;

   switch(message)
   {
      case WM_INITDIALOG :
      {
         // The timer is for the flipping book
         SetTimer(hDlg, TIMERID, 150, NULL);

         return TRUE;
      }


      case WM_TIMER :
```

```
        {
            HICON hIcon;

            if (wParam == TIMERID)
            {
                HWND hIconWnd;

                hIconWnd = GetDlgItem(hDlg, IDD_ICON);

                if (IconNumber > 4)
                    IconNumber=1;

                hIcon = LoadIcon(ghInstance,
                        MAKEINTRESOURCE(IconNumber++));

                SendDlgItemMessage(hDlg, IDD_ICON,
                                STM_SETICON,
                                (WPARAM)hIcon, 0L);

                InvalidateRect(hIconWnd, NULL, TRUE);
                break;
            }

            return TRUE;

        }


        case WM_COMMAND :
        {
            return (BOOL)HANDLE_WM_COMMAND(hDlg, wParam,
                    lParam, WM_Command_Dlg_Handler);
        }

        case WM_DESTROY :
        {
            KillTimer(hDlg, TIMERID);
            return FALSE;
        }
    }

    return FALSE;
}


/********************************************/
#pragma argsused
```

continues

Listing 2.19. continued

```
void WM_CommandHandler(HWND hWnd, int id, HWND
hWndCtl, UINT codeNotify)
{

    switch (id)
    {
        case IDM_EXIT :
        {
            SendMessage(hWnd, WM_CLOSE, 0, 0L);
            break;
        }

        case IDM_ANIMATE :
        {
            DLGPROC DlgProc;

            DlgProc = (DLGPROC)MakeProcInstance(
                    (FARPROC)MainDlgProc, ghInstance);
            DialogBox(ghInstance, "MAINDIALOG", hWnd,
                    DlgProc);
            FreeProcInstance((FARPROC)DlgProc);
            break;
        }

    }
}


/***********************************************/
LRESULT CALLBACK _export MainWndProc(HWND hWnd, UINT
                        message, WPARAM wParam,
                        LPARAM lParam)
{
    switch (message)
    {
        case WM_DESTROY :
        {
            PostQuitMessage(0);
            return 0;
        }

        case WM_COMMAND :
        {
            return (BOOL)HANDLE_WM_COMMAND(hWnd, wParam,
                    lParam, WM_CommandHandler);
```

```
        }

    }
    return DefWindowProc (hWnd, message, wParam,
                          lParam);
}
```

Listing 2.20. ANIMDLG.H header file.

```
/*
 * ANIMDLG.H header file
 *
 */

#define IDM_EXIT     111
#define IDM_ANIMATE  222
#define IDD_ICON     333
#define IDD_GROUP    444
```

Listing 2.21. ANIMDLG.RC resource script.

```
/*
 * ANIMDLG.RC resource script
 *
 */

#include "animdlg.h"

1 ICON "book1.ico"

2 ICON "book2.ico"

3 ICON "book3.ico"

4 ICON "book4.ico"


MAINMENU MENU
BEGIN
    POPUP "&File"
    BEGIN
        MENUITEM "E&xit", IDM_EXIT
    END
```

continues

Listing 2.21. continued

```
        POPUP "&More..."
        BEGIN
                MENUITEM "&Animation Dialog", IDM_ANIMATE
        END

END


MAINDIALOG DIALOG 23, 38, 142, 92
STYLE DS_MODALFRAME ¦ WS_POPUP ¦ WS_CAPTION ¦
WS_SYSMENU
CAPTION "Animation Festival"
BEGIN
        PUSHBUTTON "&Ok", IDOK, 103, 10, 28, 10, WS_CHILD
¦ WS_VISIBLE ¦ WS_TABSTOP
        PUSHBUTTON "&Cancel", IDCANCEL, 103, 25, 28, 10,
WS_CHILD ¦ WS_VISIBLE ¦ WS_TABSTOP
        ICON 1, IDD_ICON, 20, 16, 16, 16, WS_CHILD ¦
WS_VISIBLE
        CONTROL "", IDD_GROUP, "button", BS_GROUPBOX ¦
WS_CHILD ¦ NOT WS_VISIBLE, 10, 53, 121, 28
END
```

Listing 2.22. ANIMDLG.DEF module definition file.

```
;
; ANIMDLG.DEF module definition file
;

DESCRIPTION     'Dialog Animation Demo'
NAME            ANIMDLG
EXETYPE         WINDOWS
STUB            'WINSTUB.EXE'
HEAPSIZE        1024
STACKSIZE       8192
CODE            PRELOAD MOVEABLE DISCARDABLE
DATA            PRELOAD MOVEABLE MULTIPLE
```

Context-Sensitive Help

How do I implement context-sensitive help in a dialog box?

DESCRIPTION

Context-sensitive help refers to the ability to display help information that is related to the action with which the user is currently working. In a dialog box, context-sensitive help is usually implemented from the user's stand-point by pressing the F1 function key.

By implementing context-sensitive help in a dialog box, the user can press the F1 key, and information about what the user is supposed to enter in the current dialog box control is displayed instantly.

II

ANSWER

Keyboard messages are not sent to the main dialog box procedure. Instead, they are sent to the control in the dialog box. Therefore, something special has to be done to check whether the key being pressed is the F1 function key.

To implement context-sensitive help in a dialog box, the programmer needs to create a hook function. This function receives all messages before they are sent to the dialog box. In the hook function, the programmer can check for the F1 keypress and send a message to the main dialog box procedure along with the identifier of the control. The dialog box procedure takes care of displaying help about the specified item.

Before the dialog box is created, a windows hook is set. The code looks like this:

```
lpfnFilterProc = (HOOKPROC)MakeProcInstance(
                 (FARPROC)HelpFilterProc,
                 ghInstance);

hHook = SetWindowsHookEx(WH_MSGFILTER, lpfnFilterProc,
                  ghInstance, (HTASK)NULL);
```

First a procedure instance of the function is created. The `SetWindowsHookEx` function is called to create the hook function instance.

A program creates the dialog box with a call to `DialogBox`, like this:

```
DialogBox(ghInstance, "CSHELPDIALOG", hWnd, DlgProc);
```

After the dialog box is done processing, the program cleans up. Code like this is used:

```
UnhookWindowsHookEx(hHook);

FreeProcInstance((FARPROC)lpfnFilterProc);
FreeProcInstance((FARPROC)DlgProc);
```

This unhooks the hook and then frees the procedure instance of both the dialog box and the hook function.

Inside the hook function, the program checks to see if the dialog box `WM_KEYDOWN` message is equal to `VK_F1`. If it is, it posts a message to the dialog box that includes the identifier of the control that had focus when the user pressed the `F1` key stored in the `wParam` of the message. The code looks like this:

```
if ((WM_KEYDOWN == ptrMsg->message) &&
    (VK_F1 == ptrMsg->wParam))
{
    PostMessage(GetParent(ptrMsg->hwnd), HelpMsg,
                GetDlgCtrlID(GetFocus()), 0L);
    return 1L;
}
```

The main dialog box procedure then responds to the registered message and displays help depending on which control was active.

COMMENTS

In most cases, a full application would call the `WinHelp` function to access the Windows Help engine. However, you can also use `MessageBox` to display a short piece of help information.

SEE ALSO

`SetWindowsHookEx` API Function
`UnhookWindowsHookEx` API Function
`WinHelp` API Function

EXAMPLE CODE

The example program displays a dialog box and allows the user to press the F1 key to display context-sensitive help for the current control (see Figure 2.11). The source code for DLGHELP.C is in Listing 2.23 the header file for DLGHELP.H is in Listing 2.24; the resource script for DLGHELP.RC is in Listing 2.25; and the module definition file for DLGHELP.DEF is in Listing 2.26.

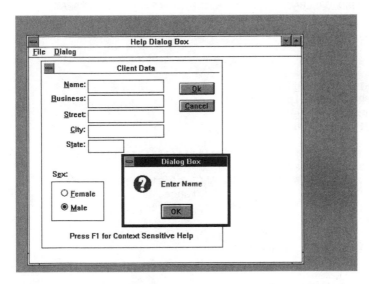

Figure 2.11. *Context-sensitive help example.*

Listing 2.23. DLGHELP.C source code.

```
// DLGHELP.C - How to add context-sensitive help to
//             a dialog box.
//
// Your Borland C++ Consultant

#define STRICT

#include <windowsx.h>
#include <stdlib.h>
#include <stdio.h>
#include "dlghelp.h"
```

continues

Listing 2.23. continued

```
// Function Prototypes
LRESULT CALLBACK _export MainWndProc(HWND, UINT,
                         WPARAM, LPARAM);
BOOL CALLBACK _export MainDlgProc(HWND, UINT, WPARAM,
                         LPARAM);
void WM_CommandHandler(HWND, int, HWND, UINT);
void WM_Command_Dlg_Handler(HWND, int, HWND, UINT);
DWORD CALLBACK _export HelpFilterProc(int, WPARAM,
                         LPARAM);


// Global Variables
HINSTANCE  ghInstance;
HOOKPROC   lpfnFilterProc;
HHOOK      hHook;
UINT       HelpMsg;

/*******************************************/
#pragma argsused
int PASCAL WinMain(HINSTANCE hInstance, HINSTANCE
                   hPrevInstance,
                   LPSTR lpCmdParam, int nCmdShow)
{
    char       ProgName[] = "Help Dialog Box";
    HWND       hWnd;
    MSG        msg;

    if (!hPrevInstance)
    {
        WNDCLASS    wndclass;

        wndclass.lpszClassName = ProgName;
        wndclass.lpfnWndProc   = (WNDPROC) MainWndProc;
        wndclass.cbClsExtra    = 0;
        wndclass.cbWndExtra    = 0;
        wndclass.hInstance     = hInstance;
        wndclass.hIcon         = LoadIcon(NULL,
                                   IDI_APPLICATION);
        wndclass.hCursor       = LoadCursor(NULL,
                                   IDC_ARROW);
        wndclass.hbrBackground = GetStockObject(
                                   WHITE_BRUSH);
        wndclass.lpszMenuName  = "MAINMENU";
        wndclass.style         = CS_VREDRAW |
                                   CS_HREDRAW;
```

```
      if (!RegisterClass(&wndclass))
          exit(1);
   }

   ghInstance = hInstance;

   hWnd = CreateWindow(ProgName, ProgName,
                       WS_OVERLAPPEDWINDOW,
                       CW_USEDEFAULT, CW_USEDEFAULT,
                       CW_USEDEFAULT, CW_USEDEFAULT,
                       NULL, NULL, hInstance, NULL);

   ShowWindow(hWnd, nCmdShow);
   UpdateWindow(hWnd);

   while (GetMessage(&msg, NULL, 0, 0))
   {
      TranslateMessage(&msg);
      DispatchMessage(&msg);
   }
   return msg.wParam;
}


/*********************************************/
BOOL CALLBACK _export MainDlgProc(HWND hDlg, UINT
                      message, WPARAM wParam, LPARAM
                      lParam)
{
   switch(message)
   {
      case WM_INITDIALOG :
      {
         HelpMsg = RegisterWindowMessage("MSG_HELP");


         return TRUE;
      }

      case WM_COMMAND :
      {
         return (BOOL)HANDLE_WM_COMMAND(hDlg, wParam,
               lParam, WM_Command_Dlg_Handler);
      }
   }
```

continues

Listing 2.23. continued

```
if (message==HelpMsg)
{
   char buf[255] = "";

   // The ID of the control is now in the wParam.
   //   In this case, we are using MessageBox to
   //   give the context-sensitive help.  In a
   //   full application you would want to use
   //   WinHelp.
   switch(wParam)
   {
      case IDD_NAME :
      {
         sprintf(buf, "Enter Name");
         break;
      }

      case IDD_BUSINESS :
      {
         sprintf(buf, "Enter Business Name");
         break;
      }

      case IDD_STREET :
      {
         sprintf(buf, "Enter Street");
         break;

      }

      case IDD_CITY :
      {
         sprintf(buf, "Enter City");
         break;
      }

      case IDD_STATE :
      {
         sprintf(buf, "Enter State");
         break;
      }

      case IDD_FEMALE :
      case IDD_MALE :
      {
         sprintf(buf, "Choose Sex");
         break;
```

```
            }

            case IDD_MOREINFO :
            {
               sprintf(buf, "Enter Additional
                       Information");
               break;
            }

            case IDOK :
            {
               sprintf(buf, "Accept the Input");
               break;
            }


            case IDCANCEL :
            {
               sprintf(buf, "Cancel the Input");
               break;
            }


        }

        MessageBox(hDlg, buf, "Dialog Box",
                   MB_OK ¦ MB_ICONQUESTION);


        return TRUE;
    }

    return FALSE;
}


/******************************************/
#pragma argsused
void WM_Command_Dlg_Handler(HWND hDlg, int id,
                            HWND hwndCtl, UINT
                            codeNotify)
{
    switch(id)
    {
        case IDOK :
        case IDCANCEL :
        {
            EndDialog(hDlg, 0);
```

continues

Listing 2.23. continued

```
        break;
      }
    }
}


/********************************************/
#pragma argsused
void WM_CommandHandler(HWND hWnd, int id, HWND
                      hWndCtl, UINT codeNotify)
{
    switch (id)
    {
        case IDM_EXIT :
        {
            SendMessage(hWnd, WM_CLOSE, 0, 0L);
            break;
        }

        case IDM_DIALOG :
        {
            DLGPROC DlgProc;

            // Create procedure instance for dialog box
procedure
            DlgProc = (DLGPROC)MakeProcInstance(
                    (FARPROC)MainDlgProc, ghInstance);
            // Create procedure instance for hook
                function
            lpfnFilterProc = (HOOKPROC)MakeProcInstance(
                    (FARPROC)HelpFilterProc,
                    ghInstance);

            // Set Windows hook
            hHook = SetWindowsHookEx(WH_MSGFILTER,
                    lpfnFilterProc, ghInstance,
                    (HTASK)NULL);

            // Go execute dialog box
            DialogBox(ghInstance, "CSHELPDIALOG", hWnd,
                    DlgProc);

            // Clean up hook function
            UnhookWindowsHookEx(hHook);
```

```
        // Clean up filter function procedure
        //   instance
        FreeProcInstance((FARPROC)lpfnFilterProc);

        // Clean up dialog function procedure
        //   instance
        FreeProcInstance((FARPROC)DlgProc);
        break;
    }

  }

}

/*********************************************/
DWORD CALLBACK _export HelpFilterProc(int nCode,
                      WPARAM wParam, LPARAM lParam)
{
   MSG FAR *ptrMsg;


   // If it is not a code we are looking for,
   //    go to next hook function
   if (nCode < 0)
       return CallNextHookEx(hHook, nCode, wParam,
                             lParam);

   // Check for press of F1 key
   if (MSGF_DIALOGBOX == nCode)
   {
      ptrMsg = (MSG FAR *)lParam;

      if ((WM_KEYDOWN == ptrMsg->message) &&
          (VK_F1 == ptrMsg->wParam))
      {
         PostMessage(GetParent(ptrMsg->hwnd), HelpMsg,
                     GetDlgCtrlID(GetFocus()), 0L);
         return 1L;
      }
      else
         return 0L;
   }
   else
   {
      // Do not handle the message
      return 0L;

   }
```

continues

Listing 2.23. continued

```c
}

/*********************************************/
LRESULT CALLBACK _export MainWndProc(HWND hWnd, UINT
                        message, WPARAM wParam,
                        LPARAM lParam)
{
   switch (message)
   {
      case WM_PAINT :
      {
         HDC          PaintDC;
         RECT         rect;
         PAINTSTRUCT ps;

         PaintDC = BeginPaint(hWnd, &ps);
         GetClientRect(hWnd, &rect);

         DrawText(PaintDC, "Make a Selection",
                  -1, &rect, DT_SINGLELINE | DT_CENTER
                  | DT_VCENTER);

         EndPaint(hWnd, &ps);
         return 0;
      }

      case WM_DESTROY :
      {
         PostQuitMessage(0);
         return 0;
      }

      case WM_COMMAND :
      {
         return HANDLE_WM_COMMAND(hWnd, wParam,
                  lParam, WM_CommandHandler);
      }

   }
   return DefWindowProc (hWnd, message, wParam,
         lParam);
}
```

Listing 2.24. DLGHELP.H header file.

```
/*
 * DLGHLP.H header file
 *
 */

#define IDD_NAME        110
#define IDD_BUSINESS    120
#define IDD_STREET      130
#define IDD_CITY        140
#define IDD_STATE       150
#define IDD_FEMALE      160
#define IDD_MALE        170
#define IDD_MOREINFO    180


#define IDM_EXIT        200
#define IDM_DIALOG      210
```

Listing 2.25. DLGHELP.RC resource script.

```
/*
 * EXPDLG.RC resource script
 *
 */

#include "dlghelp.h"

CSHELPDIALOG DIALOG 7, 20, 165, 161
STYLE DS_MODALFRAME ¦ WS_POPUP ¦ WS_CAPTION ¦
WS_SYSMENU
CAPTION "Client Data"
BEGIN
     EDITTEXT IDD_NAME, 42, 6, 71, 12
     EDITTEXT IDD_BUSINESS, 42, 20, 71, 12
     EDITTEXT IDD_STREET, 42, 34, 71, 12
     EDITTEXT IDD_CITY, 42, 48, 71, 12
     EDITTEXT IDD_STATE, 42, 62, 34, 12
     CONTROL "&Female", IDD_FEMALE, "BUTTON",
BS_AUTORADIOBUTTON ¦ WS_CHILD ¦ WS_VISIBLE ¦
WS_TABSTOP, 16, 106, 34, 12
     CONTROL "&Male", IDD_MALE, "BUTTON",
BS_AUTORADIOBUTTON ¦ WS_CHILD ¦ WS_VISIBLE ¦
WS_TABSTOP, 16, 119, 28, 12
     CONTROL "", IDD_MOREINFO, "EDIT", ES_LEFT ¦
```

continues

Listing 2.25. continued

```
ES_MULTILINE ¦ ES_AUTOVSCROLL ¦ WS_CHILD ¦ WS_VISIBLE
¦ WS_BORDER ¦ WS_VSCROLL ¦ WS_TABSTOP, 81, 102, 77, 37
    DEFPUSHBUTTON "&Ok", IDOK, 127, 9, 33, 11,
WS_CHILD ¦ WS_VISIBLE ¦ WS_TABSTOP
    PUSHBUTTON "&Cancel", IDCANCEL, 127, 25, 33, 11,
WS_CHILD ¦ WS_VISIBLE ¦ WS_TABSTOP
    LTEXT "&Name:", -1, 19, 6, 23, 8, WS_CHILD ¦
WS_VISIBLE ¦ WS_GROUP
    LTEXT "&Business:", -1, 7, 19, 35, 8
    LTEXT "&Street:", -1, 19, 34, 22, 8
    LTEXT "&City:", -1, 25, 48, 16, 8
    LTEXT "S&tate:", -1, 21, 62, 20, 8
    LTEXT "S&ex:", -1, 8, 90, 16, 8, WS_CHILD ¦
WS_VISIBLE ¦ WS_GROUP
    LTEXT "More &Information:", -1, 81, 90, 60, 8
    CONTROL "", 108, "button", BS_GROUPBOX ¦ WS_CHILD
¦ WS_VISIBLE, 7, 97, 50, 41
    LTEXT "", -1, 163, 80, 10, 8, WS_CHILD ¦
WS_VISIBLE ¦ WS_GROUP
    LTEXT "Press F1 for Context-sensitive Help", -1,
24, 148, 117, 8, WS_CHILD ¦ WS_VISIBLE ¦ WS_GROUP
END


MAINMENU MENU
BEGIN
    POPUP "&File"
    BEGIN
        MENUITEM "E&xit", IDM_EXIT
    END

    POPUP "&Dialog"
    BEGIN
        MENUITEM "Enter Information", IDM_DIALOG
    END

END
```

Listing 2.26. DLGHELP.DEF module definition file.

```
;
; DLGHLP.DEF module definition file
;

DESCRIPTION    'Context-sensitive Dialog Box Help'
NAME           DLGHELP
EXETYPE        WINDOWS
STUB           'WINSTUB.EXE'
HEAPSIZE       1024
STACKSIZE      8192
CODE           PRELOAD MOVEABLE DISCARDABLE
DATA           PRELOAD MOVEABLE MULTIPLE
```

II

In This Chapter

■ How to create your own custom SOUND resources that will allow you to embed .WAV files inside an executable program.

■ How to access the joystick from a Windows program.

■ How to use the MCI (media control interface) to send high-level commands to multimedia devices.

■ How to access the MIDI (Musical Instrument Digital Interface) from a Windows program.

Multimedia

All the example programs in this chapter use the multimedia features that were added to Windows 3.1. In order to use the multimedia functions, a program must include the multimedia system header file at the beginning of the program. For example:

```
#include <mmsystem.h>
```

is necessary. Furthermore, if you look for documentation for the multimedia functions, you may find that it is somewhat sparse. This is unfortunately true. The documentation that comes with Borland C++ is a help (.HLP) file named C:\BORLANDC\BIN\WIN31MWH.HLP. A program item is initially installed in Borland C++ with the title "Multimedia Reference." Another one is C:\BORLANDC\BIN\MCISTRWH.HLP, which contains information on the media control interface. It is available in the program item titled "MCI Reference."

If you become involved in using the multimedia functions and desire more information, you might want to look into the three-volume reference set published by Microsoft Press and available at most bookstores. The set includes:

Microsoft Windows Multimedia Authoring and Tools Guide, ISBN: 1-55615-391-0.

Microsoft Windows Multimedia Programmer's Workbook, ISBN: 1-55615-390-2.

Microsoft Windows Multimedia Programmer's Reference, ISBN: 1-55615-389-9.

Embedding Sounds in a Program

How do I embed .WAV sound files inside my application?

DESCRIPTION

The sndPlaySound function is used to play a binary .WAV file. The function makes it easy to create .WAV files that relate to certain sounds inside your program. However, the function takes the filename of the .WAV file as one of its parameters. In other words, the function requires that a separate .WAV file be distributed with the program.

In certain applications it would be nice to embed the .WAV file inside the executable file for the application as a Windows resource. The advantage of this is that you don't have to distribute any extra program files along with your application.

NOTE   In order for a program to play sound, it must first have the proper drivers. If the program is running on a system with a Sound Blaster or Pro

Audio Spectrum, the board should have come with the appropriate drivers and the sound board's manuals should be consulted for help on installing Windows drivers.

However, if the program is being run on a computer without a sound board, the user is not totally out of luck. A driver for the PC speaker is available (in fact, it is included on the disk that comes with this book). However, the sound produced by the speaker is certainly nothing special. At least it is usually enough to get an idea of the sounds created by a program.

To install the speaker driver, load control panel (see Figure 3.1) and click on the Drivers icon. Click on the Add button. Now double-click on Unlisted or Updated driver (see Figure 3.2). When you are asked for the path of the driver, specify A:\ or B:\ (depending on which drive the program disk is in) and click on the OK button.

The Add Unlisted or Updated Driver dialog box will come up with the words "Sound Driver for PC-Speaker." Click OK, and the PC-Speaker Setup dialog box will be displayed (see Figure 3.3). Set any options necessary on your system. When done, select the OK button to complete the installation.

A dialog box will be displayed telling you that in order for the new driver to take effect, the system must be restarted. Go ahead and restart the system to ensure that the PC Speaker driver will take effect.

III

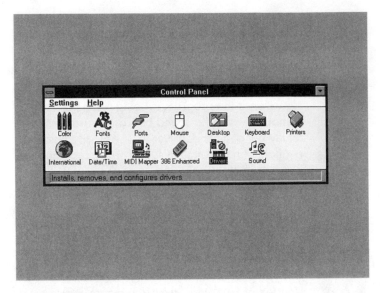

Figure 3.1. *Control panel main window.*

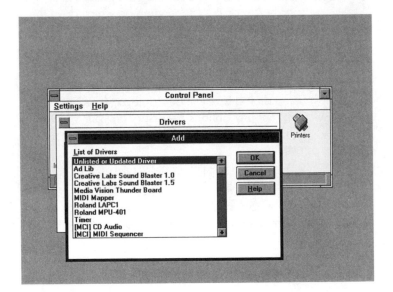

Figure 3.2. *Unlisted or updated driver.*

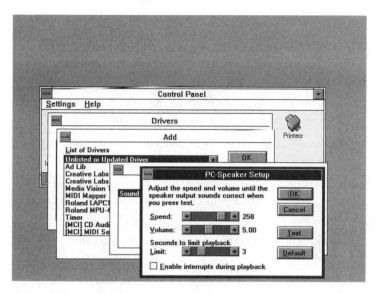

Figure 3.3. *PC-Speaker Setup dialog box.*

ANSWER

The solution is to create a custom resource type. Windows provides built-in resources such as accelerator keys, menus, dialog boxes, bitmaps, icons, and cursors. However, thanks to the extendibility of Windows, the programmer is not limited to just these types of resources. You can create your own resources as needed or desired.

The first step is to include a line in the resource script that specifies the .WAV file. For example:

```
BUZZER SOUND "buzzer.wav"
```

This creates a new resource of type SOUND with a name of BUZZER. It references the file BUZZER.WAV. The line forces the resource compiler to include the specified .WAV resource inside your executable. At this point, the program needs a way to access the sound data.

Inside the source code for the program, the first thing to be done is to get a handle to the sound resource. This is accomplished with the FindResource function. The code looks like this:

```
hSndResource = FindResource(hInstance, "BUZZER", "SOUND");
```

The FindResource function returns a handle to the specified resource. In this case, it searches for the resource of type SOUND with the name BUZZER.

Next, the program loads the resource and gets a handle to the global memory where the resource is loaded. An example is this:

```
hGlobalMem = LoadResource(hInstance, hSndResource);
```

The LoadResource function returns a handle to the global memory. With this global memory handle, the program can use LockResource to fetch a pointer to the memory. It can be done like this:

```
lpMemSound = (LPCSTR)LockResource(hGlobalMem);
```

With a pointer to the memory of the sound data, the sndPlaySound function can be called. The call looks like this:

```
sndPlaySound(lpMemSound, SND_MEMORY);
```

The SND_MEMORY identifier is passed as an option to the function, which tells the function that a pointer to the memory is being passed, rather than the filename of the binary sound file. Other flags that can be used are listed in Table 3.1.

Table 3.1. sndPlaySound **Options.**

Option	Description
SND_SYNC	Forces the sound to be played before the function returns.
SND_ASYNC	The function returns immediately after beginning to play the sound.
SND_NODEFAULT	If the sound can't be found, no sounds are played.
SND_MEMORY	Specifies that the lpszSoundName parameter points to an in-memory image of a waveform sound.

Option	Description
SND_LOOP	The sound continues to play repeatedly until the function is called again with the `lpszSoundName` parameter set to `NULL`. You must also specify the `SND_ASYNC` flag when using this option.
SND_NOSTOP	If a sound is currently playing, the function will immediately return `FALSE` without playing the requested sound.

Once the function returns, the only thing the program has to do is clean up the resource by calling the `FreeResource` function along with a handle to the global memory. It looks like this:

```
FreeResource(hGlobalMem);
```

The `FreeResource` function frees the memory occupied by the sound resource.

COMMENTS

Sounds stored in .WAV files can create large executables. If your program has many sounds, you might want to check to make sure they don't add too much to the size of the EXE file.

Also, any program that is going to use the multimedia functions of Windows 3.1 should check to make sure that the system has the necessary hardware drivers installed. To make sure that a computer system can play .WAV files, the program calls the `waveOutGetNumDevs` function. If the return value is `zero`, no wave output devices are available. Sample code looks like this:

```
if (waveOutGetNumDevs() < 1)
{
```

```
MessageBox(NULL, "No .WAV output device",
            NULL, MB_OK | MB_ICONSTOP);
exit(1);

}
```

This code checks to see if there are zero wave output devices available. If there is less than one, the program displays a message box and terminates the program. The `waveOutGetNumDevs` function will return only a count of the number of devices available. In other words, if a device is installed but being accessed by another program, the test will still fail.

SEE ALSO

`FindResource` Multimedia API Function
`FreeResource` Multimedia API Function
`LoadResource` Multimedia API Function
`LockResource` Multimedia API Function
`sndPlaySound` Multimedia API Function
`waveOutGetNumDevs` Multimedia API Function

EXAMPLE CODE

The example program creates three buttons on the screen (see Figure 3.4). Each button sounds a different .WAV file that has been embedded into the program (EXE) file. A function, `PlayWaveResource`, is included in the listing. It takes a handle to the instance of the program and the name of the SOUND resource in the resource script. It then finds the resource in the executable, loads the resource, and locks the resource, at which time it calls `sndPlaySound` to play the sound. It also does the necessary cleanup work.

Listing 3.1. contains the C source code for WAVRES.C. Listing 3.2. is the resource script for WAVRES.RC. Listing 3.3. contains the module definition file for WAVRES.DEF. The program also requires the BUZZER.WAV, CHIME.WAV, and LASER.WAV files in order to be compiled.

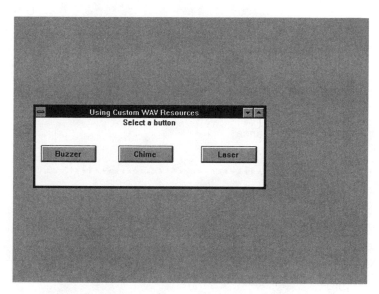

Figure 3.4. *Sample WAVRES program.*

Listing 3.1. WAVRES.C source code.

```
// WAVRES.C - Example of using a .WAV file as a
//            custom resource
//
// Help Desk Companion by Paul J. Perry
//

#define STRICT
#define IDB_BUZZER 10
#define IDB_CHIME  20
#define IDB_LASER  30


#include <windowsx.h>
#include <mmsystem.h>
#include <stdlib.h>


// Function Prototypes
LRESULT CALLBACK export MainWndProc (HWND, UINT,
                                          WPARAM, LPARAM)
```

continues

Listing 3.1. continued

```
void WM_CommandHandler(HWND, int, HWND, UINT);
BOOL PlayWaveResource(HINSTANCE, LPSTR);



// Global Variables
HINSTANCE ghInstance;


/*********************************************/
#pragma argsused
int PASCAL WinMain(HINSTANCE hInstance, HINSTANCE
                   hPrevInstance, LPSTR lpCmdParam,
                   int nCmdShow)
{
    char       ProgName[] = "Using Custom .WAV
                            Resources";
    HWND       hWnd;
    MSG        msg;


    if (waveOutGetNumDevs() < 1)
    {
        MessageBox(NULL, "No .WAV output device",
                   NULL, MB_OK | MB_ICONSTOP);
        exit(1);

    }


    if (!hPrevInstance)
    {
        WNDCLASS    wndclass;

        wndclass.lpszClassName = ProgName;
        wndclass.lpfnWndProc   = (WNDPROC) MainWndProc;
        wndclass.cbClsExtra    = 0;
        wndclass.cbWndExtra    = 0;
        wndclass.hInstance     = hInstance;
        wndclass.hIcon         = LoadIcon(NULL,
                                 IDI_APPLICATION);
        wndclass.hCursor       = LoadCursor(NULL,
                                 IDC_ARROW);
        wndclass.hbrBackground = GetStockBrush
                                 (WHITE_BRUSH);
```

```
        wndclass.lpszMenuName  = NULL;
        wndclass.style         = CS_VREDRAW |
                                 CS_HREDRAW;

        if (!RegisterClass(&wndclass))
            exit(1);
    }

    ghInstance = hInstance;

    hWnd = CreateWindow(ProgName, ProgName,
                        WS_OVERLAPPEDWINDOW,
                        CW_USEDEFAULT, CW_USEDEFAULT,
                        420, 150,
                        NULL, NULL, hInstance, NULL);

    ShowWindow(hWnd, nCmdShow);
    UpdateWindow(hWnd);

    while (GetMessage(&msg, NULL, 0, 0))
    {
        TranslateMessage(&msg);
        DispatchMessage(&msg);
    }
    return msg.wParam;
}


/*********************************************/
BOOL PlayWaveResource(HINSTANCE hInstance, LPSTR
                      lpSoundName)
{
    LPCSTR    lpMemSound;
    HGLOBAL   hGlobalMem;
    BOOL      result;
    HRSRC     hSndResource;


    // First, we get a handle to the sound resource
    hSndResource = FindResource(hInstance, lpSoundName,
                                "SOUND");

    // Next, we load the resource and get a handle
    //    to global memory.
    hGlobalMem = LoadResource(hInstance, hSndResource);

    // Now, we lock the global memory, thereby returning
    //    a pointer to the actual memory location
    //    that has the resource.
```

III

continues

Listing 3.1. continued

```
    lpMemSound = (LPCSTR)LockResource(hGlobalMem);

    // Go ahead and play the wave file
    result = sndPlaySound(lpMemSound, SND_MEMORY);

    // Clean up
    FreeResource(hGlobalMem);

    return result;

}


/*******************************************/
#pragma argsused
void WM_CommandHandler(HWND hWnd, int id, HWND
                        hWndCtl, UINT codeNotify)
{

    switch (id)
    {
        case IDB_BUZZER :
        {
            PlayWaveResource(ghInstance, "BUZZER");
            break;
        }

        case IDB_CHIME :
        {
            PlayWaveResource(ghInstance, "CHIME");
            break;
        }

        case IDB_LASER :
        {
            PlayWaveResource(ghInstance, "LASER");
            break;
        }
    }

}


/*******************************************/
LRESULT CALLBACK _export MainWndProc(HWND hWnd, UINT
                        message,WPARAM
                        wParam, LPARAM
                        lParam)
```

```
{
    static HWND hButton1;
    static HWND hButton2;
    static HWND hButton3;

    switch (message)
    {
        case WM_CREATE :
        {
            hButton1 = CreateWindow("BUTTON", "Buzzer",
                                    WS_CHILD |
                                    WS_VISIBLE |
                                    BS_PUSHBUTTON,
                                    10, 50, 100, 30, hWnd,
                                    (HMENU) IDB_BUZZER,
                                    ghInstance, NULL);

            hButton2 = CreateWindow("BUTTON", "Chime",
                                    WS_CHILD |
                                    WS_VISIBLE |
                                    BS_PUSHBUTTON,
                                    150, 50, 100, 30, hWnd,
                                    (HMENU) IDB_CHIME,
                                    ghInstance, NULL);

            hButton3 = CreateWindow("BUTTON", "Laser",
                                    WS_CHILD |
                                    WS_VISIBLE |
                                    BS_PUSHBUTTON,
                                    300, 50, 100, 30, hWnd,
                                    (HMENU) IDB_LASER,
                                    ghInstance, NULL);

            return 0;
        }

        case WM_PAINT :
        {
            HDC         PaintDC;
            RECT        rect;
            PAINTSTRUCT ps;

            PaintDC = BeginPaint(hWnd, &ps);
            GetClientRect(hWnd, &rect);

            DrawText(PaintDC, "Select a button",
                     -1, &rect, DT_BOTTOM | DT_SINGLELINE
                     |DT_CENTER | DT_VCENTER);
```

III

continues

Listing 3.1. continued

```
        EndPaint(hWnd, &ps);
        return 0;
    }

    case WM_COMMAND :
    {
        return HANDLE_WM_COMMAND(hWnd, wParam,
            lParam, WM_CommandHandler);
    }

    case WM_DESTROY :
    {
        PostQuitMessage(0);
        return 0;
    }
    }

    return DefWindowProc (hWnd, message, wParam,
                          lParam);
}
```

Listing 3.2. WAVRES.RC source code.

```
/*
 * WAVRES.RC resource script
 *
 */


BUZZER SOUND "buzzer.wav"
CHIME SOUND "chime.wav"
LASER SOUND "laser.wav"
```

Listing 3.3. WAVRES.DEF module definition file.

```
;
; WAVRES.DEF module definition file
;
```

```
DESCRIPTION    'Wav files as a resource'
NAME           WAVRES
EXETYPE        WINDOWS
STUB           'WINSTUB.EXE'
HEAPSIZE       1024
STACKSIZE      8192
CODE           PRELOAD MOVEABLE DISCARDABLE
DATA           PRELOAD MOVEABLE MULTIPLE
```

Accessing the Joystick

How does a program access the joystick input device?

DESCRIPTION

Although the joystick is less common than a mouse, it is more appropriate for certain applications—most notably for games. In DOS, a program can make a couple of interrupt calls and get information about the joystick. What about in a Windows program?

III

> **NOTE** In order to use the joystick with Windows, the joystick device driver must be installed. The driver is included on the disk that comes with this book.
>
> The first step is to copy the file IBMJOY.DRV to the Windows system directory (usually C:\WINDOWS\SYSTEM). Next, you must add a line to the SYSTEM.INI initialization file. Open the file in an editor, and search for the [drivers] section. Add a line that reads:
>
> Joystick=ibmjoy.drv
>
> Now, restart Windows. To make sure the driver was installed, load Control Panel and select the Drivers option (see Figure 3.5).

The Installed Drivers dialog box should be displayed (see Figure 3.6). This dialog shows all device drivers that have been installed.

Find the entry titled "Microsoft game adapter joystick driver," and double-click on it. The Game Adapter dialog box will be displayed (see Figure 3.7). It allows you to set the driver depending on what type of joystick you have installed. In most cases, the default option for "One or two 2-dimensional joysticks" is the proper setting. If it does not work with your system, try the other option for "Single 3-Dimensional joystick."

After these steps, the joystick driver has been installed, and you can use the program and functions presented.

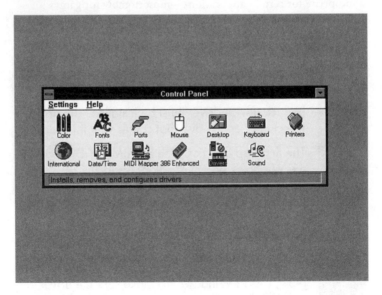

Figure 3.5. *Selecting the Drivers option of Control Panel.*

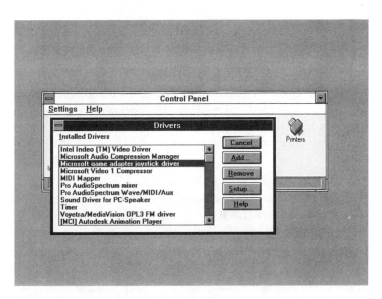

Figure 3.6. *The Installed Drivers dialog box.*

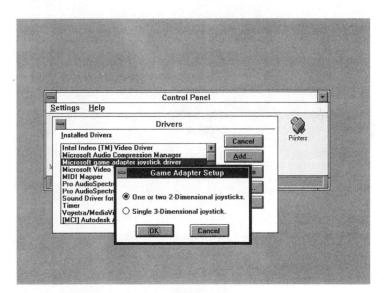

Figure 3.7. *Game Adapter Setup dialog box.*

ANSWER

With the advent of Windows 3.1 and the inclusion of multimedia functions, it's fairly easy to access the joystick. There are actually two methods that can be used. The first method calls for the program to capture all mouse input. The mouse input is then sent to the program as a series of messages (all Windows programmers should be familiar with messages). The second method allows the program to call a function that returns the coordinates of the mouse.

The first method is the most useful. You first use the joySetCapture function to capture the joystick. You must specify to capture either JOYSTICKID1 or JOYSTICKID2 (a maximum of two joysticks are supported). If the function was not successful, it returns an error code (for which your program should check).

Once the joystick has been captured, all joystick messages are sent to the window procedure associated with the specified window. Table 3.2. specifies the joystick messages that can be received.

Table 3.2. Joystick messages.

Message	Description
MM_JOY1BUTTONDOWN	The button has been pressed for joystick #1.
MM_JOY1BUTTONUP	The button has been released for joystick #1.
MM_JOY1MOVE	The position has changed for joystick #1.
MM_JOY1ZMOVE	The z-axis position has changed for joystick #1.
MM_JOY2BUTTONDOWN	The button has been pressed for joystick #2.
MM_JOY2BUTTONUP	The button has been released for joystick #2.
MM_JOY2MOVE	The position has changed for joystick #2.
MM_JOY2ZMOVE	The z-axis position has changed for joystick #2.

When a program is finished using the joystick, it must release the joystick. This is done with a call to the `joyReleaseCapture` function.

The second method of accessing the joystick does not capture the joystick. Instead, a program can call the `joyGetPos` function, which returns the position and button status of the joystick. This method has an advantage in that the joystick does not need to be captured, thereby theoretically using less of the system's resources. However, in most cases it is much easier to capture the joystick and then take actions based on which messages are received by the window procedure of the program.

COMMENTS

As the number of Windows games increases, the joystick multimedia functions should be used more frequently. It is probably a good idea to make joystick support an extra option because not everyone has a joystick connected. If joystick input is the sole method of interacting with a game, you might leave out some users who would like to play your game, but don't have a joystick.

III

SEE ALSO

`joyGetDevCaps` Multimedia API Function
`joyGetNumDevs` Multimedia API Function
`joyGetPos` Multimedia API Function
`joyGetThreshold` Multimedia API Function
`joyReleaseCapture` Multimedia API Function
`joySetCapturejoy` Multimedia API Function
`joySetThreshold` Multimedia API Function

All functions that interact with the mouse are all prefixed with the letters `joy`. This makes it easy to find which functions allow the program to work with a mouse. Full documentation is found on-line in the help file titled "Multimedia Reference," which is included in the Borland C++ Program Manager group.

EXAMPLE CODE

The example program captures the joystick and forces it to emulate the mouse. By moving the joystick, the user causes the mouse cursor to move. Pressing the joystick buttons causes the client area of the program to flash. Notice that even if the cursor moves outside the client area of the program, the joystick movement will still cause the mouse cursor to move. The reason is that the program uses the joySetCapture function. Therefore, even if the mouse cursor is moved over a different program, it still causes the cursor to move.

Listing 3.4 contains the C source code. Listing 3.5 contains the resource script. Listing 3.6 contains the module definition file. The other files necessary to run this program include JOYSTICK.ICO and JOYSTICK.CUR (see Figure 3.8).

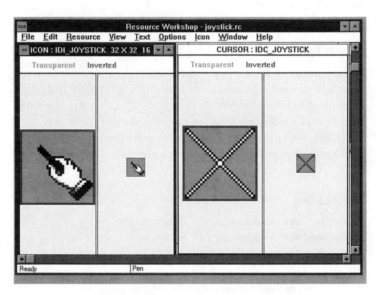

Figure 3.8. *Icon and Cursor for the JOYSTICK example program.*

Listing 3.4. JOYSTICK.C source code.

```
// JOYSTICK.C - Demonstration program showing how
//              to use a joystick input device.
//
// Help Desk Companion by Paul J. Perry
//

#define STRICT
```

```
#include <windowsx.h>
#include <mmsystem.h>
#include <stdio.h>
#include <stdlib.h>

// Function Prototypes
LRESULT CALLBACK _export MainWndProc(HWND, UINT,
                                     WPARAM, LPARAM);
BOOL InitializeJoystick(HWND);

/*********************************************/
#pragma argsused
int PASCAL WinMain(HINSTANCE hInstance, HINSTANCE
                   hPrevInstance,LPSTR lpCmdParam, int
                   nCmdShow)
{
    char        ProgName[] = "Joystick Demo";
    HWND        hWnd;
    MSG         msg;


    if (!hPrevInstance)
    {
        WNDCLASS        wndclass;

        wndclass.lpszClassName = ProgName;
        wndclass.lpfnWndProc   = (WNDPROC) MainWndProc;
        wndclass.cbClsExtra    = 0;
        wndclass.cbWndExtra    = 0;
        wndclass.hInstance     = hInstance;
        wndclass.hIcon         = LoadIcon(hInstance,
                                    "IDI_JOYSTICK");
        wndclass.hCursor       = LoadCursor(hInstance,
                                    "IDC_JOYSTICK");
        wndclass.hbrBackground = GetStockBrush
                                    (WHITE_BRUSH);
        wndclass.lpszMenuName  = NULL;
        wndclass.style         = CS_VREDRAW | CS_HREDRAW;

        if (!RegisterClass(&wndclass))
            exit(1);
    }

    hWnd = CreateWindow(ProgName, ProgName,
                        WS_OVERLAPPEDWINDOW,
                        CW_USEDEFAULT, CW_USEDEFAULT,
                        CW_USEDEFAULT, CW_USEDEFAULT,
                        NULL, NULL, hInstance, NULL);
```

III

continues

Listing 3.4. continued

```
    ShowWindow(hWnd, nCmdShow);
    UpdateWindow(hWnd);

    while (GetMessage(&msg, NULL, 0, 0))
    {
        TranslateMessage(&msg);
        DispatchMessage(&msg);
    }
    return msg.wParam;
}


/*********************************************/
BOOL InitializeJoystick(HWND hWnd)
{
    UINT result;
    char buf[255] = "";

    result = joySetCapture(hWnd, JOYSTICKID1, 0, FALSE);

    if (result == JOYERR_NOERROR)
        return TRUE;

    switch (result)
    {

        case MMSYSERR_NODRIVER :
        {
            sprintf(buf, "Joystick Driver not Present");
            break;
        }

        case JOYERR_PARMS :
        {
            sprintf(buf, "Invalid joySetCapture
                    Parameters");
            break;
        }

        case JOYERR_NOCANDO :
        {
            sprintf(buf, "Cannot Capture Joystick");
            break;
        }

        case JOYERR_UNPLUGGED :
        {
```

```
                sprintf(buf, "Joystick not Connected to
                        System");
                break;
            }

        }

        MessageBox(hWnd, buf, NULL, MB_OK | MB_ICONSTOP);

        return FALSE;

    }

    /********************************************/
    LRESULT CALLBACK _export MainWndProc(HWND hWnd, UINT
                                                message, WPARAM
                                                wParam, LPARAM
                                                lParam)
    {
        switch (message)
        {
            case WM_CREATE :
            {
                InitializeJoystick(hWnd);
                return 0;
            }

            case MM_JOY1BUTTONDOWN :
            {
                HDC    hDC;
                RECT   rect;
                HBRUSH hBrush;


                hDC = GetDC(hWnd);
                GetClientRect(hWnd, &rect);


                if (wParam & JOY_BUTTON1)
                {
                    SetROP2(hDC, R2_NOT);
                    SelectBrush(hDC,
    GetStockBrush(BLACK_BRUSH));
                    Rectangle(hDC, rect.left, rect.top,
                            rect.right, rect.bottom);

                }
                else if (wParam & JOY_BUTTON2)
                {
```

continues

Listing 3.4. continued

```
        SetROP2(hDC, R2_COPYPEN);
        hBrush = CreateSolidBrush(RGB(255, 0, 0));

        SelectBrush(hDC, hBrush);

        Rectangle(hDC, rect.left, rect.top,
                  rect.right, rect.bottom);

        SelectBrush(hDC, GetStockBrush
                   (BLACK_BRUSH));

        DeleteBrush(hBrush);
    }


    ReleaseDC(hWnd, hDC);

    return 0;
}

case MM_JOY1BUTTONUP :
{
    InvalidateRect(hWnd, NULL, TRUE);

    return 0;
}

case MM_JOY1MOVE :
{
    WORD x, y;
    POINT pt;

    GetCursorPos(&pt);

    // The joystick coordinates are expressed in
    //   coordinates with a range from 0 to 65535.
    //   Therefore, we take the 5 most significant
    //   bits, so the position is translated to
    //   screen coordinates (MM_TEXT).
    x = LOWORD(lParam) >> 11;
    y = HIWORD(lParam) >> 11;

    // If the joystick is to the left of the
    //   center then move the cursor position to
    //   the left. Otherwise, if the joystick is
    //   to the right of the center position,
    //   then move the cursor position to the
    //   right.
```

```
   if (x <= 12)
      pt.x = pt.x + x - 17;
   else if (x >= 20)
      pt.x = pt.x + x - 15;

   // If the joystick is below the center
   //    position, then move the cursor down.
   //    Otherwise, if the joystick is above the
   //    center position, then move the cursor
   //    position up.
   if (y <= 12)
      pt.y = pt.y + y - 17;
   else if (y >= 20)
      pt.y = pt.y + y - 15;

   // Go ahead and set the mouse cursor
   //    position.
   SetCursorPos(pt.x, pt.y);

   return 0;
}


case WM_PAINT :
{
   HDC          PaintDC;
   RECT         rect;
   PAINTSTRUCT  ps;

   PaintDC = BeginPaint(hWnd, &ps);
   GetClientRect(hWnd, &rect);

   DrawText(PaintDC, "Move Joystick to Position
            Cursor. "
                      "Press mouse buttons to
                      flash window",
            -1, &rect, DT_SINGLELINE | DT_CENTER
                      | DT_VCENTER);

   EndPaint(hWnd, &ps);
   return 0;
}

case WM_DESTROY :
{
   // It is necessary to release the joystick.
   //    Otherwise, the joystick is locked out
   //    until the user restarts Windows.
```

III

continues

Listing 3.4. continued

```
        joyReleaseCapture(JOYSTICKID1);
        PostQuitMessage(0);
        return 0;
    }
  }
  return DefWindowProc (hWnd, message, wParam,
lParam);
}
```

Listing 3.5. JOYSTICK.RC resource script.

```
/*
 * JOYSTICK.RC resource script
 *
 */

IDI_JOYSTICK ICON "joystick.ico"

IDC_JOYSTICK CURSOR "joystick.cur"
```

Listing 3.6. JOYSTICK.DEF module definition file.

```
;
; JOYSTICK.DEF module definition file
;

DESCRIPTION     'Joystick demonstration program'
NAME            JOYSTICK
EXETYPE         WINDOWS
STUB            'WINSTUB.EXE'
HEAPSIZE        1024
STACKSIZE       8192
CODE            PRELOAD MOVEABLE DISCARDABLE
DATA            PRELOAD MOVEABLE MULTIPLE
```

Using the Media Control Interface

What is the MCI (Media Control Interface), and how does a program access MCI commands?

DESCRIPTION

Many programs advertise that they are MCI-compliant; however, they don't explain what MCI is or how to use it.

ANSWER

The media control interface provides Windows programs with high-level, device-independent commands for controlling multimedia devices. Examples of devices that can be controlled by the media control interface include audio compact disks, video disks, .WAV (sound) files, and MIDI sequencers (a sequencer is a device for recording and playing back MIDI information).

The media control interface is a high-level method of accessing multimedia devices. The term *high-level* refers to the way the commands are accessed. Instead of having to call a large number of functions to access the device, command strings are passed to the media control interface. These strings are comprised of commands that act on the multimedia device.

The commands are at a level you might expect if you were standing in front of a stand-alone device with a row of buttons to control the device. For example, suppose you were in front of an audio compact disk player. You would see buttons for Play, Pause, Stop, and Eject. The media control interface includes command strings which mimic these buttons.

The first action that must be carried out for accessing any multimedia device through the media control interface is to open the device. For example,

```
open cdaudio
```

III

The word open is followed by a device identifier. Examples of different device identifiers are listed in Table 3.3.

Table 3.3. Device identifiers used with Media Control Interface.

Type	Description
cdaudio	Compact disk audio player
dat	Digital audio tape player
digitalvideo	Digital video in a window
mmmovie	Multimedia movie player
scanner	Image scanner
sequencer	MIDI sequencer
vcr	Videotape recorder or player
videodisc	Video disc player
waveaudio	Audio device that plays .WAV files

Now, to play the device, we use another command. For example, to open a CD-ROM device to play an audio compact disk, a command like this would be used:

```
play cdaudio
```

Assuming the compact disk is in the player and there are no problems with accessing the device, the compact disk would start playing.

To pause or stop the compact disk, use the command:

```
pause cdaudio
```

With the CD-ROM player, stopping and pausing an audio compact disk is considered the same operation.

When a program is done accessing the multimedia device, the device should be closed. This is a simple matter of a command like this one:

```
close cdaudio
```

All the MCI commands can be passed to the media control interface with the mciSendString Multimedia API function. The function takes an MCI command string, passes it to the MCI driver, and then returns any error messages or codes in a user supplied buffer. The prototype for the function looks like this:

```
DWORD mciSendString( LPSTR lpstrCommand,
                     LPSTR lpstrReturnString,
                     WORD wReturnLength,
                     HANDLE hCallback);
```

The first parameter is the MCI command string, and the second parameter is the address of the buffer in which to store the return code. The third parameter is the length of the buffer. The fourth parameter is the address of the callback function. Although you can tell the media control interface to use a callback function, it is not usually used.

```
An example of calling the mciSendString function
follows:
```

```
char buff[55];

mciSendString("open cdaudio", buff, strlen(buff), NULL);
```

This command opens the cdaudio CD-ROM player. Any error codes are returned in the buff string (for example, if no audio compact disk is present in the drive).

COMMENTS

There are actually two methods of accessing the media control interface. You have just learned about the first. The other method is message-based, and uses messages that equate to command strings. The method described above is the easiest one to use.

SEE ALSO

mciExecute Multimedia API Function
mciGetDeviceID Multimedia API Function
mciGetErrorString Multimedia API Function
mciSendCommand Multimedia API Function
mciSendString Multimedia API Function
mciSetYieldProc Multimedia API Function

> **TIP**   As is common with the functions in the multimedia extensions, the functions that work with the media control interface are prefixed by a special code—the three letters *mci*.

EXAMPLE CODE

The example program accesses the CD-ROM drive to play audio compact disks (see Figure 3.9) using the media control interface. Listing 3.7 contains the CDPLAYER.C source code; Listing 3.8 contains the CDPLAYER.H header file; Listing 3.9 contains the CDPLAYER.RC resource script; and Listing 3.10 contains the CDPLAYER.DEF module definition file. The other file required to compile the program is the CDPLAYER.ICO icon resource file.

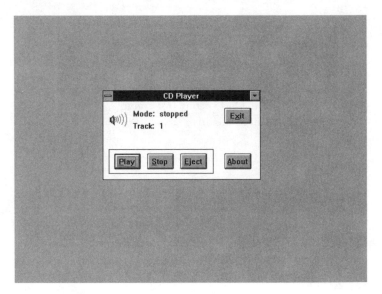

Figure 3.9. *CDPLAYER example program.*

Listing 3.7. CDPLAYER.C source code.

```
// CDPLAYER.C - Program showing how to access a
//              CD-ROM drive to play audio CDs
```

```
//               using the media control interface(MCI).
//
// Help Desk Companion by Paul J. Perry
//

#define STRICT
#define TIMERID 111

#include <windowsx.h>
#include <mmsystem.h>
#include <stdlib.h>
#include <string.h>
#include "cdplayer.h"


// Function Prototypes
BOOL CALLBACK _export MainDlgProc(HWND, UINT, UINT,
                                          LONG);
void WM_Command_Dlg_Handler(HWND, int, HWND, UINT);


// Global Variables
HINSTANCE   ghInstance;

/*********************************************/
#pragma argsused
int PASCAL WinMain(HINSTANCE hInstance, HINSTANCE
                     hPrevInstance, LPSTR lpCmdParam,
                     int nCmdShow)
{
   DLGPROC   lpfnDialog;

   if (hPrevInstance)
   {
      MessageBox(NULL, "Can Only Run One Instance of
                  CD Player",NULL, MB_OK | MB_ICONSTOP);
      exit(1);
   }


   ghInstance = hInstance;

   lpfnDialog =(DLGPROC)MakeProcInstance((FARPROC)
                MainDlgProc,hInstance);
   DialogBox(hInstance, "CDDIALOG",
              NULL, (DLGPROC)lpfnDialog);
   FreeProcInstance((FARPROC)lpfnDialog);

   return 0;
```

continues

Listing 3.7. continued

```
}

/********************************************/
#pragma argsused
void WM_Command_Dlg_Handler(HWND hDlg, int id,
                            HWND hwndCtl, UINT
                            codeNotify)
{
   char buff[55] = "";

   switch(id)
   {
      case IDD_PLAY :
      {
         mciSendString("open cdaudio",
                       buff, strlen(buff), NULL);
         mciSendString("set cdaudio time format tmsf",
                       buff, strlen(buff), NULL);
         mciSendString("play cdaudio", buff,
                       strlen(buff), NULL);
         break;
      }

      case IDD_STOP :
      {
         mciSendString("pause cdaudio", NULL, 0, NULL);
         mciSendString("close cdaudio", NULL, 0, NULL);
         break;
      }

      case IDD_EJECT :
      {
         mciSendString("set cdaudio door open",
                       NULL, 0, NULL);
         break;
      }

      case IDD_ABOUT :
      {
         MessageBox(hDlg, "CD Player\n\n"
                          "uses Media Control "
                          "Interface (MCI)\n"
                          "by Paul J. Perry",
                          "About...",
                          MB_OK | MB_ICONINFORMATION);
         break;
```

```
        }

        case IDCANCEL : // This is if the user closes
                        // down with the system menu.

        case IDD_EXIT :
        {
            mciSendString("close cdaudio", NULL, 0, NULL);

            KillTimer(hDlg, TIMERID);

            EndDialog(hDlg, 0);
            break;
        }

    }
}


/*********************************************/
BOOL CALLBACK _export MainDlgProc(HWND hDlg, UINT
                                  message,UINT wParam,
                                  LONG lParam)
{
    switch(message)
    {
        case WM_INITDIALOG :
        {
            RECT rc, rcDTop;
            int NewX, NewY, CenterX, CenterY;
            HWND hDTopWnd;

            hDTopWnd = GetDesktopWindow();

            // desktop rectangle size
            GetWindowRect(hDTopWnd, &rcDTop);

            // dialog box rectangle size
            GetWindowRect(hDlg, &rc);

            // Do some calculations
            CenterX = (rcDTop.left + rcDTop.right)/2;
            CenterY = (rcDTop.top + rcDTop.bottom)/2;

            NewX = CenterX - ((rc.right - rc.left)/2);
            NewY = CenterY - ((rc.bottom - rc.top)/2);

            // Give it a new location
```

III

continues

Listing 3.7. continued

```
        SetWindowPos(hDlg, NULL, NewX, NewY, 0, 0,
                    SWP_NOSIZE ¦ SWP_NOACTIVATE);

        SetTimer(hDlg, TIMERID, 1000, NULL);

        return TRUE;
    }

    case WM_PAINT :
    {
        PAINTSTRUCT ps;
        HDC         PaintDC;

        if (!IsIconic(hDlg))
            return FALSE;

        // We need to paint the minimized icon
        //   ourselves
        PaintDC = BeginPaint(hDlg, &ps);

        DefWindowProc (hDlg, WM_ICONERASEBKGND,
                    (WPARAM)PaintDC, 0L);
        DrawIcon(PaintDC, 0, 0, LoadIcon(ghInstance,
                                  "CDICON") );

        EndPaint(hDlg, &ps);
        return TRUE;
    }

    case WM_TIMER :
    {
        char buff[255];
        HWND hTextWnd;

        // Retrieve status information about the
        //   current mode of the CD-ROM drive.
        //   It can be not ready, open, paused,
        //   playing, seeking, or stopped.
        mciSendString("status cdaudio mode",
                    buff, sizeof(buff), NULL);

        // Change the static text control inside the
        //   dialog box.
        hTextWnd = GetDlgItem(hDlg, IDD_PLAYINFO);
```

```
        SendMessage(hTextWnd, WM_SETTEXT, 0,
                    (LPARAM)buff);


        // Get status information about the current
        //    track
        mciSendString("status cdaudio current track",
                    buff, sizeof(buff), NULL);

        // Change the static text control inside the
        //    dialog box.
        hTextWnd = GetDlgItem(hDlg, IDD_TRACKINFO);
        SendMessage(hTextWnd, WM_SETTEXT, 0,
                    (LPARAM)buff);

        return TRUE;
    }


    case WM_COMMAND :
    {
        return (BOOL)HANDLE_WM_COMMAND(hDlg, wParam,
                                        lParam,
                                        WM Command
                                        Dlg_Handler);
    }

  }
  return FALSE;
}
```

III

Listing 3.8. CDPLAYER.H header file.

```
/*
 * CDPLAYER.H header file
 *
 */


#define IDD_PLAY   110
#define IDD_STOP   120
#define IDD_ABOUT 130
#define IDD_EJECT 140
#define IDD_EXIT   150

#define IDD_TRACKINFO 160
#define IDD_PLAYINFO  170
```

Listing 3.9. CDPLAYER.RC resource script.

```
/*
 * CDPLAYER.RC resource script
 *
 */

#include "cdplayer.h"

CDICON ICON "cdplayer.ico"

CDDIALOG DIALOG 7, 15, 142, 70
STYLE WS_POPUP ¦ WS_CAPTION ¦ WS_SYSMENU ¦
WS_MINIMIZEBOX
CAPTION "CD Player"
BEGIN
    PUSHBUTTON "&Play", IDD_PLAY, 10, 47, 24, 14,
WS_CHILD ¦ WS_VISIBLE ¦ WS_TABSTOP
    PUSHBUTTON "&Stop", IDD_STOP, 40, 47, 24, 14,
WS_CHILD ¦ WS_VISIBLE ¦ WS_TABSTOP
    PUSHBUTTON "&About", IDD_ABOUT, 110, 47, 24, 14,
WS_CHILD ¦ WS_VISIBLE ¦ WS_TABSTOP
    PUSHBUTTON "&Eject", IDD_EJECT, 70, 47, 24, 14,
WS_CHILD ¦ WS_VISIBLE ¦ WS_TABSTOP
    CONTROL "", -1, "static", SS_BLACKFRAME ¦
WS_CHILD ¦ WS_VISIBLE, 5, 43, 95, 22
    LTEXT "Track:", -1, 27, 18, 21, 8
    LTEXT "", IDD_TRACKINFO, 51, 18, 40, 8
    PUSHBUTTON "E&xit", IDD_EXIT, 110, 6, 24, 14,
WS_CHILD ¦ WS_VISIBLE ¦ WS_TABSTOP
    LTEXT "Mode:", -1, 27, 7, 22, 8
    LTEXT "", IDD_PLAYINFO, 51, 7, 40, 8
    ICON "CDICON", -1, 6, 9, 16, 16, WS_CHILD ¦
WS_VISIBLE
END
```

Listing 3.10. CDPLAYER.DEF module definition file.

```
;
; CDPLAYER.DEF module definition file
;

DESCRIPTION    'Audio CD-ROM Player'
NAME           CDPLAYER
EXETYPE        WINDOWS
STUB           'WINSTUB.EXE'
```

```
HEAPSIZE      1024
STACKSIZE     8192
CODE          PRELOAD MOVEABLE DISCARDABLE
DATA          PRELOAD MOVEABLE MULTIPLE
```

Accessing the Musical Instrument Digital Interface (MIDI)

Intermediate

DESCRIPTION

III

The musical instrument digital interface (MIDI) is a common method of tying electronic instruments together. MIDI is both a software and a hardware specification for controlling musical instruments. It is a musical industry standard which has been around about ten years.

Recently *Electronic Musician* magazine named Windows 3.1 as one of the best products of 1992 (see the January 1993 issue). Now, it doesn't surprise those of us involved in the computer field when computer publications give Windows all sorts of awards. However, why would a publication devoted to music give Windows any sort of award?

The award was given because of the inclusion of MIDI support directly into Windows. Other platforms (Apple and Atari) have had great MIDI integration since the very start. Now, Windows users are afforded the luxury of easy integration with MIDI. It has made the PC equivalent to other hardware platforms, and studios are welcoming the use of PCs.

The MIDI software interface was agreed on in 1982 by a meeting of synthesizer manufacturers. It is actually a standard for the transmitting and receiving of digital musical performance information between all types of electronic musical instruments.

The creators of MIDI decided to use a serial transmission model which uses 5 pin DIN plugs as connectors. MIDI does not send sound over wires like audio components in a stereo system. Instead, it sends digital codes that represent what is being played on the instrument. For example, a digital code that corresponds to the press of middle C is sent by a musical instrument.

The codes that MIDI sends should sound familiar to Windows programmers. It is almost like Windows borrowed some of its conventions from the MIDI interface. MIDI provides codes for pressing a key, releasing a key, and for other controls that are built into synthesizers. Therefore, when a musician presses a key on the piano, a message is sent telling the MIDI interface that a key has been pressed. Then when the key is released, another message is sent to tell the system that the key has been released. This is an oversimplification, because piano keys are also sensitive to how hard the key is pressed and other factors, but you should see the similarity to the way Windows sends messages.

ANSWER

The main idea behind MIDI is to allow what is performed on one instrument to be played by any other instrument, or to record a performance and play it again later. MIDI has the added benefit of being able to record and play back a performance simultaneously.

Although MIDI is used on a wide range of instruments, such as drums and guitars, its design is based on the electronic keyboard (piano). There is a computer in most keyboards that senses when a key is pressed or when it is released and immediately converts the player's actions into MIDI information in the form of MIDI codes.

To Windows, MIDI appears as a device. In fact, a MIDI device driver must be set up in Control Panel before any of the MIDI features can be accessed. Assuming a device driver has been installed, the first step in accessing the MIDI features to play sounds is to use the `midiOutGetDevCaps` function to find the capabilities of the current MIDI device.

There are a great number of MIDI output devices, ranging in price from $400 and up to professional equipment in the price range of $5,000 and up. When accessing a MIDI device through Windows, it is important to find the capabilities of the current MIDI device. Not all MIDI devices support the same functions.

NOTE The Windows Control Panel includes another option (see Figure 3.10) for the MIDI Mapper. The MIDI Mapper is a filtering level that allows the user to redirect MIDI output.

Although the MIDI Mapper is nice, most often the user should be presented with the ability to output MIDI information to either the MIDI Mapper or directly to the MIDI driver.

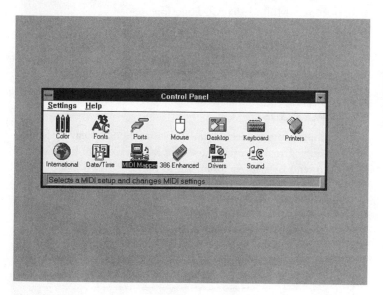

Figure 3.10. *The Control Panel MIDI mapper.*

To open the MIDI output device, use the `midiOutOpen` function. It takes the address of a handle to the MIDI device (of type `HMIDIOUT`) and the identifier of the MIDI device. If this function returns `TRUE`, the MIDI device is available.

MIDI messages can be sent with two functions: `midiOutShortMsg` and `midiOutLongMsg`. The first function is used most commonly. The second one can be used at all times; however, it is usually reserved for something called system exclusive (`SYSEX`) data. SYSEX data is comprised of user defined messages that differ depending on which manufacturer's keyboard is being used.

COMMENTS

Two functions are provided that control the volume level of MIDI devices: midiOutGetVolume and midiOutSetVolume. They provide the programmer with the ability to get and set the volume level of the MIDI device. It is important to remember that not all MIDI devices support all the MIDI messages. For example, some MIDI devices don't respond to changing the volume.

SEE ALSO

midiOutGetDevCaps Multimedia API Function
MidiOutOpen Multimedia API Function
midiOutShortMsg Multimedia API Function
midiOutLongMsg Multimedia API Function
midiOutGetVolume Multimedia API Function
midiOutSetVolume Multimedia API Function

EXAMPLE CODE

The example program demonstrates two methods of playing MIDI information. The first method uses the Media Control Interface (MCI) to send high-level commands to play a .MID file (see Figure 3.11). The other method displays a dialog box and allows the user to enter MIDI messages directly (see Figure 3.12).

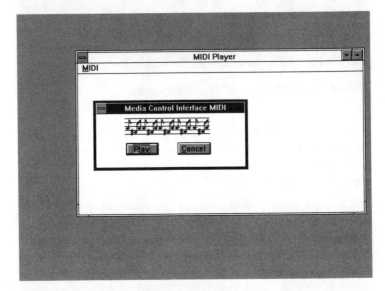

Figure 3.11. *Playing MIDI information using the Media Control Interface.*

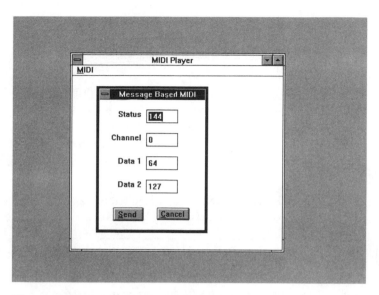

Figure 3.12. *Playing MIDI message information.*

Finally, there is also an option for selecting the configuration of the
MIDI device (see Figure 3.13).

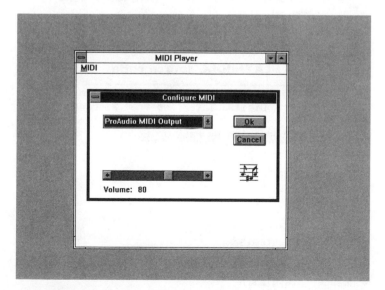

Figure 3.13. *Configuring the MIDI device.*

The configuration options don't affect playback when using the media control interface. Furthermore, because of differences with MIDI drivers, the volume setting does not always affect the output level of the MIDI device.

The program PLAYMIDI is made up of four source files. Listing 3.11 is the C source code (PLAYMIDI.C); Listing 3.12 is the header file (PLAYMIDI.H); Listing 3.13 is the resource script (PLAYMIDI.RC); and Listing 3.14 is the module definition file (PLAYMIDI.DEF). The program's icon is stored in PLAYMIDI.ICO.

At runtime, the PLAYMIDI.MID file is required to access the MIDI device through the Media Control Interface.

> **NOTE**   When sending messages directly to the MIDI device, the dialog box is initially filled with data values. The value you probably want to experiment with the most is data1. This contains an integer value describing an actual note that should be played. It is initially 64, which corresponds to middle C. Try entering larger or smaller numbers and see what happens to the sound played.

Listing 3.11. PLAYMIDI.C source code.

```
// PLAYMIDI.C - Accessing the Musical Instrument
//              Digital Interface from Windows.
//
// Help Desk Companion by Paul J. Perry
//

#define STRICT
#define VOL_MIN 0
#define VOL_MAX 127

#include <windowsx.h>
#include <mmsystem.h>
#include <stdlib.h>
#include <string.h>
#include "playmidi.h"
```

```
// Function Prototypes
LRESULT CALLBACK _export MainWndProc(HWND, UINT,
                                WPARAM, LPARA-);
void WM_CommandHandler(HWND, int, HWND, UINT);
BOOL CALLBACK _export ConfigDlgProc(HWND, UINT,
                                WPARAM, LPARAM);
void WM_Command_Config_Handler(HWND, int, HWND, UINT);
BOOL CALLBACK _export MCIDlgProc(HWND, UINT, WPARAM,
                                LPARAM);
void WM_Command_MCIDlg_Handler(HWND, int, HWND, UINT);
BOOL CALLBACK _export MSGDlgProc(HWND, UINT, WPARAM,
                                LPARAM);
void WM_Command_MSGDlg_Handler(HWND, int, HWND, UINT);
WORD SendMIDIEvent(HMIDIOUT, BYTE, BYTE, BYTE);


// Global Variables
HINSTANCE ghInstance;
int       CurrentDevice = 0;
int       CurrentVolume = 80;
HMIDIOUT  hMidiOut = 0;


/*********************************************/
#pragma argsused
int PASCAL WinMain(HINSTANCE hInstance, HINSTANCE
                   hPrevInstance,LPSTR lpCmdParam, int
                   nCmdShow)
{
   char      ProgName[] = "MIDI Player";
   HWND      hWnd;
   MSG       msg;


   if (!hPrevInstance)
   {
      WNDCLASS    wndclass;

      wndclass.lpszClassName = ProgName;
      wndclass.lpfnWndProc   = (WNDPROC) MainWndProc;
      wndclass.cbClsExtra    = 0;
      wndclass.cbWndExtra    = 0;
      wndclass.hInstance     = hInstance;
      wndclass.hIcon         = LoadIcon(hInstance,
                               "MIDICON");
      wndclass.hCursor       = LoadCursor(NULL,
                               IDC_ARROW);
```

III

continues

Listing 3.11. continued

```
        wndclass.hbrBackground = GetStockBrush
                                 (WHITE_BRUSH);
        wndclass.lpszMenuName  = "MAINMENU";
        wndclass.style         = CS_VREDRAW | CS_HREDRAW;

        if (!RegisterClass(&wndclass))
            exit(1);
    }

    hWnd = CreateWindow(ProgName, ProgName,
                        WS_OVERLAPPEDWINDOW,
                        CW_USEDEFAULT, CW_USEDEFAULT,
                        CW_USEDEFAULT, CW_USEDEFAULT,
                        NULL, NULL, hInstance, NULL);

    ghInstance = hInstance;

    ShowWindow(hWnd, nCmdShow);
    UpdateWindow(hWnd);

    while (GetMessage(&msg, NULL, 0, 0))
    {
        TranslateMessage(&msg);
        DispatchMessage(&msg);
    }
    return msg.wParam;
}


/**********************************************/
WORD SendMIDIEvent(HMIDIOUT hMidiOut, BYTE Status,
                   BYTE Data1, BYTE Data2)
{

union
{
    DWORD   dwData;
    BYTE    bData[4];
} Midi;

    Midi.bData[0] = Status;
    Midi.bData[1] = Data1;
    Midi.bData[2] = Data2;
    Midi.bData[3] = 0;

    return midiOutShortMsg(hMidiOut, Midi.dwData);
```

```
}

/*******************************************/
#pragma argsused
BOOL CALLBACK _export MCIDlgProc(HWND hDlg, UINT
                                 message,WPARAM
                                 wParam, LPARAM
                                 lParam)
{
   switch(message)
   {
      case WM_INITDIALOG :
      {
         return TRUE;
      }

      case WM_COMMAND :
      {
         return (BOOL)HANDLE_WM_COMMAND(hDlg, wParam,
                                 lParam,
                                 WM_Command
                                 MCIDlg Handler);
      }

   }

   return FALSE;
}


/*******************************************/
#pragma argsused
void WM_Command_MCIDlg_Handler(HWND hDlg, int id,
                               HWND hwndCtl, UINT
                               codeNotify)
{
   char buff[55] = "";

   switch(id)
   {
      case IDD_PLAY :
      {
         mciSendString("open playmidi.mid type
                       sequencer alias song",buff,
                       strlen(buff), NULL);
```

III

continues

Listing 3.11. continued

```
        mciSendString("play song",
                      buff, strlen(buff), NULL);
        break;

    }

    case IDCANCEL :
    {
        mciSendString("close song",
                      buff, strlen(buff), NULL);

        EndDialog(hDlg, 0);
        break;
    }
  }
}


/*********************************************/
BOOL CALLBACK _export MSGDlgProc(HWND hDlg, UINT
                                 message,WPARAM
                                 wParam, LPARAM
                                 lParam)
{

    switch(message)
    {
      case WM_INITDIALOG :
      {
          midiOutOpen(&hMidiOut, 0, NULL, 0L, 0L);

          SetDlgItemInt(hDlg, IDD_STATUS, 0x90, FALSE);
          SetDlgItemInt(hDlg, IDD_CHANNEL, 0, FALSE);
          SetDlgItemInt(hDlg, IDD_DATA1, 64, FALSE);
          SetDlgItemInt(hDlg, IDD_DATA2, 127, FALSE);

          return TRUE;
      }


      case WM_COMMAND :
      {
          return (BOOL)HANDLE_WM_COMMAND(hDlg, wParam,
                                         lParam,
                                         WM_Command
                                         MSGDlg
                                         Handler);
```

```
        }

    }

    return FALSE;
}


/*********************************************/
#pragma argsused
void WM_Command_MSGDlg_Handler(HWND hDlg, int id,
                               HWND hwndCtl, UINT
                               codeNotify)
{
    switch(id)
    {
        case IDD_SEND :
        {
            BYTE status, data1, data2;
            BOOL result;

            status = GetDlgItemInt(hDlg, IDD_STATUS,
                                   &result, FALSE);
            data1 = GetDlgItemInt(hDlg, IDD_DATA1,
                                   &result, FALSE);
            data2 = GetDlgItemInt(hDlg, IDD_DATA2,
                                   &result, FALSE);

            SendMIDIEvent(hMidiOut, status, data1, data2);
            break;
        }

        case IDCANCEL :
        {
            midiOutClose(hMidiOut);

            EndDialog(hDlg, 0);
            break;
        }
    }
}


/*********************************************/
BOOL CALLBACK _export ConfigDlgProc(HWND hDlg, UINT
    message,WPARAM wParam, LPARAM lParam)
{
```

III

continues

Listing 3.11. continued

```c
HWND    hCtrl;
static int Volume;

switch(message)
{
   case WM_INITDIALOG :
   {
      MIDIOUTCAPS MidiCaps;
      WORD        NumDevs;
      char        buff[55];
      int         count;

      hCtrl = GetDlgItem(hDlg, IDD_TYPE);

      wsprintf(buff, "%s", (LPSTR)"MIDI Mapper");
      SendMessage(hCtrl, CB_ADDSTRING, 0,
                     (LONG)(LPSTR)buff);

      NumDevs = midiOutGetNumDevs();

      // Fill the items in the "Type" combo box
      for (count=0; count<NumDevs; count++)
      {
         midiOutGetDevCaps(count, &MidiCaps,
                        sizeof(MidiCaps));
         SendMessage(hCtrl, CB_ADDSTRING, 0,
                        (LPARAM)MidiCaps.szPname);
      }

      SendMessage(hCtrl, CB_SETCURSEL,
                     (CurrentDevice), 0);

      SetDlgItemInt(hDlg, IDD_VOLUME,
                     CurrentVolume, FALSE);

      // Set the "volume" scroll bar range
      hCtrl=GetDlgItem(hDlg, IDD_VOLUME);
      SetScrollRange(hCtrl, SB_CTL, 0, VOL_MAX,
                     FALSE);
      SetScrollPos(hCtrl, SB_CTL, CurrentVolume,
                     FALSE);
      Volume = CurrentVolume;

      // Set the dialog item that contains the
      //   integer number of the volume control.
      SetDlgItemInt(hDlg, IDD_VOLTEXT,
                     CurrentVolume, FALSE);
```

```
      return TRUE;
}

case WM_HSCROLL :
{
   hCtrl = (HWND)HIWORD(lParam);

   switch (wParam)
   {
      case SB_PAGEDOWN :
      {
         Volume = min(VOL_MAX, Volume + 20);
         break;
      }

      case SB_LINEDOWN :
      {
         Volume = min(VOL_MAX, Volume + 1);
         break;
      }

      case SB_PAGEUP :
      {
         Volume = max(VOL_MIN, Volume - 20);
         break;
      }

      case SB_LINEUP :
      {
         Volume = max(VOL_MIN, Volume - 1);
         break;
      }

      case SB_TOP :
      {
         Volume = VOL_MIN;
         break;
      }

      case SB_BOTTOM :
      {
         Volume = VOL_MAX;
         break;
      }

      case SB_THUMBPOSITION :
      case SB_THUMBTRACK :
```

III

continues

Listing 3.11. continued

```
                {
                    Volume = LOWORD(lParam);
                    break;
                }

                default :
                {
                    return FALSE;
                }

            }

            SetScrollPos(hCtrl, SB_CTL, Volume, TRUE);
            SetDlgItemInt(hDlg, IDD_VOLTEXT, Volume,
                        FALSE);

            return TRUE;

        }

        case WM_COMMAND :
        {
            return (BOOL)HANDLE_WM_COMMAND(hDlg, wParam,
                                        lParam,
                                        WM_Command
                                        Config Handler);
        }

    }

    return FALSE;
}

/********************************************/
#pragma argsused
void WM_Command_Config_Handler(HWND hDlg, int id,
                                HWND hwndCtl, UINT
                                codeNotify)
{
    HWND   hCtrl;
    BOOL   result = FALSE;

    switch(id)
    {

        case IDOK :
        {
```

```
            CurrentVolume = (int)GetDlgItemInt(hDlg,
                                        IDD_VOLTEXT,
                                        &result,
                                        FALSE);

            hCtrl = GetDlgItem(hDlg, IDD_TYPE);
            CurrentDevice = (int)SendMessage(hCtrl, CB
                                        GETCURSEL,
                                        0, 0L);

            midiOutSetVolume(CurrentDevice, CurrentVolume);


        }

        case IDCANCEL :
        {
            EndDialog(hDlg, 0);
            break;
        }
    }
}


/*******************************************/
#pragma argsused
void WM_CommandHandler(HWND hWnd, int id, HWND hWndCtl,
                    UINT codeNotify)
{

    switch (id)
    {
        case IDM_USEMCI :
        {
            DLGPROC DlgProc;

            DlgProc =
(DLGPROC)MakeProcInstance((FARPROC)MCIDlgProc,
                        ghInstance);
            DialogBox(ghInstance, "MCIDIALOG", hWnd,
                    DlgProc);
            FreeProcInstance((FARPROC)DlgProc);

            break;
        }

        case IDM_MSGBASED :
        {
            DLGPROC DlgProc;
```

continues

Listing 3.11. continued

```
            DlgProc = (DLGPROC)MakeProcInstance(
                    (FARPROC)MSGDlgProc, ghInstance);
            DialogBox(ghInstance, "MSGDIALOG", hWnd,
                    DlgProc);
            FreeProcInstance((FARPROC)DlgProc);

            break;
        }

        case IDM_CONFIGURE :
        {
            DLGPROC DlgProc;

            DlgProc = (DLGPROC)MakeProcInstance(
                    (FARPROC)ConfigDlgProc,
                    ghInstance);
            DialogBox(ghInstance, "CONFIGDIALOG", hWnd,
                    DlgProc);
            FreeProcInstance((FARPROC)DlgProc);

            break;
        }

        case IDM_EXIT :
        {
            SendMessage(hWnd, WM_CLOSE, 0, 0L);
            break;
        }

    }
}

/*********************************************/
LRESULT CALLBACK _export MainWndProc(HWND hWnd, UINT
                                    message, WPARAM
                                    wParam, LPARAM
                                    lParam)
{
    switch (message)
    {
        case WM_PAINT :
        {
            HDC         PaintDC;
            RECT        rect;
            PAINTSTRUCT ps;
```

```
            PaintDC = BeginPaint(hWnd, &ps);
            GetClientRect(hWnd, &rect);

            DrawText(PaintDC, "MIDI Player",
                     -1, &rect, DT_SINGLELINE ¦ DT_CENTER
                     ¦ DT_VCENTER);

            EndPaint(hWnd, &ps);
            return 0;
        }

        case WM_COMMAND :
        {
            return HANDLE_WM_COMMAND(hWnd, wParam,
                                     lParam, WM_Command
                                     Handler);
        }


        case WM_DESTROY :
        {
            PostQuitMessage(0);
            return 0;
        }
    }
    return DefWindowProc (hWnd, message, wParam, lParam);
}
```

Listing 3.12. PLAYMIDI.H header file.

```
/*
 * PLAYMIDI.H header file
 *
 */

// Main Menu Items
#define IDM_USEMCI      100
#define IDM_MSGBASED    110
#define IDM_CONFIGURE   120
#define IDM_EXIT        130

// MCI Dialog Items
#define IDD_PLAY     200

// MSG Dialog Items
#define IDD_STATUS   300
```

continues

Listing 3.12. continued

```
#define IDD_CHANNEL  310
#define IDD_DATA1    320
#define IDD_DATA2    330
#define IDD_SEND     340

// Configure Dialog Items
#define IDD_TYPE     400
#define IDD_VOLUME   410
#define IDD_VOLTEXT  420
```

Listing 3.13. PLAYMIDI.RC resource script.

```
/*
 * PLAYMIDI.RC resource script
 *
 */

#include "playmidi.h"

MIDICON ICON "playmidi.ico"

MAINMENU MENU
BEGIN
     POPUP "&MIDI"
     BEGIN
          MENUITEM "&Using MCI", IDM_USEMCI
          MENUITEM "&Message Based", IDM_MSGBASED
          MENUITEM "&Configure...", IDM_CONFIGURE
          MENUITEM SEPARATOR
          MENUITEM "E&xit", IDM_EXIT
     END

END

CONFIGDIALOG DIALOG 20, 39, 169, 86
STYLE DS_MODALFRAME ¦ WS_POPUP ¦ WS_CAPTION ¦
WS_SYSMENU
CAPTION "Configure MIDI"
BEGIN
     CONTROL "", IDD_TYPE, "COMBOBOX",
CBS_DROPDOWNLIST ¦ WS_CHILD ¦ WS_VISIBLE ¦ WS_TABSTOP,
12, 11, 99, 38
     PUSHBUTTON "&Ok", IDOK, 130, 11, 29, 11, WS_CHILD
¦ WS_VISIBLE ¦ WS_TABSTOP
     PUSHBUTTON "&Cancel", IDCANCEL, 130, 27, 29, 11,
```

```
WS_CHILD ¦ WS_VISIBLE ¦ WS_TABSTOP
    SCROLLBAR IDD_VOLUME, 12, 61, 99, 9
    ICON "MIDICON", -1, 136, 55, 16, 16, WS_CHILD ¦
        WS_VISIBLE
    LTEXT "Volume:", -1, 13, 74, 26, 8, WS_CHILD ¦
        WS_VISIBLE ¦ WS_GROUP
    LTEXT "", IDD_VOLTEXT, 44, 74, 16, 8, WS_CHILD ¦
        WS_VISIBLE ¦ WS_GROUP
END

MCIDIALOG DIALOG 10, 36, 135, 48
STYLE DS_MODALFRAME ¦ WS_POPUP ¦ WS_CAPTION ¦
WS_SYSMENU
CAPTION "Media Control Interface MIDI"
BEGIN
    PUSHBUTTON "&Play", IDD_PLAY, 27, 26, 30, 11
    PUSHBUTTON "&Cancel", IDCANCEL, 74, 26, 30, 11
    ICON "MIDICON", -1, 26, 4, 16, 16, WS_CHILD ¦
        WS_VISIBLE
    ICON "MIDICON", -1, 41, 4, 16, 16, WS_CHILD ¦
        WS_VISIBLE
    ICON "MIDICON", -1, 56, 4, 16, 16, WS_CHILD ¦
        WS_VISIBLE
    ICON "MIDICON", -1, 71, 4, 16, 16, WS_CHILD ¦
        WS_VISIBLE
    ICON "MIDICON", -1, 87, 4, 16, 16, WS_CHILD ¦
        WS_VISIBLE
END


MSGDIALOG DIALOG 19, 33, 96, 117
STYLE DS_MODALFRAME ¦ WS_POPUP ¦ WS_CAPTION ¦
        WS_SYSMENU
CAPTION "Message Based MIDI"
BEGIN
    EDITTEXT IDD_STATUS, 42, 9, 29, 12
    EDITTEXT IDD_CHANNEL, 42, 30, 29, 12
    EDITTEXT IDD_DATA1, 42, 51, 29, 12
    EDITTEXT IDD_DATA2, 42, 72, 29, 12
    PUSHBUTTON "&Send", IDD_SEND, 13, 97, 27, 12,
WS_CHILD ¦ WS_VISIBLE ¦ WS_TABSTOP
    PUSHBUTTON "&Cancel", IDCANCEL, 52, 97, 30, 11,
WS_CHILD ¦ WS_VISIBLE ¦ WS_TABSTOP
    LTEXT "Status", -1, 17, 9, 23, 8
    LTEXT "Channel", -1, 11, 30, 29, 8
    LTEXT "Data 1", -1, 17, 51, 23, 8
    LTEXT "Data 2", -1, 17, 72, 23, 8
END
```

III

Listing 3.14. PLAYMIDI.DEF module definition file.

```
;
; PLAYMIDI.DEF module definition file
;

DESCRIPTION     'MIDI Player'
NAME            PLAYMIDI
EXETYPE         WINDOWS
STUB            'WINSTUB.EXE'
HEAPSIZE        1024
STACKSIZE       8192
CODE            PRELOAD MOVEABLE DISCARDABLE
DATA            PRELOAD MOVEABLE MULTIPLE
```

III

In This Chapter

- How to display a bitmap inside the main window of a program.

- How to display an image on the Windows desktop as a program is being loaded from disk.

- How to read in a .BMP file on-the-fly and display its contents in the main window of a program.

- How to display graphics items in the main menu of a program.

- How to draw graphics items inside a listbox by creating owner-draw controls.

- How to create a gradient fill pattern as a background for a window.

- What the graphics device interface (GDI) mapping modes are and how to use them.

Graphics

Displaying a Bitmap

How do I display a bitmap within the main window of my program?

DESCRIPTION

You have undoubtedly already seen bitmaps used in a Windows program. In fact, it would be a surprise if you had not. Bitmaps are used quite frequently within Windows programs. A bitmap is binary information which describes the pixels that comprise images on the screen. An application can use bitmaps to display pictures, give a visual flair to a program, and to display graphical status information.

Because Windows is a GUI (graphical user interface), there must be a method to include a bitmap file in an application and display it within the window of an application.

ANSWER

Windows bitmap files most commonly take the extension .BMP.
You must reference the .BMP file in the resource script of the
program. Do it the same way you reference a cursor or an icon. For
example, to use the bitmap named cars.bmp inside a program,
assuming the identifier is FASTCAR, include a statement like this in
your resource script (.RC) file:

```
FASTCAR BITMAP "fastcar.bmp"
```

This statement associates the filename FASTCAR.BMP with the
identifier FASTCAR in your program. The filename of the bitmap
does not need to correspond to the identifier in any way. For
example, you could use the following statement just as easily:

```
SLOWCAR BITMAP "fastcar.bmp"
```

Usually, however, you want to associate descriptive identifiers with
the appropriate bitmap filename. This first step includes the bitmap
file with the executable file. The next part of displaying bitmaps is
to modify your source code to access the bitmap resource.

To obtain a handle to the bitmap, use the LoadBitmap function,
specifying the instance of the program, and the bitmap identifier.
For example:

```
HBITMAP hBitmap;

hBitmap = LoadBitmap(hInstance, "FASTCAR");
```

Your program now has a handle to the bitmap.

At this point, displaying a bitmap in the client area of a program
gets a little complicated. The reason being that there is no function
to simply display the bitmap in the client area of the window. A
function like:

```
DrawBitmap(HDC hDC, HBITMAP hBitmap, int x, int y)
// Fictitious
```

would be ideal. With a function like this, we could specify the
handle to the display context, the handle to the bitmap, and a
starting x and y location at which to display the bitmap. However,
no such function exists in Windows.

Instead, a program must go through the process of creating a compatible display context, selecting the bitmap into the compatible display context, copying the bitmap from one display context to the other, then cleaning up afterwards by deleting the compatible display context, and then deleting the bitmap. Let's take a closer look at these steps.

First, as just described, use `LoadBitmap` to receive a handle to the bitmap.

```
hBitmap = LoadBitmap(hInstance, "MYBITMAPNAME");
```

Next, create a compatible display context with the statement:

```
hCompatDC = CreateCompatibleDC(PaintDC);
```

With a compatible display context created, select the bitmap into it with the following statement:

```
hOldBitmap = SelectBitmap(hCompatDC, hBitmap);
```

Notice that we save the handle to the previously selected bitmap (which was returned by the `SelectBitmap` function). Finally, we use the `BitBlt` (which stands for bit block transfer) function to copy the bitmap from the source display context (the compatible DC) to the destination display context (the `PaintDC`). The statement looks something like this:

```
BitBlt(PaintDC, 0, 0, BitmapWidth, BitmapHeight,
       hCompatDC, 0, 0, SRCCOPY);
```

The last parameter is the ROP (raster operation) code to use for the bit block transfer. It defines how the graphics device interface combines colors when it displays the bitmap in the destination display context. Some common values are listed in Table 4.1.

Table 4.1. Common ROP codes.

ROP Code	Description
BLACKNESS	Turns all output black.
DSTINVERT	Inverts the destination bitmap.
MERGECOPY	Combines the pattern and the source bitmap by using the Boolean AND operator.

continues

Table 4.1. continued

ROP Code	Description
MERGEPAINT	Combines the inverted source bitmap with the destination bitmap by using the Boolean OR operator.
NOTSRCCOPY	Copies the inverted source bitmap to the destination.
NOTSRCERASE	Inverts the result of combining the destination and source bitmaps by using the Boolean OR operator.
PATCOPY	Copies the pattern to the destination bitmap.
PATINVERT	Combines the destination bitmap with the pattern by using the Boolean XOR operator.
PATPAINT	Combines the inverted source bitmap with the pattern by using the Boolean OR operator. Combines the result of this operation with the destination bitmap by using the Boolean OR operator.
SRCAND	Combines pixels of the destination and source bitmaps by using the Boolean AND operator.
SRCCOPY	Copies the source bitmap to the destination bitmap.
SRCERASE	Inverts the destination bitmap and combines the result with the source bitmap by using the Boolean AND operator.
SRCINVERT	Combines pixels of the destination and source bitmaps by using the Boolean XOR operator.
SRCPAINT	Combines pixels of the destination and source bitmaps by using the Boolean OR operator.
WHITENESS	Turns all output white.

Now that the image has appeared in the client area of your window, you need to select the old bitmap back into the compatible display context before you can clean up. To do this, use the statement:

```
SelectBitmap(hCompatDC, hOldBitmap);
```

Finally, use the following commands to clean up:

```
DeleteDC(hCompatDC);
DeleteBitmap(hBitmap);
```

Although this may sound like a lot of programming, consider trying to do this from inside a DOS program. Having to work with bitmaps would require assembly language programming and would require much more code than what is required here.

COMMENTS

It is important to remember to delete both the display context and the memory instance of the bitmap once your program is done with them. Neglecting this rule leaves blocks of memory locked within Windows that cannot be accessed again until Windows is restarted. You don't want your program to use up resources and not return them to the system.

SEE ALSO

```
BitBlt  Windows API Function
CreateCompatibleDC  Windows API Function
LoadBitmap  Windows API Function
SelectBitmap  Macro in WINDOWSX.H
```

EXAMPLE CODE

The example program displays a bitmap using one of three methods: tiling the bitmap, centering the bitmap, or displaying the bitmap in the upper-left corner of the window. The user can select the method by which to display the bitmap through a menu option. The method that is initially selected is tiling the bitmap (see Figure 4.1).

Remember that Windows does not provide any single function to display a bitmap. Well, the example program has a function, called `DisplayBitmap`, which will take care of the steps necessary for

displaying a bitmap. You can cut and paste it into your own
programs. It is prototyped like this:

```
BOOL DisplayBitmap(HDC hDC, HBITMAP hBitmap,
                    int x, int y, DWORD RopCode);
```

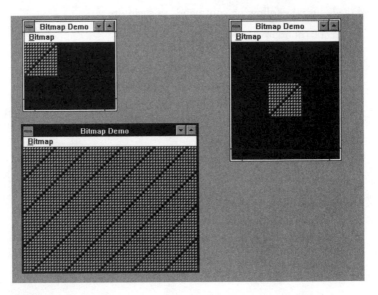

Figure 4.1. *The BITMAP demonstration program, tiling the bitmap.*

It takes a handle to the display context, a handle to a bitmap, the *x*
and *y* location at which to display the bitmap, and the ROP code.

Listing 4.1 contains the BITMAP.C source file; Listing 4.2.
contains the BITMAP.H header file; Listing 4.3. contains the
BITMAP.RC resource script; and Listing 4.4. contains the
BITMAP.DEF module definition file. In order to compile the
program, you will also need a bitmap with the filename
BITMAP.BMP.

Listing 4.1. BITMAP.C source code.

```
// BITMAP.C - Demonstrates displaying bitmaps in a
//            Windows program.
//
// Your Borland C++ Consultant by Paul J. Perry
//
```

```
#define STRICT

#include <windowsx.h>
#include <stdlib.h>
#include "bitmap.h"

// Function Prototypes
LRESULT CALLBACK _export MainWndProc(HWND, UINT,
                         WPARAM, LPARAM);
void WM_CommandHandler(HWND, int, HWND, UINT);
BOOL DisplayBitmap(HDC, HBITMAP, int, int, DWORD);

// Global Variables
HINSTANCE ghInstance;
int PaintOffset = IDM_TILE;

/******************************************/
#pragma argsused
int PASCAL WinMain(HINSTANCE hInstance, HINSTANCE
           hPrevInstance, LPSTR lpCmdParam, int
           nCmdShow)
{
    char        ProgName[] = "Bitmap Demo";
    HWND        hWnd;
    MSG         msg;
    HMENU       hMenu;

    if (!hPrevInstance)
    {
        WNDCLASS    wndclass;

        wndclass.lpszClassName = ProgName;
        wndclass.lpfnWndProc   = (WNDPROC) MainWndProc;
        wndclass.cbClsExtra    = 0;
        wndclass.cbWndExtra    = 0;
        wndclass.hInstance     = hInstance;
        wndclass.hIcon         = LoadIcon(NULL,
                                 IDI_APPLICATION);
        wndclass.hCursor       = LoadCursor(NULL,
                                 IDC_ARROW);
        wndclass.hbrBackground = GetStockBrush(
                                 BLACK_BRUSH);
        wndclass.lpszMenuName  = "MAINMENU";
        wndclass.style         = CS_VREDRAW |
                                 CS_HREDRAW;

        if (!RegisterClass(&wndclass))
            exit(1);
```

IV

continues

Listing 4.1. continued

```
    }

    ghInstance = hInstance;

    hWnd = CreateWindow(ProgName, ProgName,
                        WS_OVERLAPPEDWINDOW,
                        CW_USEDEFAULT, CW_USEDEFAULT,
                        CW_USEDEFAULT, CW_USEDEFAULT,
                        NULL, NULL, hInstance, NULL);


    hMenu = GetMenu(hWnd);
    CheckMenuItem(hMenu, IDM_TILE, MF_CHECKED);

    ShowWindow(hWnd, nCmdShow);
    UpdateWindow(hWnd);

    while (GetMessage(&msg, NULL, 0, 0))
    {
        TranslateMessage(&msg);
        DispatchMessage(&msg);
    }
    return msg.wParam;
}

/**********************************************/
BOOL DisplayBitmap(HDC hDC, HBITMAP hBitmap,
                   int X, int Y, DWORD RopCode)
{
/*
 * Steps to displaying a bitmap:
 *
 * 1. Create a compatible display context.
 * 2. Select bitmap into compatible display context.
 * 3. Do a bit-block-transfer (BitBlt) command.
 * 4. Clean-up afterwards.
 *
 */

    HDC      hCompatDC;
    HBITMAP  hOldBitmap;
    BITMAP   BM;
    BOOL     result;

    // Create compatible display context
    hCompatDC = CreateCompatibleDC(hDC);
```

```
   // Select bitmap into compatible display context
   hOldBitmap = SelectBitmap(hCompatDC, hBitmap);

   // Get dimensions of bitmap
   GetObject(hBitmap, sizeof(BM), &BM);

   // Blast those bits to the screen
   result = BitBlt(hDC, X, Y, BM.bmWidth, BM.bmHeight,
                   hCompatDC, 0, 0, RopCode);

   // De-select the bitmap
   SelectBitmap(hCompatDC, hOldBitmap);

   // Clean up after we are done
   DeleteDC(hCompatDC);

   return result;

}

/*******************************************/
#pragma argsused
void WM_CommandHandler(HWND hWnd, int id, HWND
                       hWndCtl, UINT codeNotify)
{
   HMENU hMenu;

   hMenu = GetMenu(hWnd);

   CheckMenuItem(hMenu, PaintOffset, MF_UNCHECKED);

   switch (id)
   {

      case IDM_TILE :
      {
         PaintOffset = IDM_TILE;
         CheckMenuItem(hMenu, IDM_TILE, MF_CHECKED);
         InvalidateRect(hWnd, NULL, TRUE);
         break;
      }

      case IDM_CENTER :
      {
         PaintOffset = IDM_CENTER;
         CheckMenuItem(hMenu, IDM_CENTER, MF_CHECKED);
         InvalidateRect(hWnd, NULL, TRUE);
```

IV

continues

Listing 4.1. continued

```
            break;
        }

        case IDM_NOOFFSET :
        {
            PaintOffset = IDM_NOOFFSET;
            CheckMenuItem(hMenu, IDM_NOOFFSET,
                        MF_CHECKED);
            InvalidateRect(hWnd, NULL, TRUE);
            break;
        }

        case IDM_EXIT :
        {
            SendMessage(hWnd, WM_CLOSE, 0, 0L);
            break;
        }

    }

}
/***********************************************/
LRESULT CALLBACK _export MainWndProc(HWND hWnd, UINT
                        message, WPARAM wParam,
                        LPARAM lParam)
{
    switch (message)
    {
        case WM_PAINT :
        {
            HDC         PaintDC;
            RECT        rect;
            PAINTSTRUCT ps;
            HBITMAP     hBitmap;
            BITMAP      BM;
            int         x, y;


            PaintDC = BeginPaint(hWnd, &ps);
            GetClientRect(hWnd, &rect);


            hBitmap = LoadBitmap(ghInstance,
                        "THEBITMAP");
```

```
   // Get the size of the bitmap
   GetObject(hBitmap, sizeof(BM), &BM);

   switch (PaintOffset)
   {
      case IDM_TILE :
      {
         for (x=0; x< rect.right;
               x=x+BM.bmWidth)
            for (y=0; y< rect.bottom;
                  y=y+BM.bmHeight)
               DisplayBitmap(PaintDC, hBitmap,
                             x, y, SRCCOPY);
         break;
      }

      case IDM_CENTER :
      {
         x = (rect.right/2) - (BM.bmWidth/2);
         y = (rect.bottom/2) - (BM.bmHeight/2);

         DisplayBitmap(PaintDC, hBitmap, x, y,
                       SRCCOPY);
         break;
      }

      case IDM_NOOFFSET :
      {
         DisplayBitmap(PaintDC, hBitmap, 0, 0,
                       SRCCOPY);
         break;
      }
   }

   DeleteBitmap(hBitmap);

   EndPaint(hWnd, &ps);
   return 0;
}

case WM_COMMAND :
{
   return HANDLE_WM_COMMAND(hWnd, wParam,
                            lParam, WM_Command-
                            Handler);
}

case WM_DESTROY :
```

IV

continues

Listing 4.1. continued

```
        {
            PostQuitMessage(0);
            return 0;
        }
    }

    return DefWindowProc (hWnd, message, wParam,
                            lParam);
}
```

Listing 4.2. BITMAP.H header file.

```
/*
 * BITMAP.H header file
 *
 */

#define IDM_TILE     10
#define IDM_CENTER   20
#define IDM_NOOFFSET 30
#define IDM_EXIT     40
```

Listing 4.3. BITMAP.RC resource script.

```
/*
 * BITMAP.RC resource script
 *
 */


#include "bitmap.h"

THEBITMAP BITMAP "bitmap.bmp"

MAINMENU MENU
BEGIN
    POPUP "&Bitmap"
    BEGIN
        MENUITEM "&Tile", IDM_TILE
        MENUITEM "&Center", IDM_CENTER
        MENUITEM "&No Offset", IDM_NOOFFSET
        MENUITEM SEPARATOR
```

```
          MENUITEM "E&xit", IDM_EXIT
     END

END
```

Listing 4.4. BITMAP.DEF module definition file.

```
;
; BITMAP.DEF module definition file
;

DESCRIPTION    'Bitmap Demo'
NAME           BITMAP
EXETYPE        WINDOWS
STUB           'WINSTUB.EXE'
HEAPSIZE       1024
STACKSIZE      8192
CODE           PRELOAD MOVEABLE DISCARDABLE
DATA           PRELOAD MOVEABLE MULTIPLE
```

IV

Creating a Splash Screen

How do I create a splash screen for my program?

DESCRIPTION

Consider another method of using bitmaps in your programs. You have probably noticed that when you load the Borland C++ for Windows (BCW) Integrated Development Environment (IDE), the Borland C++ for Windows logo is displayed as a bitmap on top of the Windows desktop. This effect is usually referred to as a splash screen.

The splash screen is a bitmap that is displayed on the screen before the main window of your program is displayed. A splash screen is often displayed when a program takes a rather long time to load. This gives the user some visual feedback indicating that the program is in fact being loaded. When your main overlapped window is displayed, it overwrites the area where the splash screen was.

ANSWER

To display the splash screen before the main window is created, you must create a display context in `WinMain`. Instead of using `GetDC`, you want to use a function called `CreateDC`. The function call looks like this:

```
hDesktopDC = CreateDC("DISPLAY", NULL, NULL, NULL);
```

This creates a handle to a display context called `DISPLAY`. It enables you to output information anywhere on the Windows desktop. Once you have a handle to the desktop, use the method described previously in this chapter to transfer the bitmap from a compatible display context to the screen display context. That is to say, load the bitmap, create a compatible display context, select the bitmap into the compatible display context, `Bitblt` the bitmap to the `DISPLAY` context, and then clean up after you are done (see the previous section in this chapter for full information on how this is done).

As part of the cleanup procedure, your program should make a call to `InvalidateRect`, as follows:

```
InvalidateRect(NULL, NULL, TRUE);
```

Notice the first parameter is set to `NULL`. This tells Windows to send a `WM_PAINT` message to every Window currently open on the desktop. This ensures that all Windows get repainted correctly and that your splash screen does not destroy any screen space occupied by the window of another program (which may occur if you don't use the previous call).

COMMENTS

When your program is done using the display context returned from `CreateDC`, the DC must be deleted with a call to `DeleteDC`. An example would go like this:

```
DeleteDC(hDesktopDC);
```

It is important to remember to delete this display context, or else system resources will slowly be drained, and Windows will start to perform poorly.

SEE ALSO

BitBlt Windows API Function
CreateCompatibleDC Windows API Function
CreateDC Windows API Function
LoadBitmap Windows API Function
SelectBitmap Macro in WINDOWSX.H

EXAMPLE CODE

The demonstration program creates a splash screen which is displayed in the center of the screen. Just before the program displays the bitmap, it determines the center of the screen. The center of the screen is calculated by finding the size of the screen, as well as the size of the bitmap, and then locating the centers of each. This ensures the bitmap is always displayed in an appropriate location on the screen, whether you are using a regular VGA 640×480 adapter or a super VGA adapter in 1268×1024 resolution. If hard-coded values were used, the image would appear offset to the upper left of the screen in the high resolution mode.

A splash screen works best when you have a program with a large EXE file that takes a while to load. On a small program like the example, you need to keep your eyes open to see the splash screen. However, the program tries to compensate for this by creating an artificial time delay. This allows you to view the image. The program uses the DisplayBitmap routine presented in the previous section of this chapter.

Listing 4.5 contains the C source code for SPLASH.C. Listing 4.6 contains the resource script for SPLASH.RC, and Listing 4.7 contains the module definition file for SPLASH.DEF. In order to compile the program, you will also need a bitmap with the filename SPLASH.BMP.

Listing 4.5. SPLASH.C source code.

```
// SPLASH.C - Display a bitmap image before the
//            main window of a program is displayed.
//            Also called a splash screen
//
// Your Borland C++ Consultant by Paul J. Perry
//
```

continues

Listing 4.5. continued

```c
#define STRICT

#include <windowsx.h>
#include <stdlib.h>

// Function Prototypes
LRESULT CALLBACK _export MainWndProc(HWND, UINT,
                        WPARAM, LPARAM);
BOOL DisplayBitmap(HDC, HBITMAP, int, int, DWORD);


/*********************************************/
#pragma argsused
int PASCAL WinMain(HINSTANCE hInstance, HINSTANCE
                   hPrevInstance, LPSTR lpCmdParam,
                   int nCmdShow)
{
    char     ProgName[] = "Splash Demo";
    HWND     hWnd;
    MSG      msg;
    HDC      hDesktopDC;
    int      x, y;
    HBITMAP  hBitmap;
    BITMAP   BM;

    if (!hPrevInstance)
    {
        WNDCLASS     wndclass;

        wndclass.lpszClassName = ProgName;
        wndclass.lpfnWndProc   = (WNDPROC) MainWndProc;
        wndclass.cbClsExtra    = 0;
        wndclass.cbWndExtra    = 0;
        wndclass.hInstance     = hInstance;
        wndclass.hIcon         = LoadIcon(NULL,
                                   IDI_APPLICATION);
        wndclass.hCursor       = LoadCursor(NULL,
                                   IDC_ARROW);
        wndclass.hbrBackground = GetStockObject(
                                   WHITE_BRUSH);
        wndclass.lpszMenuName  = NULL;
        wndclass.style         = CS_VREDRAW |
                                   CS_HREDRAW;

        if (!RegisterClass(&wndclass))
            exit(1);
```

```
}

hWnd = CreateWindow(ProgName, ProgName,
                    WS_OVERLAPPEDWINDOW,
                    CW_USEDEFAULT, CW_USEDEFAULT,
                    CW_USEDEFAULT, CW_USEDEFAULT,
                    NULL, NULL, hInstance, NULL);

// First, we get a handle to the screen DC.
hDesktopDC = CreateDC("DISPLAY", NULL, NULL, NULL);


// Now load the bitmap into memory.
hBitmap = LoadBitmap(hInstance, "SPLASH");

// Find the dimensions of the bitmap.
GetObject(hBitmap, sizeof(BM), &BM);

// Find out the size of the desktop.  Then
//    calculate the center of the desktop, so that
//    the bitmap can be displayed correctly in the
//    center of the screen. It is best to calculate
//    it from system metrics so that it will always
//    display correctly no matter what type of
//    driver the user is running.
x = (GetSystemMetrics(SM_CXSCREEN)/2) -
    (BM.bmWidth/2);
y = (GetSystemMetrics(SM_CYSCREEN)/2) -
    (BM.bmHeight/2);


DisplayBitmap(hDesktopDC, hBitmap, x, y, SRCCOPY);
DeleteBitmap(hBitmap);

// Clean up.
DeleteDC(hDesktopDC);


// The following code is a delay loop which ensures
//    that we see the splash screen.  This is only
//    necessary because of the small size of the
//    program.  Usually, because the program would
//    take longer to load, this would not be
//    necessary.
//
// In fact, the following delay loop is considered
//    bad programming style in the Windows world.
```

IV

continues

Listing 4.5. continued

```
//   The reason is that while our program sits in
//   this little loop, no other programs will
//   receive messages.
{
    DWORD  BeginTick, Ticks;


    Ticks = BeginTick = GetTickCount();

    while (Ticks < BeginTick+1000)
        Ticks = GetTickCount();
}

// The next statement refreshes the entire
//   screen.  This ensures that the screen
//   area where the bitmap was displayed is
//   invalidated and redisplayed correctly.
InvalidateRect(NULL, NULL, TRUE);


    ShowWindow(hWnd, nCmdShow);
    UpdateWindow(hWnd);

    while (GetMessage(&msg, NULL, 0, 0))
    {
        TranslateMessage(&msg);
        DispatchMessage(&msg);
    }
    return msg.wParam;
}


/**********************************************/
BOOL DisplayBitmap(HDC hDC, HBITMAP hBitmap,
                   int X, int Y, DWORD RopCode)
{
/*
 * Steps to displaying a bitmap:
 *
 * 1. Create a compatible display context.
 * 2. Select bitmap into compatible display context.
 * 3. Do a bit-block-transfer (BitBlt) command.
 * 4. Clean-up afterwards.
 *
 */
```

```
HDC      hCompatDC;
HBITMAP  hOldBitmap;
BITMAP   BM;
BOOL     result;

// Create compatible display context
hCompatDC = CreateCompatibleDC(hDC);

// Select bitmap into compatible display context
hOldBitmap = SelectBitmap(hCompatDC, hBitmap);

// Get dimensions of bitmap
GetObject(hBitmap, sizeof(BM), &BM);

// Blast those bits to the screen
result = BitBlt(hDC, X, Y, BM.bmWidth, BM.bmHeight,
                hCompatDC, 0, 0, RopCode);

// De-select the bitmap
SelectBitmap(hCompatDC, hOldBitmap);

// Clean up after we are done
DeleteDC(hCompatDC);

return result;

}
/***********************************************/
LRESULT CALLBACK _export MainWndProc(HWND hWnd, UINT
                         message, WPARAM wParam,
                         LPARAM lParam)
{
    switch (message)
    {
        case WM_PAINT :
        {
            HDC         PaintDC;
            RECT        rect;
            PAINTSTRUCT ps;

            PaintDC = BeginPaint(hWnd, &ps);
            GetClientRect(hWnd, &rect);

            DrawText(PaintDC, "Did you see the Splash
                     Screen?", -1, &rect, DT_SINGLELINE |
                     DT_CENTER | DT_VCENTER);
```

IV

continues

Listing 4.5. continued

```
        EndPaint(hWnd, &ps);
        return 0;
    }

    case WM_DESTROY :
    {
        PostQuitMessage(0);
        return 0;
    }
}

    return DefWindowProc (hWnd, message, wParam,
                          lParam);
}
```

Listing 4.6. SPLASH.RC resource script.

```
/*
 * SPLASH.RC resource script
 *
 */

SPLASH BITMAP "splash.bmp"
```

Listing 4.7. SPLASH.DEF module definition file.

```
;
; SPLASH.DEF module definition file
;

DESCRIPTION     'Splash Screen Demo'
NAME            SPLASH
EXETYPE         WINDOWS
STUB            'WINSTUB.EXE'
HEAPSIZE        1024
STACKSIZE       8192
CODE            PRELOAD MOVEABLE DISCARDABLE
DATA            PRELOAD MOVEABLE MULTIPLE
```

Displaying a .BMP File in a Program

How do I display a .BMP file (in other words, one that is not a resource) from within my Windows program?

DESCRIPTION

It is not always reasonable to expect bitmaps used by a program to be stored as resources inside the .EXE file. In these cases, it is necessary to read the .BMP file directly from disk and display the bitmap bits directly to those that have been read in from disk.

Bitmaps saved as .BMP files are actually referred to as *device independent bitmaps* (DIBs). The reasoning behind this terminology is that the bitmap should (in theory) look the same no matter what output device it is displayed upon. This is accomplished by including a color table inside the file describing how the pixel values correspond to actual RGB values. Of course, in actuality, there is no way to make an image appear the same on every device that displays it. There will always be minor differences. However, with device-independent bitmaps these differences can be kept to a minimum.

ANSWER

A Windows bitmap (.BMP) file is made up of several structures that are declared in the WINDOWS.H header file. The .BMP file begins with a header defined by the **BITMAPHEADER** structure. It looks like this:

```
typedef struct tagBITMAPFILEHEADER
{
    UINT    bfType;            // The identifier "BM"
    DWORD   bfSize;            // Total size of the
                               //  file
    UINT    bfReserved1;
    UINT    bfReserved2;
    DWORD   bfOffBits;         // Offset to bitmap
                               //  bytes in file
} BITMAPFILEHEADER;
```

The bfType member includes an identifier, which can be checked to ensure that the file is actually a bitmap file and not a different type of file with the .BMP extension.

That structure is followed by another header, defined by the BITMAPINFOHEADER structure, as follows:

```
typedef struct tagBITMAPINFOHEADER
{
    DWORD   biSize;          // Size of structure
    LONG    biWidth;         // Width of bitmap
    LONG    biHeight;        // Height of bitmap
    WORD    biPlanes;        // Number of planes
    WORD    biBitCount;      // Color bits per pixel
    DWORD   biCompression;   // Compression method
    DWORD   biSizeImage;     // Size of bitmap in
                             // bytes
    LONG    biXPelsPerMeter; // Horizontal resolution
    LONG    biYPelsPerMeter; // Vertical resolution
    DWORD   biClrUsed;       // Number of colors
    DWORD   biClrImportant;  // Number of important
                             // colors
} BITMAPINFOHEADER;
```

The biBitCount member is set to either 1, 4, 8, or 24, depending on the number of bits per pixel. Usually, .BMP files don't contain any compression. In this case, the biCompression member should be set to 0 (for no compression).

If biClrUsed is 0 and biBitCount is set to 1, 4, or 8, the next structure is the color table. The color table consists of two or more RGBQUAD structures. They look like this:

```
typedef struct tagRGBQUAD
{
    BYTE    rgbBlue;
    BYTE    rgbGreen;
    BYTE    rgbRed;
    BYTE    rgbReserved;
} RGBQUAD;
```

If the biBitCount member is 24, then the actual color RGB values are part of the bitmap data. If the file has a color table, it is followed by an array of bits that define the bitmap image. This array starts at the bottom row of pixels. Each pixel can have 1, 4, 8, or 24 bits.

In order to read in a .BMP file on-the-fly, it is necessary to read in the structures we have discussed. A global memory block must be allocated to store the bitmap bits. Then, at the time the bitmap is to be displayed, you use the `SetDIBitsToDevice` function to display the bitmap on the screen.

COMMENTS

Usually .BMP files contain data that is greater than 64K in length. Therefore, your program should use huge pointers so the compiler generates proper code for accessing the bits within the bitmap data. Also, with the Borland compiler it is always best to use the large memory model.

SEE ALSO

`SetDIBitsToDevice` Windows API Function

EXAMPLE CODE

The example program uses the File Open common dialog box to get the name of a bitmap (.BMP) file from the user. It then reads the bitmap data and displays it in the client area of the screen (see Figure 4.2).

Figure 4.2. *The BMPVIEW example program.*

Because the program is already lengthy, it does not include any logic to display scroll bars on the left or bottom sides of the windows; therefore, if a bitmap cannot fit in the window, it is clipped to the size of the window.

Listing 4.8 contains the C Source Code; Listing 4.9 contains the resource script; and Listing 4.10 contains the module definition file.

Listing 4.8. BMPVIEW.C source code.

```
// BMPVIEW.C - .BMP file viewer
//
// Your Borland C++ Consultant by Paul J. Perry
//

#define STRICT
#define IDM_FILEOPEN   100
#define IDM_EXIT       110

#include <windowsx.h>
#include <commdlg.h>
#include <string.h>
#include <stdlib.h>


// Function Prototypes
LRESULT CALLBACK _export MainWndProc(HWND, UINT,
                         WPARAM, LPARAM);
void WM_CommandHandler(HWND, int, HWND, UINT);
DWORD GetBitmapInfoHeaderSize(BYTE huge*);
WORD GetBitmapHeight(BYTE huge *);
WORD GetBitmapWidth(BYTE huge *);
BYTE huge *GetBitmapAddress(BYTE huge *);
BYTE huge *ReadBitmap(char *);


//Global Variables
BYTE huge *lpBitmap = NULL;
BYTE huge *lpBitmapBits = NULL;


/**********************************************/
#pragma argsused
int PASCAL WinMain(HINSTANCE hInstance, HINSTANCE
          hPrevInstance, LPSTR lpCmdParam, int
          nCmdShow)
{
```

```
char        ProgName[] = "BMP File Viewer";
HWND        hWnd;
MSG         msg;


if (!hPrevInstance)
{
   WNDCLASS    wndclass;

   wndclass.lpszClassName = ProgName;
   wndclass.lpfnWndProc   = (WNDPROC) MainWndProc;
   wndclass.cbClsExtra    = 0;
   wndclass.cbWndExtra    = 0;
   wndclass.hInstance     = hInstance;
   wndclass.hIcon         = LoadIcon(NULL,
                              IDI_APPLICATION);
   wndclass.hCursor       = LoadCursor(NULL,
                              IDC_ARROW);
   wndclass.hbrBackground = GetStockObject(
                              WHITE_BRUSH);
   wndclass.lpszMenuName  = "MAINMENU";
   wndclass.style         = CS_VREDRAW |
                              CS_HREDRAW;

   if (!RegisterClass(&wndclass))
      exit(1);
}

hWnd = CreateWindow(ProgName, ProgName,
                 WS_OVERLAPPEDWINDOW,
                 CW_USEDEFAULT, CW_USEDEFAULT,
                 CW_USEDEFAULT, CW_USEDEFAULT,
                 NULL, NULL, hInstance, NULL);

ShowWindow(hWnd, nCmdShow);
UpdateWindow(hWnd);

while (GetMessage(&msg, NULL, 0, 0))
{
   TranslateMessage(&msg);
   DispatchMessage(&msg);
}
return msg.wParam;
}

/**********************************************/
DWORD GetBitmapInfoHeaderSize(BYTE huge *lpBitmap)
```

IV

continues

Listing 4.8. continued

```
{
    // Return the size of the BITMAPINFOHEADER
    //  structure.
    return ((BITMAPINFOHEADER huge *) lpBitmap)->
            biSize;
}

/**********************************************/
WORD GetBitmapHeight(BYTE huge *lpBitmap)
{
    // Return the height of the bitmap, in pixels
    if (GetBitmapInfoHeaderSize(lpBitmap) ==
        sizeof(BITMAPCOREHEADER))
        return (WORD) (((BITMAPCOREHEADER huge*)
                    lpBitmap)->bcHeight);
    else
        return (WORD) (((BITMAPINFOHEADER huge*)
                    lpBitmap)->biHeight);
}

/**********************************************/
WORD GetBitmapWidth(BYTE huge * lpBitmap)
{
    // Return the width of the bitmap, in pixels
    if (GetBitmapInfoHeaderSize(lpBitmap) ==
        sizeof(BITMAPCOREHEADER))
        return (WORD) (((BITMAPCOREHEADER huge*)
                    lpBitmap)->bcWidth);
    else
        return (WORD) (((BITMAPINFOHEADER huge*)
                    lpBitmap)->biWidth);
}

/**********************************************/
BYTE huge *GetBitmapAddress(BYTE huge *lpBitmap)
{
    DWORD NumberOfColors, ColorTableSize;
    WORD  BitCount;

    if (GetBitmapInfoHeaderSize(lpBitmap)
        == sizeof(BITMAPCOREHEADER))
    {
        BitCount = ((BITMAPCOREHEADER huge*)
                    lpBitmap)->bcBitCount;

        if (BitCount != 24)
            NumberOfColors = 1L << BitCount;
```

```
     else
        NumberOfColors = 0;

     ColorTableSize = NumberOfColors*sizeof(
                   RGBTRIPLE);
  }
  else
  {
     BitCount = ((BITMAPINFOHEADER huge *)
               lpBitmap)->biBitCount;

     if (GetBitmapInfoHeaderSize(lpBitmap) >= 36)
        NumberOfColors = ((BITMAPINFOHEADER huge *)
                      lpBitmap)->biClrUsed;
     else
        NumberOfColors = 0;

     if (NumberOfColors == 0)
     {
        if (BitCount != 24)
           NumberOfColors = 1L << BitCount;
        else
           NumberOfColors = 0;
     }

     ColorTableSize = NumberOfColors *
                   sizeof(RGBQUAD);
  }

  return lpBitmap+ColorTableSize+
               GetBitmapInfoHeaderSize(lpBitmap);
}


/********************************************/
BYTE huge *ReadBitmap(char *Filename)
{
   BITMAPFILEHEADER  bfh;

   BYTE huge *lpBitmap;
   DWORD      BitmapSize, Offset, HeaderSize;
   HFILE      hFile;
   WORD       BitmapRead;
   int        result;


   // Open file for reading
   hFile = _lopen(Filename, READ ¦
```

continues

Listing 4.8. continued

```
            OF_SHARE_DENY_WRITE);

   // Could not read file.  Exit out of function
   if (hFile == -1)
      return NULL;

   // Read in the file header.  If it is not read in,
   //   then close file and return.
   result = _lread(hFile, (LPSTR)&bfh,
                   sizeof(BITMAPFILEHEADER));
   if (result != sizeof(BITMAPFILEHEADER))
   {
      _lclose(hFile);
      return NULL;
   }

   // Make sure that the file is actually a .BMPfile.
   //   All .BMPfiles have the BM identifier in them.
   if(bfh.bfType != 0x4d42)  // BM identifier
   {
      _lclose(hFile);
      return NULL;
   }

   // Calculate the size of the bitmap
   BitmapSize = bfh.bfSize - sizeof(BITMAPFILEHEADER);

   lpBitmap = (BYTE huge * ) GlobalAllocPtr(
              GMEM_MOVEABLE, BitmapSize);

   if (lpBitmap == NULL)
   {
      _lclose(hFile);
      return NULL;
   }

   Offset = 0;

   // Read bitmap information in
   while (BitmapSize > 0)
   {
      BitmapRead = (WORD) min (32768ul, BitmapSize);

      if (BitmapRead != _lread(hFile, (LPSTR)
                        (lpBitmap+Offset),
                        BitmapRead))
      {
         _lclose(hFile);
```

```
            GlobalFreePtr(lpBitmap);
            return NULL;
      }

      BitmapSize = BitmapSize-BitmapRead;
      Offset    = Offset + BitmapRead;
   }

   // Done, close file.
   _lclose(hFile);

   HeaderSize = GetBitmapInfoHeaderSize(lpBitmap);

   if (HeaderSize < 12 || (HeaderSize > 12 &&
      HeaderSize < 16))
   {
      GlobalFreePtr(lpBitmap);
      return NULL;
   }

   return lpBitmap;
}


/*********************************************/
#pragma argsused
void WM_CommandHandler(HWND hWnd, int id, HWND
                       hWndCtl, UINT codeNotify)
{
   switch (id)
   {
      case IDM_FILEOPEN :
      {
         OPENFILENAME OpenFileName;
         char Filters[] = "Bitmap Files
                          (*.BMP)\0*.BMP\0"
                          "All Files (*.*)\0*.*\0";
         char FileName[255] = "\0";

         memset(&OpenFileName, 0,
                sizeof(OPENFILENAME));

         OpenFileName.lpstrTitle    = "Open Bitmap
                                       File";
         OpenFileName.hwndOwner     = hWnd;
         OpenFileName.lpstrFilter   = (LPSTR)Filters;
         OpenFileName.nFilterIndex  = 1;
         OpenFileName.lpstrFile     = (LPSTR)FileName;
```

IV

continues

Listing 4.8. continued

```
          OpenFileName.nMaxFile      = sizeof(FileName);
          OpenFileName.Flags         = OFN_FILEMUSTEXIST
                                       ¦ \
                                       OFN_HIDEREADONLY
                                       ¦ \
                                       OFN_PATHMUSTEXIST;
          OpenFileName.lpstrDefExt   = "*";
          OpenFileName.lStructSize   = sizeof(
                                       OPENFILENAME);

          if (GetOpenFileName(&OpenFileName))
          {
             // If there is already a bitmap that was
             //   previously loaded, then clear it out.
             if (lpBitmap != NULL)
             {
                GlobalFreePtr(lpBitmap);
                lpBitmap = NULL;
             }

             // Go and read the bitmap in.
             lpBitmap = ReadBitmap(
                        OpenFileName.lpstrFile);

             // Program was unable to read bitmap file
             //   in
             if (lpBitmap == NULL)
                MessageBox(hWnd, "Could not open file",
                           NULL, MB_ICONEXCLAMATION ¦
                           MB_OK);

             // Re-paint client area of program.
             InvalidateRect(hWnd, NULL, TRUE);

          }

          break;
       }

       case IDM_EXIT :
       {
          SendMessage(hWnd, WM_CLOSE, 0, 0L);
          break;
       }

    }
}
```

```
/*********************************************/
LRESULT CALLBACK _export MainWndProc(HWND hWnd, UINT
                         message, WPARAM wParam,
                         LPARAM lParam)
{
   switch (message)
   {
      case WM_PAINT :
      {

         HDC           PaintDC;
         RECT          rect;
         PAINTSTRUCT   ps;
         static short  Width, Height;

         PaintDC = BeginPaint(hWnd, &ps);
         GetClientRect(hWnd, &rect);

         if (lpBitmap == NULL)
         {
            DrawText(PaintDC, "No .BMPcurrently
                     loaded", -1, &rect, DT_SINGLELINE
                     ¦ DT_CENTER ¦ DT_VCENTER);
         }
         else
         {
            lpBitmapBits = GetBitmapAddress(lpBitmap);
            Width = GetBitmapWidth(lpBitmap);
            Height = GetBitmapHeight(lpBitmap);

            SetStretchBltMode(PaintDC, COLORONCOLOR);

            SetDIBitsToDevice(PaintDC, 0, 0, Width,
                           Height, 0, 0, 0, Height,
                           (LPSTR) lpBitmapBits,
                           (LPBITMAPINFO) lpBitmap,
                           DIB_RGB_COLORS);
         }


         EndPaint(hWnd, &ps);
         return 0;
      }

      case WM_COMMAND :
      {
```

IV

continues

Listing 4.8. continued

```
        return HANDLE_WM_COMMAND(hWnd, wParam,
                                 lParam, WM_Command-
                                 Handler);
    }

    case WM_DESTROY :
    {
        if (lpBitmap != NULL)
            GlobalFreePtr(lpBitmap);

        PostQuitMessage(0);
        return 0;
    }
  }
  return DefWindowProc (hWnd, message, wParam,
                        lParam);
}
```

Listing 4.9. BMPVIEW.RC resource script.

```
/*
 * BMPVIEW.RC resource script
 *
 */


MAINMENU MENU
BEGIN
    POPUP "&File"
    BEGIN
        MENUITEM "&Open Bitmap...", 100
        MENUITEM SEPARATOR
        MENUITEM "E&xit", 110
    END

END
```

Listing 4.10. BMPVIEW.DEF module definition file.

```
;
; BMPVIEW.DEF module definition file
;

DESCRIPTION    'BMP Viewer'
NAME           BMPVIEW
EXETYPE        WINDOWS
STUB           'WINSTUB.EXE'
HEAPSIZE       1024
STACKSIZE      8192
CODE           PRELOAD MOVEABLE DISCARDABLE
DATA           PRELOAD MOVEABLE MULTIPLE
```

Displaying Graphics in Menus

How do I display graphics within menu items?

DESCRIPTION

Windows makes it easy to add a main menu to any program. All that is necessary is to specify the name of the menu resource within the class declaration, as in this:

```
wndclass.lpszMenuName  = "MENUNAME";
```

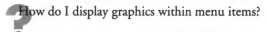

However, many programmers don't realize that Windows also provides the ability to add graphics items to menus. The graphics items give more flair to a program by actually displaying graphical information inside the menus.

ANSWER

Adding graphics items to menus must be done within the code of the program. It takes a little more effort than just specifying a resource name to the `lpszMenuName` member of the window class.

IV

Windows provides hooks to allow you to use bitmaps for any menu items you like. You can add as many bitmap items as you require. The first thing a program must do is obtain a handle to the bitmap, this is done with the following:

```
hBitmap = LoadBitmap(hInstance, "PICTURE");
```

Then, you need to create a menu. This is done with the `CreateMenu` function call:

```
hMenu = CreateMenu();
```

The `CreateMenu` function returns a handle to the newly created menu. The menu is initially empty. Now, to add a graphics item to the menu, use the `AppendMenu` function, like this:

```
AppendMenu(hMenu, MF_BITMAP, IDENTIFIER,
(LPSTR)hBitmap);
```

You can add as many bitmaps as necessary with this call. The `IDENTIFIER` value is a constant which is sent to the window procedure of your program along with the `WM_COMMAND` message. It is how your program would process menu commands selected by the user.

Now, it is a matter of associating the newly created menu with the main window of the program. A simple call to `SetMenu` is all that is necessary, like this:

```
SetMenu(hWnd, hMenu);
```

where hWnd is a handle to the window and hMenu is a handle to the newly created menu. These steps are most often carried out within the `WM_CREATE` message.

When the program shuts down, you must delete the bitmap resources that were previously loaded. Use `DeleteBitmap` within the `WM_DESTROY` message to clean up the graphics once the program is done with them.

COMMENTS

You should use some common sense when adding bitmaps to menus. Large bitmaps probably will not make the most attractive menu items. There is also good argument for not using color bitmaps, because Windows inverts the bitmap when it is selected, and inverted color bitmaps can cause some rather strange color combinations.

SEE ALSO

`AppendMenu` Windows API Function
`LoadBitmap` Macro in WINDOWSX.H File
`DeleteBitmap` Macro in WINDOWSX.H File

EXAMPLE CODE

The program uses bitmaps within the main menu (see Figure 4.3). Listing 4.11 contains the MENUGRAF.C source code; Listing 4.12 contains the MENUGRAF.RC resource script; and Listing 4.13 contains the MENUGRAF.DEF module definition file. The bitmap files MENUOPEN.BMP, MENUSAVE.BMP, and MENUEXIT.BMP are required to compile the program (see Figure 4.4).

IV

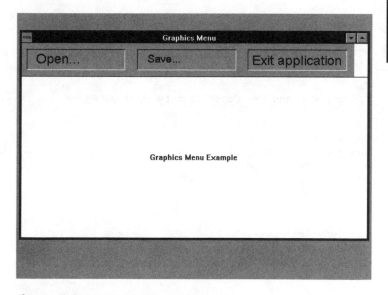

Figure 4.3. *MENUGRAF example program.*

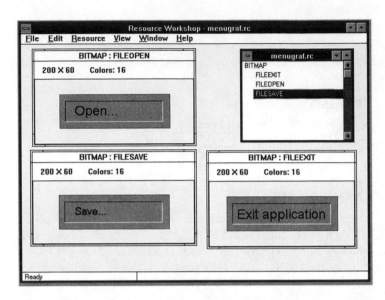

Figure 4.4. *The graphics used for the MENUGRAF example.*

Listing 4.11. MENUGRAF.C source code.

```
// MENUGRAF.C - Example of displaying graphics
//              inside menus.
//
// Your Borland C++ Consultant by Paul J. Perry
//

#define STRICT
#define IDM_FILE 10
#define IDM_OPEN 20
#define IDM_SAVE 30
#define IDM_EXIT 40


#include <windowsx.h>
#include <commdlg.h>
#include <stdlib.h>
#include <string.h>

// Function Prototypes
LRESULT CALLBACK _export MainWndProc(HWND, UINT,
                         WPARAM, LPARAM);
```

```
void WM_CommandHandler(HWND, int, HWND, UINT);

// Global Variables
HINSTANCE ghInstance;


/********************************************/
#pragma argsused
int PASCAL WinMain(HINSTANCE hInstance, HINSTANCE
          hPrevInstance, LPSTR lpCmdParam, int
          nCmdShow)
{
    char        ProgName[] = "Graphics Menu";
    HWND        hWnd;
    MSG         msg;

    if (!hPrevInstance)
    {
        WNDCLASS    wndclass;

        wndclass.lpszClassName = ProgName;
        wndclass.lpfnWndProc   = (WNDPROC) MainWndProc;
        wndclass.cbClsExtra    = 0;
        wndclass.cbWndExtra    = 0;
        wndclass.hInstance     = hInstance;
        wndclass.hIcon         = LoadIcon(NULL,
                                 IDI_APPLICATION);
        wndclass.hCursor       = LoadCursor(NULL,
                                 IDC_ARROW);
        wndclass.hbrBackground = GetStockObject(
                                 WHITE_BRUSH);
        wndclass.lpszMenuName  = NULL;
        wndclass.style         = CS_VREDRAW |
                                 CS_HREDRAW;

        if (!RegisterClass(&wndclass))
            exit(1);
    }

    ghInstance = hInstance;

    hWnd = CreateWindow(ProgName, ProgName,
                        WS_OVERLAPPEDWINDOW,
                        CW_USEDEFAULT, CW_USEDEFAULT,
                        CW_USEDEFAULT, CW_USEDEFAULT,
                        NULL, NULL, hInstance, NULL);

    ShowWindow(hWnd, SW_MAXIMIZE);
```

IV

continues

Listing 4.11. continued

```
    UpdateWindow(hWnd);

    while (GetMessage(&msg, NULL, 0, 0))
    {
        TranslateMessage(&msg);
        DispatchMessage(&msg);
    }
    return msg.wParam;
}


/*********************************************/
#pragma argsused
void WM_CommandHandler(HWND hWnd, int id, HWND
                       hWndCtl, UINT codeNotify)
{
    switch (id)
    {
        case IDM_OPEN :
        {
            OPENFILENAME OpenFileName;
            char Filters[] = "All Files (*.*)\0*.*\0";
            char FileName[255] = "\0";

            memset(&OpenFileName, 0,
                   sizeof(OPENFILENAME));

            OpenFileName.lpstrTitle   = "Open Bitmap
                                         File";
            OpenFileName.hwndOwner    = hWnd;
            OpenFileName.lpstrFilter  = (LPSTR)Filters;
            OpenFileName.nFilterIndex = 1;
            OpenFileName.lpstrFile    = (LPSTR)FileName;
            OpenFileName.nMaxFile     = sizeof(FileName);
            OpenFileName.Flags        = OFN_FILEMUSTEXIST
                                         | \
                                        OFN_HIDEREADONLY
                                         | \
                                        OFN_PATHMUSTEXIST;
            OpenFileName.lpstrDefExt  = "*";
            OpenFileName.lStructSize  = sizeof(
                                         OPENFILENAME);

            GetOpenFileName(&OpenFileName);

            break;
```

```
        }

        case IDM_SAVE :
        {
            OPENFILENAME SaveFileName;
            char Filters[] = "All Files (*.*)\0*.*\0";
            char FileName[255] = "\0";

            memset(&SaveFileName, 0,
                    sizeof(OPENFILENAME));

            SaveFileName.lpstrTitle    = "File Save";
            SaveFileName.hwndOwner      = hWnd;
            SaveFileName.lpstrFilter    = (LPSTR)Filters;
            SaveFileName.nFilterIndex  = 1;
            SaveFileName.lpstrFile      = (LPSTR)FileName;
            SaveFileName.nMaxFile       = sizeof(FileName);
            SaveFileName.Flags          = OFN_FILEMUSTEXIST
                                          | \
                                          OFN_HIDEREADONLY
                                          | \
                                          OFN_PATHMUSTEXIST;
            SaveFileName.lpstrDefExt    = "*";
            SaveFileName.lStructSize    = sizeof(
                                          OPENFILENAME);

            GetSaveFileName(&SaveFileName);

            break;
        }


        case IDM_EXIT :
        {
            SendMessage(hWnd, WM_CLOSE, 0, 0L);
            break;
        }

    }

}

/*********************************************/
LRESULT CALLBACK _export MainWndProc(HWND hWnd, UINT
                        message, WPARAM wParam,
                        LPARAM lParam)
{
    HBITMAP hBmpOpen;
    HBITMAP hBmpSave;
```

continues

Listing 4.11. continued

```
HBITMAP hBmpExit;

switch (message)
{
    case WM_CREATE :
    {
        HMENU    hMenu;

        hMenu = CreateMenu();

        // File Open bitmap
        hBmpOpen = LoadBitmap(ghInstance,
                    "FILEOPEN");
        AppendMenu(hMenu, MF_BITMAP, IDM_OPEN,
                    (LPSTR)hBmpOpen);

        // File Save bitmap
        hBmpSave = LoadBitmap(ghInstance,
                        "FILESAVE");
        AppendMenu(hMenu, MF_BITMAP, IDM_SAVE,
                    (LPSTR)hBmpSave);

        // File Exit bitmap
        hBmpExit = LoadBitmap(ghInstance,
                        "FILEEXIT");
        AppendMenu(hMenu, MF_BITMAP, IDM_EXIT,
                    (LPSTR)hBmpExit);

        SetMenu(hWnd, hMenu);

        return 0;
    }

    case WM_COMMAND :
    {
        return HANDLE_WM_COMMAND(hWnd, wParam,
                lParam, WM_CommandHandler);
    }

    case WM_PAINT :
    {
        HDC         PaintDC;
        RECT        rect;
        PAINTSTRUCT ps;

        PaintDC = BeginPaint(hWnd, &ps);
```

```
        GetClientRect(hWnd, &rect);

        DrawText(PaintDC, "Graphics Menu Example",
                 -1, &rect, DT_SINGLELINE ¦ DT_CENTER
                 ¦ DT_VCENTER);

        EndPaint(hWnd, &ps);
        return 0;
    }

    case WM_DESTROY :
    {
        // Remember to clean up before program
        //   terminates.
        DeleteBitmap(hBmpOpen);
        DeleteBitmap(hBmpSave);
        DeleteBitmap(hBmpExit);
        PostQuitMessage(0);
        return 0;
    }
    }
    return DefWindowProc (hWnd, message, wParam,
                          lParam);
}
```

IV

Listing 4.12. MENUGRAF.RC resource script.

```
/*
 * MENUGRAF.RC resource script
 *
 */


FILEOPEN BITMAP "menuopen.bmp"
FILESAVE BITMAP "menusave.bmp"
FILEEXIT BITMAP "menuexit.bmp"
```

Listing 4.13. MENUGRAF.DEF module definition file.

```
;
; MENUGRAF.DEF module definition file
;
```

continues

Listing 4.13. continued

```
DESCRIPTION    'Graphics items in a menu'
NAME           MENUGRAF
EXETYPE        WINDOWS
STUB           'WINSTUB.EXE'
HEAPSIZE       1024
STACKSIZE      8192
CODE           PRELOAD MOVEABLE DISCARDABLE
DATA           PRELOAD MOVEABLE MULTIPLE
```

 # An Owner-Draw Listbox

How do I display graphics items within a listbox?

DESCRIPTION

Although there is no direct way to add bitmaps to a listbox, Windows does provide something called *owner-draw* controls, of which there is an over-draw listbox. These controls allow the application (rather than Windows) to display the contents inside the listbox. Through the use of owner-draw listboxes, a programmer can display bitmap items inside a listbox.

ANSWER

The first step to creating an owner-draw listbox is to specify the correct listbox style. This can be done inside Resource Workshop (see Figure 4.5) or by adding one of the styles in Table 4.2 to the resource script.

Table 4.2. Owner-draw styles.

Style	Description
LBS_OWNDRAWFIXED	Fixed-size owner draw
LBS_OWNDRAWVARIABLE	Variable-size owner draw

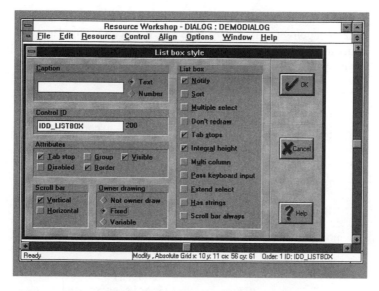

Figure 4.5. *Specifying the owner-draw style in Resource Workshop.*

The difference between the two owner-draw styles is that `LBS_OWNDRAWFIXED` forces all items in the listbox to be the same size, and `LBS_OWNDRAWVARIABLE` allows items to be of different sizes.

With the appropriate style bit set, and the dialog box created, the first task the code must take care of is trapping the `WM_DRAWITEM` message. Whenever the listbox needs updating, Windows sends the control's owner a `WM_DRAWITEM` message. The best method is to use a message cracker declared in WINDOWSX.H, like this:

```
case WM_DRAWITEM :
{

   return HANDLE_WM_DRAWITEM(hDlg, wParam, lParam,
                             WM_DrawItem_Handler);
}
```

Then, when the message is sent to the program, the `WM_DrawItem_Handler` function will be called. The prototype for this function looks like:

```
void WM_DrawItem_Handler(HWND, const DRAWITEMSTRUCT
                         FAR*);
```

When Windows sends the WM_DRAWITEM message, it sets the lParam equal to a pointer to the DRAWITEMSTRUCT structure. This data structure provides information the owner needs in order to update the control. The structure is declared in WINDOWS.H like this:

```
typedef struct tagDRAWITEMSTRUCT
{
    UINT      CtlType;      // Specifies control type
    UINT      CtlID;        // Specifies control
                            //   identifier
    UINT      itemID;       // Specifies index of item
                            //   in list
    UINT      itemAction;   // Specifies drawing
                            //   action
    UINT      itemState;    // Specifies visual state
                            //   of item
    HWND      hwndItem;     // Contains hWnd of
                            //   control
    HDC       hDC;          // Contains hDC for
                            //   control
    RECT      rcItem;       // Specifies control
                            //   boundaries
    DWORD     itemData;     // Value last assigned to
                            //   item
} DRAWITEMSTRUCT;
```

The CtlType member can be one of ODT_BUTTON, ODT_COMBOBOX, ODT_LISTBOX, or ODT_MENU. This specifies for which type of control this message is intended.

The itemAction member can be:

■ ODA_DRAWENTIRE when the entire control needs to be drawn.

■ ODA_FOCUS when the control gains or loses input focus. The itemState structure member should be checked to determine whether the control has focus.

■ ODA_SELECT when only the selection status has changed. The itemState member should be checked to determine the new selection state.

The itemState structure member can be one or more of the following flags:

■ ODS_CHECKED if the menu item is to be checked. This is used only in owner-draw menus.

■ ODS_DISABLE if the item is to be drawn as disabled.

- ODS_FOCUS if the item has input focus.

- ODS_GRAYED if the item is to be grayed. This is used only in owner-draw menus.

- ODS_SELECTED if the item's status is selected.

Another important member of the data structure is the hDC member. It actually contains a handle to the device context of the owner-draw control. This means that your program does not have to go to the bother of using BeginPaint and EndPaint to get a handle to the display context.

The itemData member contains a DWORD which specifies the item within the listbox that is to be acted upon. All items in the listbox are numbered starting at 1.

The dialog box must also specify the size of the listbox items. This is done by trapping the WM_MEASUREITEM message within the dialog box window procedure. By setting the itemHeight member of the LPMEASUREITEMSTRUCT (which is passed in the lParam), the program can specify the size of the listbox data items. Code would look like this:

IV

```
LPMEASUREITEMSTRUCT lpMeasureItem;

lpMeasureItem = (LPMEASUREITEMSTRUCT)lParam;

if (lpMeasureItem->CtlType == ODT_LISTBOX &&
    lpMeasureItem->CtlID == IDD_LISTBOX)
    lpMeasureItem->itemHeight =
    GetSystemMetrics(SM_CYICON)+2;
```

The previous code checks to make sure the WM_MEASUREITEM message is meant for the type of control with which we are working. It then changes the height of the listbox items to the current height of an icon plus two pixels (for spacing considerations).

COMMENTS

Although this discussion has focused mostly on owner-draw listboxes (as you have seen), Windows also allows for owner-draw buttons, comboboxes, and menus. The methodology used for working with these other controls is similar to the techniques presented here for owner-draw listboxes.

Through the use of owner-draw controls, you can build controls that display more data than can be handled by Windows' built-in controls. The maximum amount of data that can be stored in a listbox or combobox is 64K. However, with an owner-draw style, the control stores only a 4-byte data-item identifier instead of the actual string data. Therefore, this opens the possibility of listboxes storing much more data.

SEE ALSO

DATAITEMSTRUCT Data Structure
WM_DRAWITEM Windows Message
WM_MEASUREITEM Windows Message

EXAMPLE CODE

The example program brings up a dialog box, which displays an owner-draw listbox (see Figure 4.6). The listbox contains icons that have been extracted from programs using the ExtractIcon function. One of the buttons in the dialog box brings up the Open File common dialog box which allows you to specify a new filename from which to extract icons.

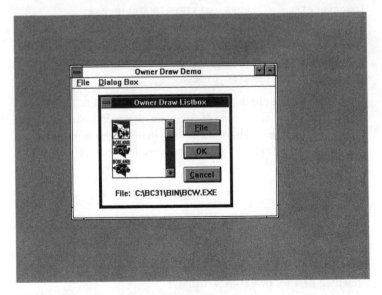

Figure 4.6. *Owner-draw list box example.*

Listing 4.14 contains the source code for OWNDRAW.C; Listing 4.15 contains the header file for OWNDRAW.H; Listing 4.16 contains the resource script for OWNDRAW.RC; and Listing 4.17 contains the module definition file for OWNDRAW.DEF.

> **NOTE** The ExtractIcon is a handy function found with Windows 3.1. It returns a handle to an icon that is located in a different file. You specify the filename, and the type of file can be either an EXE, ICO, or DLL. The prototype for the function is
>
> ```
> HICON WIPI ExtractIcon(HINSTANCE hInst,
>                        LPCSTR lpszExeFileName,
>                        UINT nIconIndex);
> ```
>
> The hInst parameter is a handle to the instance of the current program. The lpszExeFilename is the actual string of the file from which you want to extract an icon. As noted above, it can be either an EXE, an ICO, or a DLL. The nIconIndex specifies which icon to extract from the file. If this is set to zero, it returns to the first icon within the specified file. Alternatively, you can pass a parameter of -1, and the function will return an integer specifying how many icons are actually in the executable.
>
> One of the files you might try to extract icons from is C:\WINDOWS\MOREICONS.DLL. It is a bonus file which comes with Windows 3.1 and contains about 45 extra icons you can use for your program groups inside Program Manager.

Listing 4.14. OWNDRAW.C source code.

```
// OWNDRAW.C - Example of using an
//             owner-draw listbox.
//
// Your Borland C++ Consultant by Paul J. Perry
//
```

continues

Listing 4.14. continued

```
#define STRICT

#include <windowsx.h>
#include <shellapi.h>
#include <commdlg.h>
#include <string.h>
#include <stdlib.h>
#include "owndraw.h"

// Function Prototypes
LRESULT CALLBACK _export MainWndProc(HWND, UINT,
                                     WPARAM, LPARAM);
void WM_CommandHandler(HWND, int, HWND, UINT);
BOOL CALLBACK _export DemoDlgProc(HWND, UINT, WPARAM,
                                  LPARAM);
void WM_Command_Dlg_Handler(HWND, int, HWND, UINT);
void WM_DrawItem_Handler(HWND, const DRAWITEMSTRUCT
                         FAR*);


// Global Variables
HINSTANCE ghInstance;
char      FileName[128] = "PROGMAN.EXE";


/**********************************************/
#pragma argsused
int PASCAL WinMain(HINSTANCE hInstance, HINSTANCE
                   hPrevInstance,
                   LPSTR lpCmdParam, int nCmdShow)
{
    char      ProgName[] = "Owner Draw Demo";
    HWND      hWnd;
    MSG       msg;


    if (!hPrevInstance)
    {
        WNDCLASS    wndclass;

        wndclass.lpszClassName = ProgName;
        wndclass.lpfnWndProc   = (WNDPROC) MainWndProc;
        wndclass.cbClsExtra    = 0;
        wndclass.cbWndExtra    = 0;
        wndclass.hInstance     = hInstance;
        wndclass.hIcon         = LoadIcon(NULL,
                                   IDI_APPLICATION);
```

```
        wndclass.hCursor       = LoadCursor(NULL,
                                   IDC_ARROW);
        wndclass.hbrBackground = GetStockObject(
                                   WHITE_BRUSH);
        wndclass.lpszMenuName  = "MAINMENU";
        wndclass.style         = CS_VREDRAW |
                                   CS_HREDRAW;

        if (!RegisterClass(&wndclass))
            exit(1);
    }

    ghInstance = hInstance;

    hWnd = CreateWindow(ProgName, ProgName,
                        WS_OVERLAPPEDWINDOW,
                        CW_USEDEFAULT, CW_USEDEFAULT,
                        CW_USEDEFAULT, CW_USEDEFAULT,
                        NULL, NULL, hInstance, NULL);

    ShowWindow(hWnd, nCmdShow);
    UpdateWindow(hWnd);

    while (GetMessage(&msg, NULL, 0, 0))
    {
        TranslateMessage(&msg);
        DispatchMessage(&msg);
    }
    return msg.wParam;
}

/*********************************************/
#pragma argsused
void WM_DrawItem_Handler(HWND hwnd,
                         const DRAWITEMSTRUCT
                         FAR* lpDrawItem)
{
    switch (lpDrawItem->itemAction)
    {
        // Redraw every item within the listbox.
        case ODA_DRAWENTIRE :
        {
            // Draw the icon in the list box
            DrawIcon(lpDrawItem->hDC,
                     lpDrawItem->rcItem.left,
                     lpDrawItem->rcItem.top+1,
                     ExtractIcon(ghInstance, FileName,
                               (UINT)lpDrawItem-
                                 >itemData));
```

IV

continues

Listing 4.14. continued

```
    // If the item has been selected by the user,
    //   make sure it is inverted.
    if (lpDrawItem->itemState & ODS_SELECTED)
        PatBlt(lpDrawItem->hDC,
                lpDrawItem->rcItem.left,
                lpDrawItem->rcItem.top,
                lpDrawItem->rcItem.right -
                lpDrawItem->rcItem.left,
                lpDrawItem->rcItem.bottom -
                lpDrawItem->rcItem.top,
                DSTINVERT);

    // If the item has the input focus
    //   draw the focus rectangle.
    if (lpDrawItem->itemState & ODS_FOCUS)
        DrawFocusRect(lpDrawItem->hDC,
                    &lpDrawItem->rcItem);

    break;
}

// Draw item to show current selection state.
case ODA_SELECT :
{
    // Set the location to white.
    PatBlt(lpDrawItem->hDC,
            lpDrawItem->rcItem.left,
            lpDrawItem->rcItem.top,
            lpDrawItem->rcItem.right - lpDrawItem-
            >rcItem.left,
            lpDrawItem->rcItem.bottom -
            lpDrawItem->rcItem.top,
            PATCOPY);

    // Draw the icon previously selected
    DrawIcon(lpDrawItem->hDC,
            lpDrawItem->rcItem.left,
            lpDrawItem->rcItem.top+1,
            ExtractIcon(ghInstance, FileName,
                    (UINT)lpDrawItem-
                    >itemData));

    // If the item has been selected, then
    //   invert it.
```

```
        if (lpDrawItem->itemState & ODS_SELECTED)
        PatBlt(lpDrawItem->hDC,
                lpDrawItem->rcItem.left,
                lpDrawItem->rcItem.top,
                lpDrawItem->rcItem.right - lpDrawItem-
                >rcItem.left,
                lpDrawItem->rcItem.bottom -
                lpDrawItem->rcItem.top,
                DSTINVERT);

        break;
        }

    // Redraw the focus rectangle if the focus state
    //   is changing.
    case ODA_FOCUS :
    {
        DrawFocusRect(lpDrawItem->hDC, &lpDrawItem-
                    >rcItem);
        break;
    }

    }

}


/********************************************/
BOOL CALLBACK _export DemoDlgProc(HWND hDlg, UINT
                    message, WPARAM wParam, LPARAM
                    lParam)
{
    switch(message)
    {
    case WM_INITDIALOG :
    {
        int     result, count;
        HWND    hCtrl;


        // Find out how many icons are in file.
        result = (int)ExtractIcon(ghInstance,
                            FileName, -1);

        SetDlgItemText(hDlg, IDD_FILENAME, FileName);

        // Let the user know the filename
        hCtrl = GetDlgItem(hDlg, IDD_LISTBOX);
```

continues

Listing 4.14. continued

```
        if (result == 0)
           MessageBox(hDlg, "No Icons in this File",
                      NULL, MB_ICONSTOP | MB_OK);

        // Make sure listbox is cleared out
        SendMessage(hCtrl, LB_RESETCONTENT, 0, 0L);

        // Add items to listbox
        for (count=0; count<result; count++)
           SendMessage(hCtrl, LB_ADDSTRING, 0,
                       (LPARAM)count);

        return TRUE;
    }

    case WM_MEASUREITEM :
    {
        LPMEASUREITEMSTRUCT lpMeasureItem;

        lpMeasureItem = (LPMEASUREITEMSTRUCT)lParam;

        // Make the height of the listbox item the
        //   same as that of an icon.
        if (lpMeasureItem->CtlType == ODT_LISTBOX &&
            lpMeasureItem->CtlID == IDD_LISTBOX)
           lpMeasureItem->itemHeight =
              GetSystemMetrics(SM_CYICON)+2;


        return TRUE;
    }


    case WM_DRAWITEM :
    {

        return (BOOL)HANDLE_WM_DRAWITEM(hDlg, wParam,
                                       lParam,
                              WM_DrawItem_Handler);
    }


    case WM_COMMAND :
    {
```

```
        return (BOOL)HANDLE_WM_COMMAND(hDlg, wParam,
                                       lParam,
                            WM_Command_Dlg_Handler);
    }

}

return FALSE;
}


/********************************************/
#pragma argsused
void WM_Command_Dlg_Handler(HWND hDlg, int id,
                            HWND hwndCtl, UINT
                            codeNotify)
{
    switch(id)
    {
        case IDD_FILE :
        {
            OPENFILENAME OpenFileName;
            char Filters[] = "Executable Files
                              (*.EXE)\0*.EXE\0"
                             "Icon Files
                              (*.ICO)\0*.ICO\0"
                             "Dynamic Link Libraries
                              (*.DLL)\0*.DLL\0";


            memset(&OpenFileName, 0, sizeof(
                   OPENFILENAME));

            OpenFileName.lpstrTitle   = "File Open";
            OpenFileName.hwndOwner     = hDlg;
            OpenFileName.lpstrFilter   = (LPSTR)Filters;
            OpenFileName.nFilterIndex = 1;
            OpenFileName.lpstrFile     = (LPSTR)FileName;
            OpenFileName.nMaxFile       = sizeof(FileName);
            OpenFileName.Flags         = OFN_FILEMUSTEXIST
                                         | \
                                         OFN_HIDEREADONLY
                                         | \
                                         OFN_PATHMUSTEXIST;
            OpenFileName.lpstrDefExt   = "*";
            OpenFileName.lStructSize   = sizeof(
                                         OPENFILENAME);
```

IV

continues

Listing 4.14. continued

```
        GetOpenFileName(&OpenFileName);

        strcpy(FileName, OpenFileName.lpstrFile);

        SendMessage(hDlg, WM_INITDIALOG, 0, 0L);

        InvalidateRect(hDlg, NULL, TRUE);

        break;
      }

    case IDOK :
    case IDCANCEL :
      {
        EndDialog(hDlg, 0);
        break;
      }
    }
}


/**********************************************/
#pragma argsused
void WM_CommandHandler(HWND hWnd, int id, HWND
hWndCtl, UINT codeNotify)
{
    switch (id)
    {
      case IDM_DIALOG :
      {
        DLGPROC DlgProc = NULL;

        DlgProc = (DLGPROC)MakeProcInstance(
                 (FARPROC)DemoDlgProc,
                 ghInstance);
        DialogBox(ghInstance, "DEMODIALOG", hWnd,
                 DlgProc);
        FreeProcInstance((FARPROC)DlgProc);

        break;
      }

      case IDM_EXIT :
      {
        SendMessage(hWnd, WM_CLOSE, 0, 0L);
        break;
      }
```

```
    }
}


/*********************************************/
LRESULT CALLBACK _export MainWndProc(HWND hWnd, UINT
                                     message, WPARAM
                                     wParam, LPARAM
                                     lParam)
{
    switch (message)
    {
        case WM_PAINT :
        {
            HDC         PaintDC;
            RECT        rect;
            PAINTSTRUCT ps;

            PaintDC = BeginPaint(hWnd, &ps);
            GetClientRect(hWnd, &rect);

            DrawText(PaintDC, "Owner-Draw Listbox
                    Example", -1, &rect, DT_SINGLELINE |
                    DT_CENTER | DT_VCENTER);

            EndPaint(hWnd, &ps);
            return 0;
        }

        case WM_COMMAND :
        {
            return HANDLE_WM_COMMAND(hWnd, wParam,
                                     lParam,
                                     WM_CommandHandler);
        }

        case WM_DESTROY :
        {
            PostQuitMessage(0);
            return 0;
        }
    }
    return DefWindowProc (hWnd, message, wParam,
                          lParam);
}
```

IV

Listing 4.15. OWNDRAW.H header file.

```
/*
 * OWNDRAW.H header file
 *
 */


#define IDM_EXIT     110
#define IDM_DIALOG   120

#define IDD_LISTBOX  200
#define IDD_FILENAME 202
#define IDD_FILE     201
```

Listing 4.16. OWNDRAW.RC resource script.

```
/*
 * OWNDRAW.RC resource script
 *
 */

#include "owndraw.h"

MAINMENU MENU
BEGIN
     POPUP "&File"
     BEGIN
          MENUITEM "E&xit", IDM_EXIT
     END

     MENUITEM "&Dialog Box", IDM_DIALOG
END


DEMODIALOG DIALOG 9, 18, 116, 87
STYLE DS_MODALFRAME ¦ WS_POPUP ¦ WS_CAPTION ¦
WS_SYSMENU
CAPTION "Owner-Draw Listbox"
BEGIN
     CONTROL "", IDD_LISTBOX, "LISTBOX", LBS_NOTIFY ¦
LBS_OWNERDRAWFIXED ¦ WS_CHILD ¦ WS_VISIBLE ¦ WS_BORDER
¦ WS_VSCROLL ¦ LBS_USETABSTOPS ¦ WS_TABSTOP, 10, 11,
56, 61
     DEFPUSHBUTTON "OK", IDOK, 74, 32, 34, 14,
WS_CHILD ¦ WS_VISIBLE ¦ WS_TABSTOP
```

```
     PUSHBUTTON "&Cancel", IDCANCEL, 74, 53, 34, 14,
WS_CHILD | WS_VISIBLE | WS_TABSTOP
     PUSHBUTTON "&File", IDD_FILE, 74, 11, 34, 14,
WS_CHILD | WS_VISIBLE | WS_TABSTOP
     LTEXT "File:", -1, 12, 72, 15, 8, WS_CHILD |
WS_VISIBLE | WS_GROUP
     LTEXT "", IDD_FILENAME, 30, 72, 75, 8, WS_CHILD |
WS_VISIBLE | WS_GROUP
END
```

Listing 4.17. OWNDRAW.DEF module definition file.

```
;
; OWNDRAW.DEF module definition file
;

DESCRIPTION    'Owner-Draw Controls'
NAME           OWNDRAW
EXETYPE        WINDOWS
STUB           'WINSTUB.EXE'
HEAPSIZE       1024
STACKSIZE      8192
CODE           PRELOAD MOVEABLE DISCARDABLE
DATA           PRELOAD MOVEABLE MULTIPLE
```

Creating a Layered Fill Pattern

How do I create a gradient fill pattern?

DESCRIPTION

A gradient fill pattern is a special pattern that starts at the top of a window and slowly changes color, so by the time it gets to the bottom of the window, the pattern is a different color. The Windows Help program (WINHELP.EXE) displays a pattern similar to this (see Figure 4.7) when it is started directly from Program Manager by choosing the Run option from the File menu (without specifying any .HLP file command-line arguments).

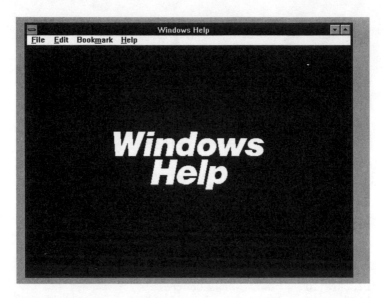

Figure 4.7. *A gradient fill pattern in WinHelp.*

ANSWER

This fancy visual effect is actually fairly easy to implement. It is a matter of splitting the screen into rows and then displaying a different color rectangle within each row. Because Windows will dither all color requests, a loop can be created that creates a new brush, displays the row with that brush, deletes the brush, and then carries on through the loop until the bottom row of the window has been painted. The actual algorithm looks like this:

```
for (i=0; i<=Steps; i++)
{
   hBrush = CreateSolidBrush(RGB(0, 0, i*colorinc));
   rect2.top = rect.top + i * Stepsize;
   rect2.bottom = rect.top + (i+1)*Stepsize;

   FillRect(hDC, &rect2, hBrush);
   DeleteBrush(hBrush);
}
```

The FillRect routine is used instead of Rectangle, because
FillRect does not require selecting the brush into the display
context. This requires fewer program statements, and it makes
cleanup easier.

COMMENTS

By incrementing the values specified within the RGB() macro, it is
easy to create a gradient fill pattern between any two colors.

SEE ALSO

CreateSolidBrush Windows API Function
FillRect Windows API Function
DeleteBrush Macro in WINDOWSX.H

EXAMPLE CODE

The program creates a gradient fill that goes from black to blue
(see Figure 4.8). Listing 4.18 contains the C source code, and
Listing 4.18 contains the module definition file.

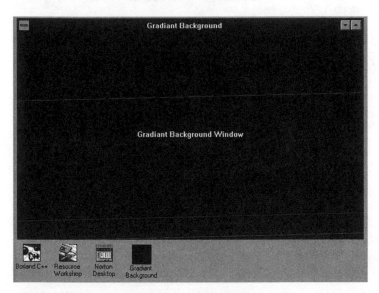

Figure 4.8. *The GRADIENT example program.*

Listing 4.18. GRADIENT.C source code.

```
// GRADIENT.C - Display gradient window background.
//
// Your Borland C++ Consultant by Paul J. Perry
//

#define STRICT

#include <windowsx.h>
#include <stdlib.h>

// Function Prototypes
LRESULT CALLBACK _export MainWndProc(HWND, UINT,
                          WPARAM, LPARAM);
void PaintGradientBackground(HWND hWnd, HDC hDC, int
                             Steps);


/*********************************************/
#pragma argsused
int PASCAL WinMain(HINSTANCE hInstance, HINSTANCE
                   hPrevInstance, LPSTR lpCmdParam,
                   int nCmdShow)
{
   char        ProgName[] = "Gradient Background";
  HWND         hWnd;
   MSG          msg;


   if (!hPrevInstance)
   {
      WNDCLASS      wndclass;

      wndclass.lpszClassName = ProgName;
      wndclass.lpfnWndProc   = (WNDPROC) MainWndProc;
      wndclass.cbClsExtra    = 0;
      wndclass.cbWndExtra    = 0;
      wndclass.hInstance     = hInstance;
      wndclass.hIcon         = NULL;
      wndclass.hCursor       = LoadCursor(NULL,
                               IDC_ARROW);
      wndclass.hbrBackground = GetStockObject(
                               BLACK_BRUSH);
      wndclass.lpszMenuName  = NULL;
      wndclass.style         = CS_VREDRAW |
                               CS_HREDRAW;

      if (!RegisterClass(&wndclass))
         exit(1);
```

```
    }

    hWnd = CreateWindow(ProgName, ProgName,
                        WS_OVERLAPPEDWINDOW,
                        CW_USEDEFAULT, CW_USEDEFAULT,
                        CW_USEDEFAULT, CW_USEDEFAULT,
                        NULL, NULL, hInstance, NULL);

    ShowWindow(hWnd, nCmdShow);
    UpdateWindow(hWnd);

    while (GetMessage(&msg, NULL, 0, 0))
    {
        TranslateMessage(&msg);
        DispatchMessage(&msg);
    }
    return msg.wParam;
}

/*******************************************/
void PaintGradientBackground(HWND hWnd, HDC hDC, int
                             Steps)
{
    int     i, colorinc, Stepsize;
    RECT    rect, rect2;
    HBRUSH  hBrush;

    GetClientRect(hWnd, &rect);

    rect2.left  = 0;
    rect2.right = rect.right;

    Stepsize = (rect.bottom/Steps) + 1;

    colorinc = 255 / (Steps);

    // Create and display the colors
    for (i=0; i<=Steps; i++)
    {
        hBrush = CreateSolidBrush(RGB(0, 0,
                                  i*colorinc));
        rect2.top = rect.top + i * Stepsize;
        rect2.bottom = rect.top + (i+1)*Stepsize;

        FillRect(hDC, &rect2, hBrush);
        DeleteBrush(hBrush);
    }

}
```

IV

continues

Listing 4.18. continued

```c
/**********************************************/
LRESULT CALLBACK _export MainWndProc(HWND hWnd, UINT
                                     message, WPARAM
                                     wParam, LPARAM
                                     lParam)
{
   switch (message)
   {
      case WM_PAINT :
      {
         HDC         PaintDC;
         RECT        rect;
         PAINTSTRUCT ps;

         PaintDC = BeginPaint(hWnd, &ps);
         GetClientRect(hWnd, &rect);

         if (IsIconic(hWnd))
         {
            PaintGradientBackground(hWnd, PaintDC,
                                    16);
         }
         else
         {
            PaintGradientBackground(hWnd, PaintDC,
                                    32);

            SetBkMode(PaintDC, TRANSPARENT);
            SetTextColor(PaintDC, RGB(255, 255, 255));

            DrawText(PaintDC, "Gradient Background
                     Window", -1, &rect, DT_SINGLELINE
                     ¦ DT_CENTER ¦ DT_VCENTER);
         }

         EndPaint(hWnd, &ps);
         return 0;
      }

      case WM_DESTROY :
      {
         PostQuitMessage(0);
         return 0;
      }
   }
```

```
      return DefWindowProc (hWnd, message, wParam,
                            lParam);
}
```

Listing 4.19. GRADIENT.DEF module definition file.

```
;
; GRADIENT.DEF module definition file
;

DESCRIPTION     'Display Gradient Background'
NAME            GRADIENT
EXETYPE         WINDOWS
STUB            'WINSTUB.EXE'
HEAPSIZE        1024
STACKSIZE       8192
CODE            PRELOAD MOVEABLE DISCARDABLE
DATA            PRELOAD MOVEABLE MULTIPLE
```

Working with Mapping Modes

IV

What are mapping modes?

DESCRIPTION

Mapping modes are special drawing coordinate systems the graphics device interface uses to make drawing easier. However, many programmers find some of the mapping modes rather difficult to use, primarily the ANISOTROPIC and ISOTROPIC modes.

ANSWER

A mapping mode refers to the units you specify when setting display coordinates. In real life, if you were to travel from your home to the supermarket, you could measure it in miles, yards, or feet. You are probably most familiar with using miles. However, if the grocery store is just around the corner, you might say that it is 100 feet away. Well, some of these same concepts creep up when working with Windows.

Windows provides eight different mapping modes, or ways of measuring display items. The default mapping mode is screen pixels. In this mode, each pixel corresponds to a coordinate in the graphics device interface. You set the mapping mode with a call to the `SetMapMode` routine. It is defined as follows:

```
int SetMapMode(HDC hDC, int MapMode);
```

The `hDC` parameter is a handle to the display context. The `MapMode` parameter is set to a constant defined in WINDOWS.H. The constants fall into one of the following groups:

Pixel Mode	To use this mode, use the `MM_TEXT` identifier. It refers to the pixel mapping mode, where there is a one-to-one mapping ratio between physical pixels and graphics device interface coordinates. Positive *x* values move to the right, and positive *y* values move down the screen.
Fixed Mode	There are five fixed modes available: `MM_LOMETRIC`, `MM_HIMETRIC`, `MM_LOENGLISH`, `MM_HIENGLISH`, and `MM_TWIPS`. You may be more familiar with these units. *Twips* is a fabricated word meaning twentieth of a point. In these units, moving to the right is a positive *x* direction, and upward is a positive *y* direction.
Isotropic Mode	In isotropic mode, `MM_ISOTROPIC`, the aspect ratio and scale can be changed. It causes the scale of the horizontal and vertical dimensions to be set equivalently.
Anisotropic Mode	In Anisotropic mode, `MM_ANISOTROPIC`, the aspect ratio and scale can be changed. This mode causes the scale of the horizontal and vertical dimensions to be set differently.

Once a specified mapping mode is selected, all graphics device interface functions are going to interpret coordinates within the new coordinate system.

COMMENTS

When a new mapping mode has been selected, it only pertains to functions associated with the graphics device interface. Therefore, coordinates that are passed when a window is resized (as in when your program receives the WM_SIZE message) are always going to be in device coordinates (which are the same as pixels).

To convert from device coordinates (pixels) to the current mapping mode, use the DPtoLP function. For example,

```
RECT rect;

SetMapMode(hdc, MM_LOENGLISH);
SetRect(&rc, 100, 100, 200, 200);
DPtoLP(hdc, (LPPOINT) &rc, 2);
```

converts the device coordinates in the rectangle rect to the coordinates specified as the current mapping mode.

The LPtoDP function does just the opposite and converts from logical coordinates to display coordinates.

SEE ALSO

DPtoLP Windows API Function
LPtoDP Windows API Function
SetMapMode Windows API Function

IV

EXAMPLE CODE

The example program shows the difference between the MM_ANISOTROPIC and MM_ISOTROPIC mapping modes. It draws a unique shape within the client area of the main window. The user can select which of the two mapping modes should be used.

Several instances of the program being run are shown in Figure 4.9. When the mapping mode is set to MM_ISOTROPIC, the size of the shape appears in its regular proportions, no matter what size the window is. If the mapping mode is set to MM_ANISOTROPIC, the figure will change in size to become distorted if the window is resized into a nonsquare shape.

Once the program is executed, the color of the shape is updated each second, and it is redisplayed in a new color. The program cycles between five colors (red, green, blue, purple, and dark gray) and then starts over again.

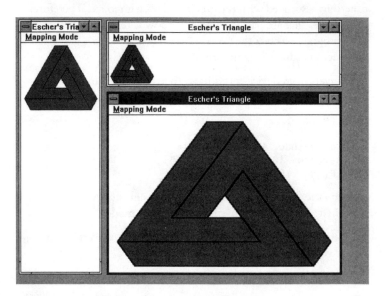

Figure 4.9. *Output of ESCHER.C program.*

Let's take a look at each element of the program and see how it is implemented. The first and most striking item is the Escher shape (duplicated from artwork by the famous artist). The end points are stored in an integer array and then drawn using the `PolyPolygon` function. The function call looks simple enough:

```
PolyPolygon (PaintDC, arr, count, 3);
```

The `arr` array contains the end points of three polygons: the bottom, right, and left-hand sides of the Escher. The `count` array contains the number of points in each array.

In order to draw the Escher shape with the specified mapping mode, we use a single line of code like this:

```
SetMapMode(PaintDC, CurrentMapMode);
```

The scale is set with the `SetWindowExt` and `SetViewportExt` functions. The `SetWindowExt` function sets the *x* and *y* extents of the window. The call to `SetWindowExt` that is used looks like this:

```
SetWindowExt(PaintDC, 260, 228);
```

It tells Windows that no matter how big the window is, the *x*-extent will go from 0 to 260, and the *y*-extent will go from 0 to 228. These numbers were chosen because they are slightly larger than the Escher shape.

The `SetViewportExt` call looks like this:

```
GetClientRect(hWnd, &rect);
SetViewportExt(PaintDC, rect.right, rect.bottom);
```

It tells Windows the extent of the viewport of the window. Therefore, every time the window size changes, we query Windows for the size of the window with the `GetClientRect` function. The viewport is then reset to the extent of the width and height of the client area of the window.

The border of the shape is specified with a pen. The call used to create a new pen is

```
hPen = CreatePen(PS_SOLID, 1, RGB(0,0,0));
hOldPen = SelectPen(PaintDC, hPen);
```

After the pen is created, it is selected into the display context with the `SelectPen` macro. Notice that the handle to the old pen is saved (it is returned from `SelectPen`). This is important so the program can clean up after it is done.

To use different colors inside the shape, the program must create a brush. These color values are stored as `COLORREF` values inside an array. To create the brush, code like this is used:

```
hBrush = CreateSolidBrush(colors[index++]);
hOldBrush = SelectBrush(PaintDC, hBrush);
```

After the brush is created, it is selected into the display context and the program saves the previously selected brush. Notice that the value of `index` is used to represent which color value to use inside the array. After it is used once, it is incremented.

At the end of the `WM_PAINT` message processing, some clean up work is carried out. Basically, the brush and pen are deleted. It looks like this:

```
SelectBrush(PaintDC, hOldBrush);
DeleteBrush(hBrush);
```

IV

```
SelectPen(PaintDC, hOldPen);
DeletePen(hPen);
```

Before the objects can be deleted, the program must first select the old brush back into the display context. The program can then safely delete the objects that we created.

Listing 4.20 contains the ESCHER.C source code; Listing 4.21 contains the ESCHER.H header file; Listing 4.22 contains the ESCHER.RC resource script; and Listing 4.23 contains the ESCHER.DEF module definition file.

Listing 4.20. ESCHER.C source code.

```
// ESCHER.C - Program to display Escher's triangle in
//            a window using mapping modes.
//
// Your Borland C++ Consultant by Paul J. Perry
//

#define STRICT
#define ID_TIMER     100
#define NUMBOFCOLORS 5


#include <windowsx.h>
#include <stdlib.h>
#include "escher.h"


// Function Prototypes
LRESULT CALLBACK _export MainWndProc(HWND, UINT,
                                WPARAM, LPARAM);
void WM_CommandHandler(HWND, int, HWND, UINT);


// Global Variables
int index;
int CurrentMapMode = MM_ISOTROPIC;

/***********************************************/
#pragma argsused
int PASCAL WinMain(HINSTANCE hInstance, HINSTANCE
                   hPrevInstance, LPSTR lpCmdParam,
                   int nCmdShow)
{
    char        ProgName[] = "Escher's Triangle";
```

```
    HWND        hWnd;
    MSG         msg;


    if (!hPrevInstance)
    {
        WNDCLASS    wndclass;

        wndclass.lpszClassName = ProgName;
        wndclass.lpfnWndProc   = (WNDPROC) MainWndProc;
        wndclass.cbClsExtra    = 0;
        wndclass.cbWndExtra    = 0;
        wndclass.hInstance     = hInstance;
        wndclass.hIcon         = LoadIcon(NULL,
                                    IDI_APPLICATION);
        wndclass.hCursor       = LoadCursor(NULL,
                                    IDC_ARROW);
        wndclass.hbrBackground = GetStockObject(
                                    WHITE_BRUSH);
        wndclass.lpszMenuName  = "MAINMENU";
        wndclass.style         = CS_VREDRAW |
                                    CS_HREDRAW;

        if (!RegisterClass(&wndclass))
            exit(1);
    }

    hWnd = CreateWindow(ProgName, ProgName,
                        WS_OVERLAPPEDWINDOW,
                        CW_USEDEFAULT, CW_USEDEFAULT,
                        CW_USEDEFAULT, CW_USEDEFAULT,
                        NULL, NULL, hInstance, NULL);

    ShowWindow(hWnd, nCmdShow);
    UpdateWindow(hWnd);

    while (GetMessage(&msg, NULL, 0, 0))
    {
        TranslateMessage(&msg);
        DispatchMessage(&msg);
    }
    return msg.wParam;
}


/*******************************************/
#pragma argsused
```

IV

continues

Listing 4.20. continued

```
void WM_CommandHandler(HWND hWnd, int id, HWND
                       hWndCtl, UINT codeNotify)
{
   HMENU hMenu;

   hMenu = GetMenu(hWnd);

   switch (id)
   {
      case IDM_ISO :
      {
         CurrentMapMode = MM_ISOTROPIC;
         CheckMenuItem(hMenu, IDM_ISO, MF_CHECKED);
         CheckMenuItem(hMenu, IDM_ANISO,
                       MF_UNCHECKED);
         InvalidateRect(hWnd, NULL, TRUE);

         break;
      }

      case IDM_ANISO :
      {
         CurrentMapMode = MM_ANISOTROPIC;
         CheckMenuItem(hMenu, IDM_ANISO, MF_CHECKED);
         CheckMenuItem(hMenu, IDM_ISO, MF_UNCHECKED);
         InvalidateRect(hWnd, NULL, TRUE);

         break;
      }

      case IDM_EXIT :
      {
         SendMessage(hWnd, WM_CLOSE, 0, 0L);
         break;
      }

   }
}


/**********************************************/
LRESULT CALLBACK _export MainWndProc(HWND hWnd, UINT
                                     message, WPARAM
                                     wParam, LPARAM
                                     lParam)
{
   switch (message)
```

```
{
   case WM_CREATE :
   {
      if (!SetTimer(hWnd, ID_TIMER, 1000, NULL))
         MessageBox(hWnd, "Too many timers set", "
                   ", MB_ICONEXCLAMATION | MB_OK);

      return 0;
   }

   case WM_TIMER :
   {
      index = index%NUMBOFCOLORS;
      InvalidateRect(hWnd, NULL, TRUE);

      return 0;
   }


   case WM_PAINT :
   {
      int   count[3] = {7,7,7};

      POINT arr[] = { {10,  183},
                  // bottom polygon
                     {30,  218},
                  {230, 218},
                  {150, 80},
                  {130, 115},
                  {170, 183},
                  {10,  183},

                  {230, 218},    // right-hand polygon
                  {250, 183},
                  {150, 10},
                  {70,  148},
                     {110, 148},
                  {150, 80},
                  {230, 218},

                  {10,  183},    // left-hand polygon
                  {170, 183},
                  {150, 148},
                  {70,  148},
                  {150, 10},
                  {110, 10},
                  {10,  183} };
```

continues

Listing 4.20. continued

```
COLORREF colors[NUMBOFCOLORS] =
      { RGB(255, 0, 0),          // red
          RGB(0, 255, 0),          // green
          RGB(0, 0, 255),          // blue
          RGB(255, 0, 255),        // purple
          RGB(128, 128, 128) };  // gray

RECT        rect;
HPEN        hPen, hOldPen;
HBRUSH      hBrush, hOldBrush;
HDC         PaintDC;
PAINTSTRUCT ps;

PaintDC = BeginPaint(hWnd, &ps);
GetClientRect(hWnd, &rect);

// Select a new pen in the display context
hPen = CreatePen(PS_SOLID, 1, RGB(0,0,0));
hOldPen = SelectPen(PaintDC, hPen);

// Select a new brush into the display
//  context
hBrush = CreateSolidBrush(colors[index++]);
hOldBrush = SelectBrush(PaintDC, hBrush);

// Set the new mapping mode
GetClientRect(hWnd, &rect);
SetMapMode(PaintDC, CurrentMapMode);
SetWindowExt(PaintDC, 260, 228);
SetViewportExt(PaintDC, rect.right,
               rect.bottom);

// draw figure and do fill
PolyPolygon (PaintDC, arr, count, 3);

// cleanup
SelectBrush(PaintDC, hOldBrush);
DeleteBrush(hBrush);

SelectPen(PaintDC, hOldPen);
DeletePen(hPen);


EndPaint(hWnd, &ps);
return 0;
}
```

```
        case WM_COMMAND :
        {
            return HANDLE_WM_COMMAND(hWnd, wParam,
                                     lParam, WM_Command-
                                     Handler);
        }


        case WM_DESTROY :
        {
            KillTimer(hWnd, ID_TIMER);

            PostQuitMessage(0);
            return 0;
        }
    }

    return DefWindowProc (hWnd, message, wParam,
                          lParam);
}
```

Listing 4.21. ESCHER.H header file.

```
/*
 * ESCHER.H header file
 *
 */


#define IDM_ISO    100
#define IDM_ANISO  110
#define IDM_EXIT   120
```

Listing 4.22. ESCHER.RC resource script.

```
/*
 * ESCHER.RC resource script
 *
 */

#include "escher.h"
```

continues

Listing 4.22. continued

```
MAINMENU MENU
BEGIN
    POPUP "&Mapping Mode"
    BEGIN
        MENUITEM "&Isotropic", IDM_ISO, CHECKED
        MENUITEM "&Anisotropic", IDM_ANISO
        MENUITEM SEPARATOR
        MENUITEM "E&xit", IDM_EXIT
    END

END
```

Listing 4.23. ESCHER.DEF module defintiion file.

```
;
; ESCHER.C module definition file
;

DESCRIPTION     'Demonstration of Mapping Modes'
NAME            ESCHER
EXETYPE         WINDOWS
STUB            'WINSTUB.EXE'
HEAPSIZE        1024
STACKSIZE       8192
CODE            PRELOAD MOVEABLE DISCARDABLE
DATA            PRELOAD MOVEABLE MULTIPLE
```

IV

In This Chapter

- How to get information about the system upon which a program is running, including the percentage of system resources available, the amount of memory available, the Windows and DOS version numbers, the presence of a math coprocessor, and the type of microprocessor upon which the system is running.

- How to use the drag-and-drop feature of Windows 3.1 to interact with File Manager.

- How to write a screen saver that integrates itself with Windows.

- How to display multiple fonts inside a main menu.

- How to output both text and bitmaps to a printer with the help of the common dialogs.

- How to write a Windows hook that allows a program to monitor system events.

- How to change the font used inside an edit control.

- How to create a program with multiple panes that can be resized with the mouse using a sizing window.

- How to implement rubberband drawing.

Miscellaneous

Getting System Information

How do I get basic information about the system upon which a program is running?

DESCRIPTION

All built-in Windows applications display the amount of memory available and the percentage of system resources in their About box (see Figure 5.1). There must be some way for an application program to get this information, as well as other information about the system under which the program is running.

ANSWER

The Windows API provides several functions that return specific information about the current system configuration. Some of these functions are new to Windows 3.1; others have been part of Windows since version 2.0.

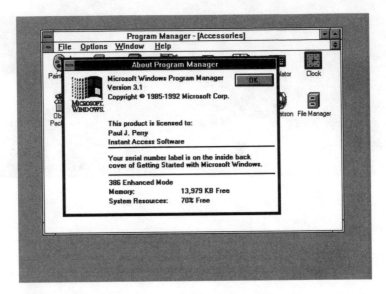

Figure 5.1. *The Program Manager About box.*

The `GetVersion` function returns the Windows and DOS version number. A version number is usually referred to as two parts: major and minor. For example, with version 3.1, the major version number is 3, and the minor version number is 1.

The low-order word of the return value from `GetVersion` contains the Windows version (of which the high-order byte contains the minor version number and the low-order byte contains the major version number). The high-order word of the return value from the `GetVersion` function contains the DOS version number, with the high-order byte containing the major version number and the low-order byte containing the minor version number.

The `LOBYTE`, `HIBYTE`, `LOWORD`, and `HIWORD` macros can be used to extract the appropriate values. The following code demonstrates how to retrieve the Windows and DOS version numbers:

```
DWORD Version;
int WinMajor, WinMinor, DOSMajor, DOSMinor;

Version = GetVersion();

WinMajor = LOBYTE(LOWORD(Version));
WinMinor = HIBYTE(LOWORD(Version));
```

```
DOSMajor = HIBYTE(HIWORD(Version));
DOSMinor = LOBYTE(HIWORD(Version));
```

To find the percentage of system resources available in the system, use the `GetFreeSystemResources` function. Likewise, to find the amount of available memory, use the `GetFreeSpace` function. These two functions are available in Windows 3.1 only.

Finally, the function `GetWinFlags` returns information about various aspects of Windows. Some of the information returned includes the type of processor, whether a math coprocessor is present, the mode under which Windows is running (standard or enhanced), and whether Windows is running on a system with paged memory. The `GetWinFlags` function returns a `DWORD` value and takes no parameters. The function sets bits within the value returned. Therefore, a program should use the logical or operator (¦) to test for the values listed in Table 5.1.

Table 5.1. `GetWinFlags` **values.**

Value	Meaning
WF_80x87	System contains a math coprocessor.
WF_CPU286	System CPU is an 80286.
WF_CPU386	System CPU is an 80386.
WF_CPU486	System CPU is an 80486.
WF_ENHANCED	Windows is running in enhanced mode.
WF_PAGING	Windows is running on a system with paged memory.
WF_PMODE	Windows is running in protected mode. In Windows 3.1, this flag is always set.
WF_STANDARD	Windows is running in standard mode.

COMMENTS

Other useful information about the system under which a program is running can be found in the WIN.INI and SYSTEM.INI files. To gain access to the entries in the WIN.INI file, use the

GetProfileString function. To access the information in the
SYSTEM.INI file, use the GetPrivateProfileString function.

SEE ALSO

GetFreeSpace Windows API Function
GetFreeSystemResources Windows API Function
GetPrivateProfileString Windows API Function
GetProfileStirng Windows API Function
GetVersion Windows API Function
GetWinFlags Windows API Function

EXAMPLE CODE

The example program displays a dialog box listing information
about the computer on which the program is run (see Figure 5.2).
Listing 5.1 contains the SYSINFO.C source code; Listing 5.2
contains the SYSINFO.H header file; Listing 5.3. contains the
SYSINFO.RC resource script; and Listing 5.4 contains the
SYSINFO.DEF module definition file. To compile the program,
you also need an icon with the filename SYSINFO.ICO.

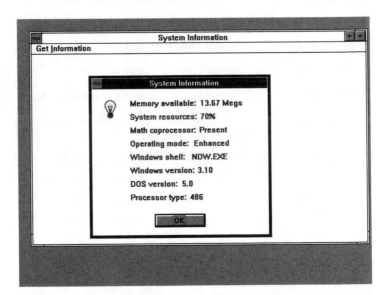

Figure 5.2. *The System Information example program.*

Listing 5.1. SYSINFO.C source code.

```c
// SYSINFO.C - Display system information.
//
// Your Borland C++ Consultant by Paul J. Perry
//

#define STRICT

#include <windowsx.h>
#include <stdlib.h>
#include <string.h>
#include <stdio.h>
#include "sysinfo.h"

// Function Prototypes
LRESULT CALLBACK _export MainWndProc(HWND, UINT,
WPARAM, LPARAM);
void WMSiDlgCommand_Handler(HWND, int, HWND, UINT);
BOOL CALLBACK _export SysInfoDlgProc(HWND, UINT,
WPARAM, LPARAM);
void DisplaySystemInformation(HWND, HINSTANCE);


// Global Variables
HINSTANCE ghInstance;


/********************************************/
#pragma argsused
int PASCAL WinMain(HINSTANCE hInstance, HINSTANCE
                   hPrevInstance, LPSTR lpCmdParam,
                   int nCmdShow)
{
    char        ProgName[] = "System Information";
    HWND        hWnd;
    MSG         msg;


    if (!hPrevInstance)
    {
        WNDCLASS    wndclass;

        wndclass.lpszClassName = ProgName;
        wndclass.lpfnWndProc   = (WNDPROC) MainWndProc;
        wndclass.cbClsExtra    = 0;
        wndclass.cbWndExtra    = 0;
        wndclass.hInstance     = hInstance;
```

continues

Listing 5.1. continued

```
    wndclass.hIcon          = LoadIcon(hInstance,
                              "MAINICON");
    wndclass.hCursor        = LoadCursor(NULL,
                              IDC_ARROW);
    wndclass.hbrBackground = GetStockBrush(
                              WHITE_BRUSH);
    wndclass.lpszMenuName   = "MAINMENU";
    wndclass.style          = CS_VREDRAW |
                              CS_HREDRAW;

    if (!RegisterClass(&wndclass))
        exit(1);
}

ghInstance = hInstance;

hWnd = CreateWindow(ProgName, ProgName,
                    WS_OVERLAPPEDWINDOW,
                    CW_USEDEFAULT, CW_USEDEFAULT,
                    CW_USEDEFAULT, CW_USEDEFAULT,
                    NULL, NULL, hInstance, NULL);

ShowWindow(hWnd, nCmdShow);
UpdateWindow(hWnd);

while (GetMessage(&msg, NULL, 0, 0))
{
    TranslateMessage(&msg);
    DispatchMessage(&msg);
}
return msg.wParam;
}

/**********************************************/
void DisplaySystemInformation(HWND hWnd, HINSTANCE
hInst)
{
    DLGPROC SiDlgProc;

    SiDlgProc = (DLGPROC)MakeProcInstance(
                (FARPROC)SysInfoDlgProc, hInst);
    DialogBox(hInst, "SYSINFODIALOG", hWnd, SiDlgProc);

    FreeProcInstance((FARPROC)SiDlgProc);
}
```

```
/**********************************************/
#pragma argsused
void WMSiDlgCommand_Handler(HWND hDlg, int id, HWND
                            hwndCtl, UINT codeNotify)
{
   switch(id)
   {
      case IDOK :
      case IDCANCEL :
      {
         EndDialog(hDlg, 0);
         break;
      }
   }

}


/**********************************************/
BOOL CALLBACK _export SysInfoDlgProc(HWND hDlg, UINT
              message, WPARAM wParam, LPARAM lParam)
{
   switch(message)
   {
      case WM_INITDIALOG :
      {
         // Local variables
         HWND hMemCtl, hSysResCtl,
         hMathCoCtl, hOpModeCtl, hWinShellCtl,
         hWinVerCtl, hProcCtl, hDOSVerCtl;
         UINT SysRes;
         DWORD MemAvail, Flags, Version;
         char buf[35];

         // Get handles to static control windows
         hMemCtl = GetDlgItem(hDlg, MEMAVAIL);
         hSysResCtl = GetDlgItem(hDlg, SYSRES);
         hMathCoCtl = GetDlgItem(hDlg, MATHCO);
         hOpModeCtl = GetDlgItem(hDlg, OPMODE);
         hWinShellCtl = GetDlgItem(hDlg, WINSHELL);
         hWinVerCtl = GetDlgItem(hDlg, WINVERS);
         hProcCtl = GetDlgItem(hDlg, PROCESSOR);
         hDOSVerCtl = GetDlgItem(hDlg, DOSVERS);

         // Reset text for "System Resources" control
         SysRes = GetFreeSystemResources(
                 GFSR_SYSTEMRESOURCES);
```

V

continues

Listing 5.1. continued

```
sprintf(buf, "%d%", SysRes);
SendMessage(hSysResCtl, WM_SETTEXT, 0,
            (LPARAM)buf);

// Reset text for Memory Available control
MemAvail = GetFreeSpace(NULL);
sprintf(buf, "%.2f Megs", MemAvail/1024.0/
        1024.0);
SendMessage(hMemCtl, WM_SETTEXT, 0,
            (LPARAM)buf);

// Reset text for Math Coprocessor control
Flags = GetWinFlags();

sprintf(buf, "%s", (Flags & WF_80x87) ?
                    "Present" : "Not
                    Present");
SendMessage(hMathCoCtl, WM_SETTEXT, 0,
            (LPARAM)buf);

// Set Control for Windows operating mode
sprintf(buf, "%s", (Flags & WF_ENHANCED) ?
                    "Enhanced" : "Standard");
SendMessage(hOpModeCtl, WM_SETTEXT, 0,
            (LPARAM)buf);

// Set Control for Processor Type
if (Flags & WF_CPU286)
   sprintf(buf, "286");
else if (Flags & WF_CPU386)
   sprintf(buf, "386");
else if (Flags & WF_CPU486)
   sprintf(buf, "486");
SendMessage(hProcCtl, WM_SETTEXT, 0,
            (LPARAM)buf);

// Set Control for Windows Version
Version = GetVersion();
sprintf(buf, "%d.%d",
        LOBYTE(LOWORD(Version)),
        HIBYTE(LOWORD(Version)));
SendMessage(hWinVerCtl, WM_SETTEXT, 0,
            (LPARAM)buf);

// Set Control for DOS Version
sprintf(buf, "%d.%d",
        HIBYTE(HIWORD(Version)),
```

```
            LOBYTE(HIWORD(Version)));
        SendMessage(hDOSVerCtl, WM_SETTEXT, 0,
                    (LPARAM)buf);


        // Set Control for Windows Shell
        GetPrivateProfileString("boot", "shell", "",
                            buf, sizeof(buf),
                            "system.ini");
        strupr(buf);
        SendMessage(hWinShellCtl, WM_SETTEXT, 0,
                    (LPARAM)buf);

        return TRUE;
    }

    case WM_COMMAND :
    {
        return (BOOL)HANDLE_WM_COMMAND(hDlg, wParam,
                                lParam, WMSi-
                                DlgCommand-
                                _Handler);
    }

    }
    return FALSE;

}


/**********************************************/
LRESULT CALLBACK _export MainWndProc(HWND hWnd, UINT
                                    message, WPARAM
                                    wParam, LPARAM
                                    lParam)
{
    switch (message)
    {
    case WM_PAINT :
    {
        HDC         PaintDC;
        RECT        rect;
        PAINTSTRUCT ps;

        PaintDC = BeginPaint(hWnd, &ps);
        GetClientRect(hWnd, &rect);
```

continues

Listing 5.1. continued

```
        DrawText(PaintDC, "System Information Demo
                Program", -1, &rect, DT_SINGLELINE ¦
                DT_CENTER ¦ DT_VCENTER);

        EndPaint(hWnd, &ps);
        return 0;
    }

    case WM_COMMAND :
    {
        DisplaySystemInformation(hWnd, ghInstance);
        return 0;
    }

    case WM_DESTROY :
    {
        PostQuitMessage(0);
        return 0;
    }

    }
    return DefWindowProc (hWnd, message, wParam,
                        lParam);

}
```

Listing 5.2. SYSINFO.H header file.

```
/*
 * SYSINFO.H header file
 *
 */

#define IDM_GETINFO 10


#define MEMAVAIL   11
#define SYSRES     22
#define MATHCO     33
#define OPMODE     44
#define WINSHELL   55
#define WINVERS    66
#define PROCESSOR  77
#define DOSVERS    88
```

Listing 5.3. SYSINFO.RC resource script.

```
/ *
 * SYSINFO.RC resource script
 *
 */

#include "sysinfo.h"


MAINICON ICON "sysinfo.ico"

SYSINFODIALOG DIALOG 39, 33, 160, 131
STYLE DS_MODALFRAME ¦ WS_POPUP ¦ WS_CAPTION ¦
WS_SYSMENU
CAPTION "System Information"
BEGIN
    LTEXT "Memory available:", -1, 35, 9, 63, 8,
WS_CHILD ¦ WS_VISIBLE ¦ WS_GROUP
    LTEXT "System resources:", -1, 35, 21, 63, 8,
WS_CHILD ¦ WS_VISIBLE ¦ WS_GROUP
    LTEXT "Math coprocessor:", -1, 35, 33, 62, 8,
WS_CHILD ¦ WS_VISIBLE ¦ WS_GROUP
    LTEXT "Operating mode:", -1, 35, 45, 57, 8,
WS_CHILD ¦ WS_VISIBLE ¦ WS_GROUP
    LTEXT "Windows shell:", -1, 35, 57, 55, 8,
WS_CHILD ¦ WS_VISIBLE ¦ WS_GROUP
    LTEXT "", MEMAVAIL, 99, 9, 39, 8, WS_CHILD ¦
WS_VISIBLE ¦ WS_GROUP
    LTEXT "", SYSRES, 99, 21, 38, 8, WS_CHILD ¦
WS_VISIBLE ¦ WS_GROUP
    LTEXT "", MATHCO, 98, 33, 37, 8, WS_CHILD ¦
WS_VISIBLE ¦ WS_GROUP
    LTEXT "", OPMODE, 93, 45, 33, 8, WS_CHILD ¦
WS_VISIBLE ¦ WS_GROUP
    LTEXT "", WINSHELL, 91, 57, 60, 8, WS_CHILD ¦
WS_VISIBLE ¦ WS_GROUP
    PUSHBUTTON "OK", IDOK, 57, 112, 46, 12, WS_CHILD
¦ WS_VISIBLE ¦ WS_TABSTOP
    LTEXT "Windows version:", -1, 35, 69, 60, 8,
WS_CHILD ¦ WS_VISIBLE ¦ WS_GROUP
    LTEXT "", WINVERS, 96, 69, 31, 8, WS_CHILD ¦
WS_VISIBLE ¦ WS_GROUP
    ICON "MAINICON", -1, 9, 10, 16, 16, WS_CHILD ¦
WS_VISIBLE
    LTEXT "Processor type:", -1, 35, 93, 53, 8,
WS_CHILD ¦ WS_VISIBLE ¦ WS_GROUP
```

V

continues

Listing 5.3. continued

```
    LTEXT "", DOSVERS, 82, 81, 47, 8, WS_CHILD |
WS_VISIBLE | WS_GROUP
    LTEXT "DOS version:", -1, 35, 81, 46, 8
    LTEXT "", PROCESSOR, 89, 93, 41, 8, WS_CHILD |
WS_VISIBLE | WS_GROUP
END

MAINMENU MENU
BEGIN
    MENUITEM "Get &Information", IDM_GETINFO
END
```

Listing 5.4. SYSINFO.DEF module definition file.

```
;
; SYSINFO.DEF module definition file
;

DESCRIPTION    'System Information'
NAME           SYSINFO
EXETYPE        WINDOWS
STUB           'WINSTUB.EXE'
HEAPSIZE       1024
STACKSIZE      8192
CODE           PRELOAD MOVEABLE DISCARDABLE
DATA           PRELOAD MOVEABLE MULTIPLE
```

Using Drag and Drop

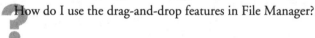

How do I use the drag-and-drop features in File Manager?

DESCRIPTION

When a program implements drag and drop, a user can select a file within File Manager, drag it to a separate application window, and

drop it there. The window into which the file was dropped receives
a message that can be used to retrieve the filenames and the coordinates of the point where the file was dropped.

ANSWER

Drag-and-drop functionality is implemented in a separate Windows
dynamic link library (DLL) module; therefore, you must include
the SHELLAPI.H header file in your program to make the function
prototypes and structure definitions available. You would use a line
like this:

```
#include <shellapi.h>
```

A program tells Windows that it is ready to accept drag-and-drop
files by calling the `DragAcceptFiles` function and passing it the
handle of the window to receive drop information. Then, whenever
a user drops a file on the application's window, the application
receives a `WM_DROPFILES` message. At this point, a program can use
the `DragQueryPoint` function to retrieve the point within the
window at which the user dropped the file, as well as use the
`DragQueryFile` function to return the name of the file the user
dropped.

A program tells Windows it is done accepting drag-and-drop files
by calling the `DragAcceptFiles` function with the same window
handle as the original call and a second parameter of `FALSE`. This is
usually done when the `WM_DESTROY` message is processed.

COMMENTS

Although drag and drop was allowed between Program Manager
and File Manager in Windows 3.0, it was not documented.
Therefore, the calls listed here are limited solely to Windows 3.1.

Drag-and-drop features are nice to implement. It is unfortunate
that Microsoft did not document how a program can begin a drag-
and-drop operation (like File Manager). With this limitation, the
drag-and-drop functionality is not as useful as it could be.

SEE ALSO

DragAcceptFiles Windows API Function
DragQueryFile Windows API Function
DragQueryPoint Windows API Function
WM_DROPFILES Windows Message

EXAMPLE CODE

The example program (see Figure 5.3) implements drag and drop by receiving files from File Manager. Once the file is dropped, its icon is displayed in the window. If the user double-clicks on the icon, the program is executed. The program stores the information about the files that have been dropped into the program in a linked list; therefore, there is no artificial limit on the number of files that can be dropped, and the main window will always be repainted correctly if it becomes invalidated.

Listing 5.5 contains the DD.C source code; Listing 5.6 contains the DD.H header file; Listing 5.7 contains the DD.RC resource script; and Listing 5.8. contains the DD.DEF module definition file.

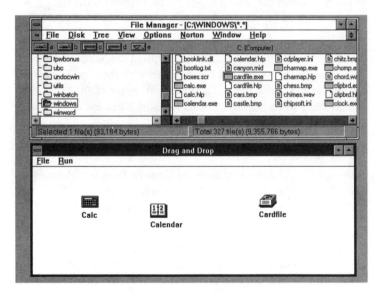

Figure 5.3. *DD.EXE demonstration drag-and-drop program.*

Listing 5.5. DD.C source code.

```c
// DD.C - Drag-and-drop demonstration program.
//
// Your Borland C++ Consultant by Paul J. Perry
//

#define STRICT

#include <shellapi.h>
#include <windowsx.h>
#include <string.h>
#include <stdlib.h>
#include <ctype.h>
#include <dir.h>
#include "dd.h"


// Function Prototypes
LRESULT CALLBACK _export MainWndProc(HWND, UINT,
                          WPARAM, LPARAM);
void WM_CommandHandler(HWND, int, HWND, UINT);
void WMDropFilesHandler(HWND, HDROP);


// Structure definition
struct ddata
{
   char FileName[MAXPATH];
   char Title[MAXFILE];
   POINT pt;
   HICON hIcon;
   struct ddata *next;
} DDATA;


// Global Variables
HINSTANCE ghInstance;
struct ddata *first = NULL;
struct ddata *current;


/*********************************************/
#pragma argsused
int PASCAL WinMain(HINSTANCE hInstance, HINSTANCE
                hPrevInstance, LPSTR lpCmdParam,
                int nCmdShow)
{
```

continues

Listing 5.5. continued

```
char        ProgName[] = "Drag and Drop";
HWND        hWnd;
MSG         msg;


if (!hPrevInstance)
{
   WNDCLASS     wndclass;

   wndclass.lpszClassName = ProgName;
   wndclass.lpfnWndProc   = (WNDPROC) MainWndProc;
   wndclass.cbClsExtra    = 0;
   wndclass.cbWndExtra    = 0;
   wndclass.hInstance     = hInstance;
   wndclass.hIcon         = LoadIcon(NULL,
                               IDI_APPLICATION);
   wndclass.hCursor       = LoadCursor(NULL,
                               IDC_ARROW);
   wndclass.hbrBackground = GetStockBrush(
                               WHITE_BRUSH);
   wndclass.lpszMenuName  = "MAINMENU";
   wndclass.style         = CS_VREDRAW ¦ CS_HREDRAW
                               ¦ CS_DBLCLKS;

   if (!RegisterClass(&wndclass))
       exit(1);
}

ghInstance = hInstance;

hWnd = CreateWindow(ProgName, ProgName,
                    WS_OVERLAPPEDWINDOW,
                    CW_USEDEFAULT, CW_USEDEFAULT,
                    CW_USEDEFAULT, CW_USEDEFAULT,
                    NULL, NULL, hInstance, NULL);

ShowWindow(hWnd, nCmdShow);
UpdateWindow(hWnd);

while (GetMessage(&msg, NULL, 0, 0))
{
   TranslateMessage(&msg);
   DispatchMessage(&msg);
}

return msg.wParam;
}
```

```
/**********************************************/
void WMDropFilesHandler(HWND hWnd, HDROP hDrop)
{
   POINT   pt;
   char    FileName[MAXPATH],
           AssocFile[MAXPATH],
   drive[MAXDRIVE],    // These constants are declared
   dir[MAXDIR],        //   in the dir.h header file
   file[MAXFILE],      //   They provide maximum
                       //   lengths for each part
   ext[MAXEXT];        //   of a filename
   HICON   hIcon;
   HDC     hDC;
   struct ddata *temp;


   hDC = GetDC(hWnd);

   // Retrieve drag-and-drop information
   DragQueryPoint(hDrop, &pt);
   DragQueryFile(hDrop, 0, FileName,
                 sizeof(FileName));

   // Split the pathname apart to get just the
   //   filename
   fnsplit(FileName, drive, dir, file, ext);
   strlwr(file);
   // Make the first character uppercase
   file[0] = (char)_toupper((int)file[0]);

   // Grab the icon out of the file
   hIcon = ExtractIcon(ghInstance, FileName, 0);

   // There was no icon in this file, maybe it has
   //   a file association (as setup in File Manager).
   if (hIcon == (HICON)1)
   {
      FindExecutable(FileName, NULL, AssocFile);
      hIcon = ExtractIcon(ghInstance, AssocFile, 0);
   }

   // Store the drag-and-drop data in a linked list
   temp = first;

   first = (struct ddata*) malloc(sizeof(DDATA));
   first->pt.x = pt.x;
   first->pt.y = pt.y;
   strcpy(first->FileName, FileName);
```

V

continues

Listing 5.5. continued

```
    strcpy(first->Title, file);
    first->hIcon = hIcon;
    first->next = temp;

    // Draw the icon
    DrawIcon(hDC, pt.x, pt.y, hIcon);

    // Display title underneath icon
    TextOut(hDC, pt.x, pt.y +
    GetSystemMetrics(SM_CYICON),
    file, strlen(file));

    // Clean up
    ReleaseDC(hWnd, hDC);

}


/*********************************************/
#pragma argsused
void WM_CommandHandler(HWND hWnd, int id, HWND
hWndCtl, UINT codeNotify)
{
    switch (id)
    {
        case IDM_EXIT :
        {
            SendMessage(hWnd, WM_CLOSE, 0, 0L);
            break;
        }

        case IDM_FILEMANAGER :
        {
            WinExec("WINFILE.EXE", SW_NORMAL);
            break;
        }

        case IDM_ABOUT :
        {
            MessageBox(hWnd, "Drag and Drop
                    Demonstration.\n\n"
                    "Use in conjunction with File\n"
                    "Manager to accept dropped
                     files.\n\n"
                    "Once file has been dropped, a\n"
                    "double click of the mouse button\n"
```

```
                    "allows for execution of specified
                    file\n",
              "About...", MB_OK ¦ MB_ICONINFORMATION);
            break;
        }

    }

}


/*********************************************/
LRESULT CALLBACK _export MainWndProc(HWND hWnd, UINT
                                     message, WPARAM
                                     wParam, LPARAM
                                     lParam)
{
    switch (message)
    {
        case WM_CREATE :
        {
            // Tell Windows that we want to
            //   receive drag and drop messages.
            DragAcceptFiles(hWnd, TRUE);
            return 0;
        }

        case WM_DROPFILES :
        {
            return HANDLE_WM_DROPFILES(hWnd, wParam,
                                       lParam, WMDrop-
                                       FilesHandler);
        }

        case WM_LBUTTONDBLCLK :
        {
            RECT  rect;
            POINT pt;


            pt.x = LOWORD(lParam);
            // Horizontal position of cursor
            pt.y = HIWORD(lParam);
            // Vertical position of cursor

            current = first;

            // Walk through the linked list in order to
            //   redisplay contents of the client area.
```

V

continues

Listing 5.5. continued

```
        while (current != NULL)
        {
            SetRect(&rect,
                current->pt.x,
                current->pt.y,
                current->pt.x+GetSystemMetrics(
                    SM_CXICON), current-
                    >pt.y+GetSystemMetrics(
                    SM_CYICON));

            if (PtInRect(&rect, pt))
        {
            ShellExecute(NULL, NULL, current-
                    >FileName, NULL, NULL,
                    SW_NORMAL);
            return 0;
        }

            current = current->next;
        }
        return 0;
    }

    case WM_PAINT :
    {
        HDC         PaintDC;
        RECT        rect;
        PAINTSTRUCT ps;

        PaintDC = BeginPaint(hWnd, &ps);
        GetClientRect(hWnd, &rect);

        current = first;

        // Walk through the linked list in order to
        //    redisplay contents of the client area.
        while (current != NULL)
        {
            DrawIcon(PaintDC, current->pt.x, current-
                    >pt.y, current->hIcon);
            TextOut(PaintDC, current->pt.x, current-
                    >pt.y + GetSystemMetrics(
                    SM_CYICON),
```

```
                    current->Title, strlen(current-
                                      >Title));
            current = current->next;
        }

        EndPaint(hWnd, &ps);
        return 0;
    }

    case WM_COMMAND :
    {
        return HANDLE_WM_COMMAND(hWnd, wParam,
                                 lParam,
                                 WM_CommandHandler);
    }

    case WM_DESTROY :
    {
        struct ddata *temp;

        // Clear up the memory associated with the
        //   linked list.  Although Windows will do
        //   this for us, it is always good program-
        //   ming style to delete any memory that is
        //   allocated.
        current = first;
        while (current != NULL)
        {
            free(current);
            current = temp;
        }

        // Tell windows that we are done accepting
        //   drag-and-drop messages
        DragAcceptFiles(hWnd, FALSE);

        PostQuitMessage(0);
        return 0;
    }

    }

    return DefWindowProc (hWnd, message, wParam,
                          lParam);
}
```

Listing 5.6. DD.H header file.

```
/*
 * DD.H header file
 *
 */


#define IDM_EXIT         100
#define IDM_FILEMANAGER  200
#define IDM_ABOUT        300
```

Listing 5.7. DD.RC resource script.

```
/*
 * DD.RC resource script
 *
 */

#include "dd.h"

MAINMENU MENU
BEGIN
     POPUP "&File"
     BEGIN
         MENUITEM "E&xit", IDM_EXIT
     END

     POPUP "&Run"
     BEGIN
         MENUITEM "&File Manager", IDM_FILEMANAGER
         MENUITEM SEPARATOR
         MENUITEM "&About", IDM_ABOUT
     END

END
```

Listing 5.8. DD.DEF module definition file.

```
;
; DD.DEF module definition file
;

DESCRIPTION    'Drag and Drop Demo'
NAME           DD
```

```
EXETYPE       WINDOWS
STUB          'WINSTUB.EXE'
HEAPSIZE      1024
STACKSIZE     8192
CODE          PRELOAD MOVEABLE DISCARDABLE
DATA          PRELOAD MOVEABLE MULTIPLE
```

Writing a Screen Saver

How do I write a Windows 3.1 screen saver?

DESCRIPTION

Screen savers are considered by many to be some of the most overrated computer programs around. Somebody once said that if as much thought were put into today's business software as is put into some of the screen savers available commercially, the state-of-the-art in software technology would be increased exponentially.

Although screen savers don't really do anything useful, they are fun to have. In programming circles, telling people you wrote your own screen saver is even more fun (especially when they ask where they can get a copy of it). Although screen savers were around before Windows 3.1, this was the version that officially integrated them into the operating system.

In Windows 3.1, you can open Control Panel, choose Desktop, and specify which screen saver you want to use (see Figure 5.4).

Within the Screen Saver section, you can choose the Test button, (which lets the screen saver run) or choose the Setup button. In this case, you can set certain options that affect the specified screen saver.

ANSWER

Screen savers are stored in the Windows subdirectory with the file extension .SCR. These files are nothing other than regular Windows EXE files that have been renamed. However, there are substantial differences within the source code for a screen saver.

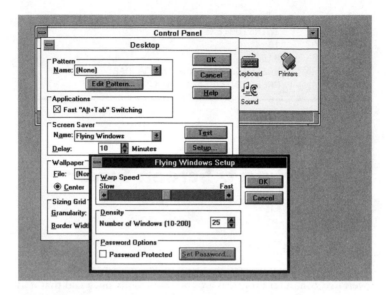

Figure 5.4. *Control Panel Screen Saver Setup.*

The first difference shows up in the module definition file. The description line must start with the string 'SCRNSAVE : followed by a description of the screen saver (and a closing quotation mark). This description is used by the Control Panel combo-box to describe the screen saver.

```
DESCRIPTION    'SCRNSAVE : Boxes'
```

A screen saver has two modes. The first mode is when the screen saver is actually executing. The other mode is when it is being configured. Windows tells the screen saver which mode it should start up in by passing a command-line argument. If the argument is /c or -c, it instructs the screen saver to go into configuration mode. If the argument is anything else, it tells the screen saver to start executing.

Therefore, a program must check the command-line parameters passed to it from WinMain. This can be done with code like this:

```
if  (((lpCmdParam[0] == '/') || (lpCmdParam[0] == '-')
) &&
     (toupper(lpCmdParam[1]) == 'C'))
```

```
{
    DLGPROC  lpfnDialog;

    lpfnDialog = (DLGPROC)MakeProcInstance(
                    (FARPROC)ConfigDlgProc, hInstance);
    DialogBox(hInstance, "CONFIGDIALOG",
                GetFocus(), (DLGPROC)lpfnDialog);
    FreeProcInstance((FARPROC)lpfnDialog);

    return 0;
}
```

If the screen saver is to go into configuration mode (the /c or -c options were passed to it), a configuration dialog box is displayed. The configuration dialog box should allow the user to modify as many options as possible. Otherwise, the screen saver starts executing like normal.

Once the user has pressed the OK button inside the configuration dialog box, the screen saver will store the options the user has set inside the control panel (CONTROL.INI) profile string.

If the screen saver did not receive any command-line parameters, it can assume that it should start executing. The screen saver first creates a pop-up window that fills the entire screen. It then starts a message loop, similar to a regular Windows program. It looks like this:

```
MessageLoop:
{
    if (PeekMessage(&msg, NULL, 0, 0, PM_REMOVE))
    {
        if (msg.message == WM_QUIT)
            return msg.wParam;

        TranslateMessage(&msg);
        DispatchMessage(&msg);
    }
    else
    {
        DoScreenSaver(hWnd);
    }

}

goto MessageLoop;
```

This message loop uses the `PeekMessage` function to check whether there are any messages inside the Windows queue. If any messages are found, the program executes the `TranslateMessage` and `DispatchMessage` function. Otherwise, the screen saver module is called.

The `DoSaver` function is called every time the screen should be updated. All the fun takes place within this function. Each time `DoSaver` is called, it should repaint the screen with a new image. As is obvious from commercial applications, many programmers have let their real creativity flow at this point.

The full-screen window still has a regular window procedure. Inside the window procedure, the mouse movement and keyboard input messages are checked. If they are pressed, the program posts a quit message and terminates.

Before displaying the screen saver, the mouse cursor is turned off, and the current mouse location is saved. Within the `WM_MOUSEMOVE` message processing, the current mouse location is checked with the previously saved mouse location. If they are the same, the message is ignored. It is ignored because mouse messages can be stored in the message queue, and the screen saver would be quickly displayed and then exited shortly afterward.

COMMENTS

Some vendors advertise screen savers as having the ability to save color monitors from phosphor burn-in. This is not true. Although burn-in can occur on monochrome monitors, it cannot happen on a color monitor. Color monitors have three beams that make up the image on the screen. The intensity of the light is dispersed in these three beams, versus the single beam used on a monochrome monitor.

SEE ALSO

`GetPrivateProfileInt` Windows API Function
`GetPrivateProfileString` Windows API Function
`InflateRect` Windows API Function

EXAMPLE CODE

The example screen saver displays a series of enlarging boxes. It allows the user to configure it by choosing the speed and specifying it as multicolor or single-color (see Figure 5.5). Listing 5.9 contains the BOXES.C source code; Listing 5.10 contains the BOXES.H header file; Listing 5.11 contains the BOXES.RC resource script; and Listing 5.12 contains the BOXES.DEF module definition file.

> **NOTE** Remember to rename the resulting executable file with the file extension .SCR before copying it to the Windows subdirectory. If this is not done, Windows won't recognize it as a screen saver.

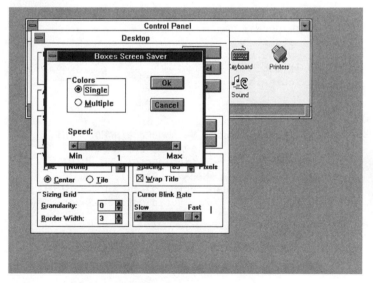

Figure 5.5. *Boxes Screen Saver Configuration dialog box.*

Listing 5.9. BOXES.C source code.

```
// BOXES.C - Example screen saver. Displays
//           pattern of rapidly expanding
```

continues

Listing 5.9. continued

```
//           rectangles.
//
// Your Borland C++ Consultant by Paul J. Perry
//

#define STRICT
#define SINGLE   1
#define MULTIPLE 2

#define TOTALCOLORS 9

#define SPEED_PAGE 2
#define SPEED_MAX  10
#define SPEED_MIN  1

#define SECTIONNAME "Screen Saver.Boxes"


#include <windowsx.h>
#include <stdlib.h>
#include <ctype.h>
#include <stdio.h>
#include "boxes.h"


// Function Prototypes
LRESULT CALLBACK _export MainWndProc(HWND, UINT,
                     WPARAM, LPARAM);
BOOL CALLBACK _export ConfigDlgProc(HWND, UINT,
                     WPARAM, LPARAM);
void WM_Command_Dlg_Handler(HWND, int, HWND, UINT);
                     void DoScreenSaver(HWND);


// Global Variables
POINT StartingCursorPosition;
int ColorOption, SpeedOption;


/*********************************************/
#pragma argsused
int PASCAL WinMain(HINSTANCE hInstance, HINSTANCE
                   hPrevInstance, LPSTR lpCmdParam,
                   int nCmdShow)
{
   char        ProgName[] = "BOXES";
   HWND        hWnd;
```

```
MSG         msg;
WNDCLASS    wndclass;

// Check to see if the configuration dialog box
//   should be displayed, or if the screen
//   saver should be started.
if  (((lpCmdParam[0] == '/') || (lpCmdParam[0] ==
                                    '-') ) &&
     (toupper(lpCmdParam[1]) == 'C'))
{
   DLGPROC lpfnDialog;

   lpfnDialog = (DLGPROC)MakeProcInstance(
                  (FARPROC)ConfigDlgProc,
                  hInstance);
   DialogBox(hInstance, "CONFIGDIALOG",
            GetFocus(), (DLGPROC)lpfnDialog);
   FreeProcInstance((FARPROC)lpfnDialog);

   return 0;
}

// It looks like the screen saver
//   should be started.  We start
//   out by registering the window
//   class.
wndclass.lpszClassName = ProgName;
wndclass.lpfnWndProc   = (WNDPROC) MainWndProc;
wndclass.cbClsExtra    = 0;
wndclass.cbWndExtra    = 0;
wndclass.hInstance     = hInstance;
wndclass.hIcon         = 0;
wndclass.hCursor       = 0;
wndclass.hbrBackground = GetStockObject(
                           BLACK_BRUSH);
wndclass.lpszMenuName  = NULL;
wndclass.style         = CS_VREDRAW | CS_HREDRAW;

if (!RegisterClass(&wndclass))
   exit(1);


// Go ahead and create the window with a
//   style of WS_POPUP and with a height
//   and width of the computer's screen.
hWnd = CreateWindow(ProgName, ProgName,
                  WS_POPUP, 0, 0,
```

continues

Listing 5.9. continued

```
                              GetSystemMetrics(SM_CXSCREEN),
                              GetSystemMetrics(SM_CYSCREEN),
                              NULL, NULL, hInstance, NULL);

    // Save the cursor position
    GetCursorPos(&StartingCursorPosition);

    // Hide the mouse cursor
    ShowCursor(FALSE);

    // Go ahead and display window as normal
    ShowWindow(hWnd, nCmdShow);
    UpdateWindow(hWnd);


    // Modified message loop.  If no messages
    //    are occuring in the system, the
    //    function DoScreenSaver is called.
    MessageLoop:
    {
        if (PeekMessage(&msg, NULL, 0, 0, PM_REMOVE))
        {
            if (msg.message == WM_QUIT)
                return msg.wParam;

            TranslateMessage(&msg);
            DispatchMessage(&msg);
        }
        else
        {
            DoScreenSaver(hWnd);
        }

    }

    goto MessageLoop;

}


/***********************************************/
void DoScreenSaver(HWND hWnd)
{
    HDC       hDC;
    HBRUSH    hBrush, hOldBrush;
    int       MaxX, MaxY;
```

```
static RECT  rect;
static BOOL  StartOver = TRUE;
static int   CurrentColor = 0;

// Array of colors to use when
//    displaying the boxes.
COLORREF Colors[TOTALCOLORS] =
{
    RGB(255,   0, 255),   // Magenta
    RGB(  0,   0, 255),   // Blue
    RGB(  0, 255,   0),   // Green
    RGB(  0, 255, 255),   // Cyan
    RGB(255,   0,   0),   // Red
    RGB(  0, 128,   0),   // Dark green
    RGB(255, 255,   0),   // Yellow
    RGB(128, 128, 128),   // Gray
    RGB(128,   0,   0)    // Dark Red
};


hDC = GetDC(hWnd);

MaxX = GetSystemMetrics(SM_CXSCREEN);
MaxY = GetSystemMetrics(SM_CYSCREEN);

if (StartOver)
{
    SetRect(&rect, (MaxX/2)-5, (MaxY/2)-5,
                   (MaxX/2)+5, (MaxY/2)+5);
    StartOver = FALSE;
    CurrentColor++;
}

if (ColorOption == MULTIPLE)
    CurrentColor++;


hBrush = CreateSolidBrush(Colors[CurrentColor]);
hOldBrush = SelectBrush(hDC, hBrush);

Rectangle(hDC, rect.left, rect.top,
          rect.right, rect.bottom);

InflateRect(&rect, SpeedOption, SpeedOption);

// The rectangle is the size of the screen,
//    redisplay the black background color
//    and then start over.
```

continues

Listing 5.9. continued

```
if ((rect.left <= 0) )
{
    InvalidateRect(hWnd, NULL, TRUE);
    StartOver = TRUE;
}

// Reset the colors to the beginning of the array.
if (CurrentColor == TOTALCOLORS)
    CurrentColor = 0;


// Cleanup
SelectBrush(hDC, hOldBrush);
DeleteBrush(hBrush);

ReleaseDC(hWnd, hDC);

}


/**********************************************/
#pragma argsused
void WM_Command_Dlg_Handler(HWND hDlg, int id,
                            HWND hwndCtl, UINT
codeNotify)
{
    switch(id)
    {
        case IDOK :
        {
            char buff[55];
            HWND hCtrl;

            hCtrl = GetDlgItem(hDlg, IDD_SINGLE);
            if (SendMessage(hCtrl, BM_GETCHECK, 0, 0L))
                ColorOption = SINGLE;
            else
                ColorOption = MULTIPLE;

            sprintf(buff, "%d", ColorOption);
            WritePrivateProfileString(SECTIONNAME,
                                      "Color", buff,
                                      "CONTROL.INI");

            sprintf(buff, "%d", SpeedOption);
            WritePrivateProfileString(SECTIONNAME,
                                      "Speed", buff,
                                      "CONTROL.INI");
```

```
              // fall through
          }


          case IDCANCEL :
          {
              EndDialog(hDlg, 0);
              break;
          }

      }
}

/*********************************************/
BOOL CALLBACK _export ConfigDlgProc(HWND hDlg, UINT
                                    message, WPARAM
                                    wParam, LPARAM
                                    lParam)
{
    switch(message)
    {
       case WM_INITDIALOG :
       {
           HWND hCtrl;

           ColorOption =
GetPrivateProfileInt(SECTIONNAME, "Color", SINGLE,
                     "CONTROL.INI");
           if (ColorOption == SINGLE)
           {
              hCtrl = GetDlgItem(hDlg, IDD_SINGLE);
              SendMessage(hCtrl, BM_SETCHECK, 1, 0L);
           }
           else
           {
              hCtrl = GetDlgItem(hDlg, IDD_MULTIPLE);
              SendMessage(hCtrl, BM_SETCHECK, 1, 0L);
           }

           SpeedOption = GetPrivateProfileInt(
                     SECTIONNAME, "Speed", 1,
                     "CONTROL.INI");

           // Set the speed scrollbar
           SetDlgItemInt(hDlg, IDD_SPEEDTXT,
                     SpeedOption, FALSE );

           hCtrl = GetDlgItem(hDlg, IDD_SPEED );
```

continues

Listing 5.9. continued

```
        SetScrollRange(hCtrl, SB_CTL, SPEED_MIN,
                       SPEED_MAX, FALSE );
        SetScrollPos( hCtrl, SB_CTL, SpeedOption,
                      FALSE );

        return TRUE;
}

case WM_HSCROLL :
{
    HWND hCtrl;

    hCtrl = (HWND)HIWORD(lParam);

    switch(wParam)
    {
        case SB_PAGEDOWN :
        {
            SpeedOption = SpeedOption + SPEED_PAGE;
            // Fall through
        }

        case SB_LINEDOWN :
        {
            SpeedOption = min(SPEED_MAX,
                          SpeedOption+1);
            break;

        }

        case SB_PAGEUP :
        {
            SpeedOption = SpeedOption - SPEED_PAGE;
            // Fall through
        }

        case SB_LINEUP :
        {
            SpeedOption = max(SPEED_MIN,
                          SpeedOption-1);
            break;
        }

        case SB_TOP :
```

```
            {
                SpeedOption = SPEED_MIN;
                break;
            }

            case SB_BOTTOM :
            {
                SpeedOption = SPEED_MAX;
                break;
            }

            case SB_THUMBPOSITION :
            case SB_THUMBTRACK :
            {
                SpeedOption = LOWORD(lParam);
                break;
            }

            default :
            {
                return FALSE;
            }


        }

        SetScrollPos(hCtrl, SB_CTL, SpeedOption,
                    TRUE);
        SetDlgItemInt(hDlg, IDD_SPEEDTXT,
                    SpeedOption, FALSE);
        return TRUE;

    }

    case WM_COMMAND :
    {
        return (BOOL)HANDLE_WM_COMMAND(hDlg, wParam,
                                    lParam,
                            WM_Command_Dlg_Handler);
    }
}

    return FALSE;
}
/*******************************************/
```

continues

Listing 5.9. continued

```
LRESULT CALLBACK _export MainWndProc(HWND hWnd, UINT
                                     message, WPARAM
                                     wParam, LPARAM
                                     lParam)
{
   switch (message)
   {
      case WM_CREATE :
      {
         ColorOption =
GetPrivateProfileInt(SECTIONNAME, "Color", SINGLE,
                     "CONTROL.INI");
         SpeedOption = GetPrivateProfileInt(
                     SECTIONNAME, "Speed", 1,
                     "CONTROL.INI");
         return 0;
      }

      case WM_MOUSEMOVE :
      {
         if ((LOWORD(lParam) ==
             StartingCursorPosition.x) &&
             (HIWORD(lParam) ==
             StartingCursorPosition.y))
            return TRUE;

         // fall through
      }

      case WM_ACTIVATEAPP :
      case WM_ACTIVATE :
      {
         if (wParam != 0)
            return TRUE;

         // fall through
      }

      case WM_KEYDOWN :
      case WM_SYSKEYDOWN :
      case WM_LBUTTONDOWN :
      case WM_RBUTTONDOWN :
      case WM_MBUTTONDOWN :
      {
         PostMessage(hWnd, WM_CLOSE, 0, 0L);
         return 0;

      }
```

```
        case WM_SYSCOMMAND :
        {
           if ((wParam & 0xFFF0) == SC_SCREENSAVE)
              return 0;

           // Otherwise, fall through
        }


        case WM_DESTROY :
        {
           ShowCursor(TRUE);

           PostQuitMessage(0);
           return 0;
        }

     }

     return DefWindowProc (hWnd, message, wParam,
                           lParam);
}
```

Listing 5.10. BOXES.H header file.

```
/*
 * BOXES.H header file
 *
 */

#define IDD_SINGLE   100
#define IDD_MULTIPLE 110
#define IDD_SPEED    120
#define IDD_SPEEDTXT 130
```

Listing 5.11. BOXES.RC resource script.

```
/*
 * BOXES.RC resource script
 *
 */

#include "boxes.h"
```

continues

Listing 5.11. continued

```
CONFIGDIALOG DIALOG 18, 18, 142, 92
STYLE DS_MODALFRAME | WS_POPUP | WS_CAPTION |
WS_SYSMENU
CAPTION "Boxes Screen Saver"
BEGIN
    CONTROL "Single", IDD_SINGLE, "BUTTON",
BS_AUTORADIOBUTTON | WS_CHILD | WS_VISIBLE |
WS_TABSTOP, 25, 19, 39, 12
    CONTROL "&Multiple", IDD_MULTIPLE, "BUTTON",
BS_AUTORADIOBUTTON | WS_CHILD | WS_VISIBLE |
WS_TABSTOP, 25, 31, 39, 12
    CONTROL "Colors", 103, "button", BS_GROUPBOX |
WS_CHILD | WS_VISIBLE, 18, 11, 53, 35
    PUSHBUTTON "Ok", IDOK, 94, 13, 31, 12, WS_CHILD |
WS_VISIBLE | WS_TABSTOP
    PUSHBUTTON "Cancel", IDCANCEL, 94, 33, 31, 12,
WS_CHILD | WS_VISIBLE | WS_TABSTOP
    SCROLLBAR IDD_SPEED, 20, 72, 102, 8, SBS_HORZ |
WS_CHILD | WS_VISIBLE
    CONTROL "Min", -1, "STATIC", SS_LEFT | WS_CHILD |
WS_VISIBLE | WS_GROUP, 20, 81, 16, 8
    LTEXT "Max", -1, 109, 81, 16, 8, WS_CHILD |
WS_VISIBLE | WS_GROUP
    CONTROL "Speed:", -1, "STATIC", SS_LEFT |
WS_CHILD | WS_VISIBLE | WS_GROUP, 19, 59, 27, 8
    LTEXT "", IDD_SPEEDTXT, 63, 83, 16, 8, WS_CHILD |
WS_VISIBLE | WS_GROUP
END
```

Listing 5.12. BOXES.DEF module definition file.

```
;
; BOXES.DEF module definition file
;

DESCRIPTION    'SCRNSAVE : Boxes'
NAME           BOXES
EXETYPE        WINDOWS
STUB           'WINSTUB.EXE'
HEAPSIZE       1024
STACKSIZE      8192
CODE           PRELOAD MOVEABLE DISCARDABLE
DATA           PRELOAD MOVEABLE MULTIPLE
```

Displaying Multiple Fonts in a Menu

How do I add different fonts to a main menu?

DESCRIPTION

Normally, the text displayed in a menu uses the default system font. However, sometimes (say within a menu that lets the user select a font) it would be nice to display the actual appearance of the font in the menu itself, thereby letting the user know exactly what a specified font looks like before selecting it.

ANSWER

As you saw in Chapter 4, *Graphics*, it is relatively easy to display a bitmap inside a menu. Using the `AppendMenu` function, you can add a bitmap to a menu with the following statement:

```
AppendMenu(hMenu, MF_BITMAP, IDM_ITEM,
(LPCSTR)hBitmap);
```

The only way to display text with a unique font is to create a bitmap on the fly. The bitmap should contain the image that is to be added to the menu. In this case, it is text displayed in a unique font. Once the bitmap is created, the bitmap can be added to the menu with code similar to the statement above.

The bitmap can be created with a call to `CreateBitmap`. If this bitmap is selected into a display context, a program can use the `TextOut` function to write text to the bitmap. When the bitmap is first created, the program must specify the size, as well as the number of colors. Once the program is done with the bitmaps, it must delete them.

With the bitmap that has been created, a call to `AppendMenu` adds the bitmap to the specified menu.

COMMENTS

Frequently a programmer wants to display a list of all the fonts available within a menu. Windows provides a font enumeration procedure to get information on all the fonts available to the system. Basically, your program calls the `EnumFontFamilies` function, passing it the procedural instance of a callback function. This callback function is called once for each font in the system.

In the callback function, a program can create a bitmap, create a font, and then display text in the specified font in the bitmap. The bitmap can then be added to the specified menu.

SEE ALSO

`CreateBitmap` Windows API Function
`CreateFont` Windows API Function
`CreateFontIndirect` Windows API Function
`DeleteBitmap` WINDOWSX.H Macro
`DeleteFont` WINDOWSX. H Macro
`EnumFontFamilies` Windows API Function
`SelectBitmap` WINDOWSX.H Macro
`SelectFont` WINDOWSX.H Macro

EXAMPLE CODE

The example program enumerates through all the system fonts. It then creates a menu containing an entry for each TrueType font installed on the system. The menu entry is displayed in the specified font (see Figure 5.6).

Listing 5.13 contains the FONTMENU.C source code, and Listing 5.14 contains the FONTMENU.DEF module definition file.

Figure 5.6. *FONTMENU.EXE example program.*

Listing 5.13. FONTMENU.C source code.

```
// FONTMENU.C - Example program showing how to
//              display fonts inside a menu.
//
// Your Borland C++ Consultant by Paul J. Perry
//

#define STRICT
#define IDM_FONT      10
#define IDM_FONTITEM  20
#define MAXITEMS      10

#include <windowsx.h>
#include <string.h>
#include <stdlib.h>

// Function Prototypes
LRESULT CALLBACK _export MainWndProc(HWND, UINT,
                        WPARAM, LPARAM);
int CALLBACK _export EnumFontFamProc(LOGFONT FAR*,
                TEXTMETRIC FAR*, int, LPARAM);
```

continues

Listing 5.13. continued

```
void WMCommandHandler(HWND, int, HWND, UINT);


// Global Variables
HINSTANCE   ghInstance;
HMENU       hMainMenu, hFontMenu;
HBITMAP     hBitmap[MAXITEMS];
HFONT       hFonts[MAXITEMS];
int         NumbItems = 0, CurrentFont = 0, PrevID;

/*********************************************/
#pragma argsused
int PASCAL WinMain(HINSTANCE hInstance, HINSTANCE
                   hPrevInstance, LPSTR lpCmdParam,
                   int nCmdShow)
{
    char    ProgName[] = "Font Menu";
    HWND    hWnd;
    MSG     msg;
    HDC     hDC;

    FONTENUMPROC lpEnumFamCallBack;


    if (!hPrevInstance)
    {
        WNDCLASS    wndclass;

        wndclass.lpszClassName = ProgName;
        wndclass.lpfnWndProc   = (WNDPROC) MainWndProc;
        wndclass.cbClsExtra    = 0;
        wndclass.cbWndExtra    = 0;
        wndclass.hInstance     = hInstance;
        wndclass.hIcon         = LoadIcon(NULL,
                                  IDI_APPLICATION);
        wndclass.hCursor       = LoadCursor(NULL,
                                  IDC_ARROW);
        wndclass.hbrBackground = GetStockBrush(
                                  WHITE_BRUSH);
        wndclass.lpszMenuName  = NULL;
        wndclass.style         = CS_VREDRAW |
                                  CS_HREDRAW;

        if (!RegisterClass(&wndclass))
            exit(1);
    }
```

```
    ghInstance = hInstance;

    // Create top-level menu
    hMainMenu = CreateMenu();

    // Create popup menu labeled "Font"
    hFontMenu = CreateMenu();

    // We want to enumerate through all the TrueType
    //   fonts available.
    hDC = CreateDC("DISPLAY", NULL, NULL, NULL);

    lpEnumFamCallBack = (FONTENUMPROC)MakeProcInstance(
                        (FARPROC) EnumFontFamProc,
                        ghInstance);
    EnumFontFamilies(hDC, NULL, lpEnumFamCallBack,
                (LPARAM) hFontMenu);

    FreeProcInstance((FARPROC)lpEnumFamCallBack);

    // Attach the popup menu item for "Font" to the
main
    //   menu.
    AppendMenu(hMainMenu, MF_POPUP, (UINT)hFontMenu,
            "&Font");


    DeleteDC(hDC);

    hWnd = CreateWindow(ProgName, ProgName,
                    WS_OVERLAPPEDWINDOW,
                    CW_USEDEFAULT, CW_USEDEFAULT,
                    CW_USEDEFAULT, CW_USEDEFAULT,
                    NULL, hMainMenu, hInstance,
NULL);

    ShowWindow(hWnd, nCmdShow);
    UpdateWindow(hWnd);

    while (GetMessage(&msg, NULL, 0, 0))
    {
        TranslateMessage(&msg);
        DispatchMessage(&msg);
    }
    return msg.wParam;
}
```

continues

Listing 5.13. continued

```
/********************************************/
#pragma argsused
int CALLBACK _export EnumFontFamProc(LOGFONT FAR
                     *lpnlf, TEXTMETRIC FAR *lpntm,
                     int FontType, LPARAM lParam)

{
    HBITMAP hOldBitmap;
    HDC     hIC, hCompatDC;
    HFONT   hOldFont;
    RECT    rect;
    DWORD   Size;
    char    FontName[80];
    TEXTMETRIC tm;


    if (FontType != TRUETYPE_FONTTYPE)
       return TRUE;

    if (NumbItems >= MAXITEMS)
      return FALSE;    // Stop Enumeration


    hIC = CreateIC("DISPLAY", NULL, NULL, NULL);
    GetTextMetrics(hIC, &tm);

    // Create Compatible DC
    hCompatDC = CreateCompatibleDC(hIC);

    // Create the font and select it into the DC
    hFonts[NumbItems] = CreateFontIndirect(lpnlf);
    hOldFont = SelectFont(hCompatDC,
                    hFonts[NumbItems]);

    // Get the face-name of the font
    strcpy(FontName, (char*)lpnlf->lfFaceName);

    // Find the size of the font as it is in the menu
    Size = GetTextExtent(hCompatDC, FontName,
                    strlen(FontName));

    // Create a device-dependant bitmap
    hBitmap[NumbItems] = CreateBitmap (LOWORD(Size),
                                HIWORD(Size), 1,
                                1, NULL);
```

```
hOldBitmap = SelectBitmap(hCompatDC,
                    hBitmap[NumbItems]);

// Set the coordinates of the rectangle
SetRect(&rect, 0, 0, LOWORD(Size), HIWORD(Size));

// Set the background color of the bitmap to white
FillRect(hCompatDC, &rect, GetStockObject(
        WHITE_BRUSH));

// Display the name of the font
TextOut(hCompatDC, 0, 0, FontName,
        strlen(FontName));

// Clean up work.  Notice that bitmaps aren't
//   deleted until processing of the  WM_DESTROY
//   message.
SelectBitmap(hCompatDC, hOldBitmap);
SelectFont(hCompatDC, hOldFont);


DeleteDC(hCompatDC);
DeleteDC(hIC);


AppendMenu(hFontMenu, MF_BITMAP,
        IDM_FONTITEM+NumbItems,
        (LPCSTR)hBitmap[NumbItems]);

NumbItems++;

return TRUE;  // Continue enumeration process
}


/*********************************************/
#pragma argsused
void WM_CommandHandler(HWND hWnd, int id, HWND
                    hWndCtl, UINT codeNotify)
{
// Uncheck the previous menu item
CheckMenuItem(hMainMenu, PrevID, MF_UNCHECKED);

// Check the new menu item
CheckMenuItem(hMainMenu, id, MF_CHECKED);

// Specify new font to use for painting
CurrentFont = id - IDM_FONTITEM;
```

continues

Listing 5.13. continued

```
    // Repaint client area
    InvalidateRect(hWnd, NULL, TRUE);

    PrevID = id;

}




/**********************************************/
LRESULT CALLBACK _export MainWndProc(HWND hWnd, UINT
                                     message, WPARAM
                                     wParam, LPARAM
                                     lParam)
{
    switch (message)
    {
        case WM_CREATE :
        {
            CheckMenuItem(hMainMenu, IDM_FONTITEM,
                          MF_CHECKED);
            PrevID = IDM_FONTITEM;
            return 0;
        }

        case WM_PAINT :
        {
            HDC          PaintDC;
            RECT         rect;
            PAINTSTRUCT  ps;
            HFONT        hOldFont;

            PaintDC = BeginPaint(hWnd, &ps);
            GetClientRect(hWnd, &rect);

            hOldFont = SelectFont(PaintDC,
                        hFonts[CurrentFont]);

            DrawText(PaintDC, "This is an example of the
                    tremendous " "use of fonts in a
                    Windows program.  " "It is evident
                    that the use of fonts " "gives a
                    program extra flair and power!", -1,
                    &rect, DT_WORDBREAK);
```

```
            SelectFont(PaintDC, hOldFont);

            EndPaint(hWnd, &ps);
            return 0;
        }

        case WM_COMMAND :
        {
            return HANDLE_WM_COMMAND(hWnd, wParam,
                                        lParam,
                                        WM_CommandHandler);
        }

        case WM_DESTROY :
        {
            int x;

            // Delete the bitmaps
            for (x=0; x < NumbItems; x++)
            {
                DeleteBitmap(hBitmap[x]);
                DeleteFont(hFonts[x]);
            }


            PostQuitMessage(0);
            return 0;
        }

    }

    return DefWindowProc (hWnd, message, wParam,
                            lParam);
}
```

Listing 5.14. FONTMENU.DEF module definition file.

```
;
; FONTMENU.DEF module definition file
;

DESCRIPTION    'Unique fonts inside a menu'
NAME           FONTMENU
EXETYPE        WINDOWS
```

continues

Listing 5.14. continued

```
STUB          'WINSTUB.EXE'
HEAPSIZE      1024
STACKSIZE     8192
CODE          PRELOAD MOVEABLE DISCARDABLE
DATA          PRELOAD MOVEABLE MULTIPLE
```

Outputting Text to a Printer

How do I display text on a printer within my Windows program?

DESCRIPTION

In a DOS program, printing to a printer is as easy as:

```
fprintf(stdprn, "Print Me\n");
```

Many programmers mistakenly assume there is an equivalent statement within Windows. Unfortunately, outputting text to a printer takes more effort. You must remember that the program is running in a non-preemptive based multitasking environment.

If a program continuously prints information, no other programs receive Windows messages. Therefore, while a program is printing, it must go into a modified message loop so that Windows messages can still be passed through the system. At the same time, it is common courtesy to provide a way for the user to cancel the print operation. This is done with a dialog box.

Each part of printing adds more complexity to the whole task. You are no longer calling a single statement (such as `fprintf(stdprn,"...")`), but you must create a revised message loop, an abort dialog box, and the associated abort dialog procedure.

ANSWER

On the surface, printing to a printer is similar to displaying text on the screen. A program obtains a handle to a device context for the printer and then uses the normal GDI functions to output information to the printer.

The Print common dialog comes in handy to obtain a handle to a printer DC. With a call to the `PrintDlg` function, the function returns a handle to printer display context. The dialog box allows the user to choose to which printer (because there can be more than one printer connected to the system) the display context should be directed. The Print common dialog also allows the user to specify a great number of options associated with printing, including the number of copies, the print quality, and whether the printed copies should be collated.

Because a printer is a multipage device, the display context returned from `PrintDlg` is a little different than a regular display context that is retrieved for the screen.

Because a printer is a shared resource, a program must use the `StartDoc` function when it is ready to start outputting text to the printer. This causes the system to cache any other print requests behind your print job. If this did not occur, pages from different documents could be printed alternately causing much confusion to the user. The `EndDoc` function is used at the end of a print job, signifying that the program is done printing and the Print Manager can continue with other printing requests.

Because the printer is a multipage output device, a program needs to specify some way of printing each page. This is done by using the `StartPage` function to specify the beginning of a page and the `EndPage` function to signify the end of a page.

A program specifies an abort procedure with the `SetAbortProc` function. The abort procedure is a function that checks the system for messages and allows other programs to execute while the job is being printed. The abort procedure includes the modified message loop, which allows other system processing to continue as the text is printed.

To display an abort dialog box, a program must call the `CreateDialog` function to create a modeless dialog box. Once the print job is underway, the program disables the main window and enables the dialog box, therefore, giving the appearance of a modal dialog box.

COMMENTS

The StartDoc, EndDoc, StartPage, EndPage, and SetAbortProc functions are new to Windows 3.1. In previous versions of Windows these functions were actually codes that were passed to the Escape function. The Escape function can still be used to gain a great degree of control over different printers; however, it is usually not necessary to call the Escape function at all.

SEE ALSO

CreateDialog Windows API Function
EndDoc Windows API Function
EndPage Windows API Function
Escape Windows API Function
PrintDlg Windows API Function
SetAbortProc Windows API Function
StartDoc Windows API Function
StartPage Windows API Function

EXAMPLE CODE

The example program is a source code lister. It lets the user specify a filename (usually a C or C++ source code listing) and prints it to the printer, numbering each line and printing a header at the top of each page which specifies the filename, date, time, and page number of the document.

Listing 5.15 contains the PRNFILE.C source code; Listing 5.16 contains the PRNFILE.H header file; Listing 5.17 contains the PRNFILE.RC resource script; and Listing 5.18 contains the PRNFILE.DEF module definition file.

Listing 5.15. PRNFILE.C source code.

```
// PRNFILE.C - Print a file.  Uses print dialog
//             which is in Windows 3.1.
//
// Your Borland C++ Consultant by Paul J. Perry
//

#define STRICT
#define MAX_LINE_LENGTH 255
#define LEFTMARGIN 1
```

```
#include <windowsx.h>
#include <commdlg.h>
#include <stdlib.h>
#include <string.h>
#include <stdio.h>
#include <time.h>
#include "prnfile.h"


// Function Prototypes
LRESULT CALLBACK _export MainWndProc(HWND, UINT,
                                     WPARAM, LPARAM);
void WMCommandHandler(HWND, int, HWND, UINT);
BOOL CALLBACK _export AbortDlgProc(HWND, UINT, WPARAM,
                                   LPARAM);
BOOL CALLBACK _export AbortProc(HDC, int);
void PrintTextFile(HDC);
void PrintPageHeader(HDC);
void PrintLine(HDC, LPSTR, int, int);



// Global Variables
char      FileName[256] = "\0";
BOOL      Abort;
HWND      hAbortDlgWnd;
HINSTANCE ghInstance;
PRINTDLG  pd;
int    FileLineNumber = 1;       // Line number within
                                 file
int    LineNumber = 0;           // Line number on
                                 current page
int    PageNumber = 1;           // Current page
                                 number
int    TextHeight, LinesPerPage;


/*********************************************/
#pragma argsused
int PASCAL WinMain(HINSTANCE hInstance, HINSTANCE
hPrevInstance,
                   LPSTR lpCmdParam, int nCmdShow)
{
   char      ProgName[] = "Print File";
   HWND      hWnd;
   MSG       msg;
```

continues

Listing 5.15. continued

```
if (!hPrevInstance)
{
    WNDCLASS    wndclass;

    wndclass.lpszClassName = ProgName;
    wndclass.lpfnWndProc   = (WNDPROC) MainWndProc;
    wndclass.cbClsExtra    = 0;
    wndclass.cbWndExtra    = 0;
    wndclass.hInstance     = hInstance;
    wndclass.hIcon         = LoadIcon(NULL,
                             IDI_APPLICATION);
    wndclass.hCursor       = LoadCursor(NULL,
                             IDC_ARROW);
    wndclass.hbrBackground = GetStockBrush(
                             WHITE_BRUSH);
    wndclass.lpszMenuName  = "MAINMENU";
    wndclass.style         = CS_VREDRAW |
                             CS_HREDRAW;

    if (!RegisterClass(&wndclass))
        exit(1);
}

ghInstance = hInstance;

hWnd = CreateWindow(ProgName, ProgName,
                    WS_OVERLAPPEDWINDOW,
                    CW_USEDEFAULT, CW_USEDEFAULT,
                    CW_USEDEFAULT, CW_USEDEFAULT,
                    NULL, NULL, hInstance, NULL);

ShowWindow(hWnd, nCmdShow);
UpdateWindow(hWnd);

while (GetMessage(&msg, NULL, 0, 0))
{
    TranslateMessage(&msg);
    DispatchMessage(&msg);
}
return msg.wParam;
}

/********************************************/
#pragma argsused
BOOL CALLBACK _export AbortDlgProc(HWND hDlg, UINT
                                   message, WPARAM
                                   wParam, LPARAM
                                   lParam)
```

```
{
    if (message == WM_COMMAND)
    {
        Abort = TRUE;

        EndDialog(hDlg, wParam);
        return TRUE;
    }
    else if (message == WM_INITDIALOG)
    {
        SetFocus(hDlg);
        // Set the dialog box static text item to
        //    contain the filename being printed.
        SetDlgItemText(hDlg, IDD_FILENAME, FileName);
        return TRUE;
    }

    return FALSE;

}


/********************************************/
#pragma argsused
BOOL CALLBACK _export AbortProc(HDC hDC, int error)
{
    MSG msg;

    while (PeekMessage((LPMSG) &msg, NULL, NULL, NULL,
                    PM_REMOVE))
        if(!IsDialogMessage(hAbortDlgWnd, (LPMSG)&msg))
        {
            TranslateMessage((LPMSG)&msg);
            DispatchMessage((LPMSG)&msg);
        }

    return (!Abort); // Continue print job (in most
                                            cases)
}


/********************************************/
#pragma argsused
void WMCommandHandler(HWND hWnd, int id, HWND hWndCtl,
                    UINT codeNotify)
{
    switch (id)
    {
```

continues

Listing 5.15. continued

```
case IDM_OPEN :
{
    OPENFILENAME OpenFileName;
    char Filters[] = "C source code (*.C)\0*.C\0"
                     "C++ Source code
                     (*.CPP)\0*.CPP\0"
                     "Text Files
                     (*.TXT)\0*.TXT\0"
                     "All Files (*.*)\0*.*\0";

    memset(&OpenFileName, 0, sizeof(
          OPENFILENAME));

    OpenFileName.lpstrTitle   = "Specify Print
                                Filename";
    OpenFileName.hwndOwner    = hWnd;
    OpenFileName.lpstrFilter  = (LPSTR)Filters;
    OpenFileName.nFilterIndex = 1;
    OpenFileName.lpstrFile    = (LPSTR)FileName;
    OpenFileName.nMaxFile     = sizeof(FileName);
    OpenFileName.Flags        = OFN_FILEMUSTEXIST
                                ¦ \
                                OFN_HIDEREADONLY
                                ¦ \
                                OFN_PATHMUSTEXIST;
    OpenFileName.lpstrDefExt  = "*";
    OpenFileName.lStructSize  = sizeof(
                                OPENFILENAME);

    GetOpenFileName(&OpenFileName);

    // Ensure that the client area is updated
    //   to show the newly entered filename.
    InvalidateRect(hWnd, NULL, TRUE);

    break;
}

case IDM_PRINT :
{
    OFSTRUCT ofs;

    // First check to make sure that a file
    //   has been selected and that it exists.
    if (OpenFile(FileName, &ofs, OF_EXIST) ==
        HFILE_ERROR)
    {
```

```
            MessageBox(hWnd, "No File Selected",
                       NULL, MB_OK ¦
                       MB_ICONSTOP);
            break;
}

// Set up the common Print dialog
memset(&pd, 0, sizeof(PRINTDLG));

pd.hwndOwner    = hWnd;
pd.Flags        = PD_RETURNDC ¦ \
                  PD_HIDEPRINTTOFILE ¦ \
                  PD_NOPAGENUMS ¦ \
                  PD_DISABLEPRINTTOFILE ¦ \
                  PD_NOSELECTION;

pd.lStructSize = sizeof(PRINTDLG);

// Call the Print Dialog box.  If it returns
//   a successful value, the file is printed
//   out.
if (PrintDlg(&pd) != NULL)
{
   DOCINFO DocInfo;
   char    buf[255];

   ABORTPROC lpAbortProc;
   DLGPROC   lpAbortDlgProc;

            // Create Abort procedure
   lpAbortProc = (ABORTPROC)MakeProcInstance(
                  (FARPROC)AbortProc,
                  ghInstance);
                  SetAbortProc(pd.hDC,
                  (ABORTPROC)lpAbortProc);

   // Create document name
   sprintf(buf, "Print File — %s",
         FileName);

   // Fill out the DOCINFO structure members
   DocInfo.cbSize      = sizeof(DOCINFO);
   DocInfo.lpszDocName = buf;
   DocInfo.lpszOutput  = NULL;

   // Try to get access to the printer.  If
   //   access is denied, then return;
```

continues

Listing 5.15. continued

```
if (StartDoc(pd.hDC, &DocInfo) < 0)
{
    // An error occured
    MessageBox(hWnd, "Unable to start print
                job", NULL, MB_OK |
                MB_ICONSTOP);
    FreeProcInstance((FARPROC)lpAbortProc);
    DeleteDC(pd.hDC);
    break;
}

    Abort = FALSE;

    // Now, we are ready to display the
    //   Abort dialog box on the screen.
    lpAbortDlgProc = (DLGPROC)
                MakeProcInstance((FARPROC)
                    AbortDlgProc,
                    ghInstance);
    hAbortDlgWnd = CreateDialog(
                ghInstance,
                "ABORTDLG", hWnd,
                (DLGPROC)
                lpAbortDlgProc);
    ShowWindow(hAbortDlgWnd, SW_NORMAL);

// Enable the cancel dialog box window
    UpdateWindow(hAbortDlgWnd);

// Disable parent window.
EnableWindow(hWnd, FALSE);

// Go and actually print the file
PrintTextFile(pd.hDC);

// Remove abort dialog box and set focus
//   back to the main window.
EnableWindow(hWnd, TRUE);
DestroyWindow(hAbortDlgWnd);


// Cleanup
FreeProcInstance((FARPROC)lpAbortProc);
FreeProcInstance((FARPROC)lpAbortDlgProc);
DeleteDC(pd.hDC);

    }
```

```
               break;
           }

         case IDM_SETUP :
         {
            memset(&pd, 0, sizeof(PRINTDLG));
            pd.hwndOwner   = hWnd;
            pd.nCopies     = -1;
            pd.Flags       = PD_PRINTSETUP;

            pd.lStructSize = sizeof(PRINTDLG);

            PrintDlg(&pd);
            DeleteDC(pd.hDC);

            break;

         }


         case IDM_EXIT :
         {
            SendMessage(hWnd, WM_CLOSE, 0, 0L);
            break;
         }

      }
}


/********************************************/
void PrintTextFile(HDC PrinterDC)
{
   FILE   *fin;
   char    buffer[MAX_LINE_LENGTH];

   TEXTMETRIC TextMetric;

   // Initialize several variables
   FileLineNumber = 1;
   LineNumber = 0;
   PageNumber = 1;


   // Open the file
   fin = fopen(FileName, "r");
```

continues

Listing 5.15. continued

```
// Get information about the size of the text and
//    the size of the page.
GetTextMetrics(PrinterDC, &TextMetric);
TextHeight = TextMetric.tmHeight+
             TextMetric.tmExternalLeading;
LinesPerPage = GetDeviceCaps(PrinterDC, VERTRES) /
             TextHeight;


while (fgets(buffer, MAX_LINE_LENGTH, fin) != NULL)
{
    if (LineNumber < 2)
    {
        StartPage(PrinterDC);
        PrintPageHeader(PrinterDC);
    }

    PrintLine(PrinterDC, buffer, LEFTMARGIN,
            LineNumber*TextHeight);
    LineNumber++;
    FileLineNumber++;

    if (LineNumber >= LinesPerPage)
    {
        EndPage(PrinterDC);
        LineNumber = 0;
        PageNumber++;
    }

}

EndPage(PrinterDC);
EndDoc(PrinterDC);

}

/**********************************************/
void PrintLine(HDC PrinterDC, LPSTR line, int x, int
y)
{
    char  buff[355];
    LPSTR ptr;

    ptr = line;

    // Replace any tab characters with a space
    while (*ptr != '\0')
```

```
    {
        if (*ptr == '\t')
            *ptr = ' ';
        ptr++;
    }

    // Add the line number to the beginning of the line
    sprintf(buff, "%4d: %s", FileLineNumber, line);
    // Send the output to the printer
    TextOut(PrinterDC, x, y, buff, strlen(buff)-1);

}

/******************************************/
void PrintPageHeader(HDC PrinterDC)
{
    char    buff[255], datebuf[9], timebuf[9];

    _strdate(datebuf);
    _strtime(timebuf);

    // Create header string which contains filename,
    //    date, time, and page number
    sprintf(buff, "%s, %s, %s      **Page %d**",
            FileName, datebuf, timebuf, PageNumber);

    // Send output to printer
    TextOut(PrinterDC, 10, LineNumber*TextHeight,
            buff, strlen(buff));

    // Increment line number
    LineNumber = LineNumber + 2;

}


/******************************************/
LRESULT CALLBACK _export MainWndProc(HWND hWnd, UINT
                                            message,
                                        WPARAM wParam,
                                        LPARAM lParam)
{
    switch (message)
    {
        case WM_PAINT :
        {
            HDC            PaintDC;
            RECT           rect;
```

V

continues

Listing 5.15. continued

```
        PAINTSTRUCT ps;
        char        buff[255];

        PaintDC = BeginPaint(hWnd, &ps);
        GetClientRect(hWnd, &rect);

        // Display in lowercase so it is easier on
        //    the eyes.
        strlwr(FileName);

        if (strlen(FileName) != 0)
            sprintf(buff, "Current filename = %s",
                    FileName);
        else
            sprintf(buff, "No file selected");

        TextOut(PaintDC, 5, 5, buff, strlen(buff));

        DrawText(PaintDC, "File Print Utility",
                -1, &rect, DT_SINGLELINE | DT_CENTER
                | DT_VCENTER);

        EndPaint(hWnd, &ps);
        return 0;
    }

    case WM_COMMAND :
    {
        return HANDLE_WM_COMMAND(hWnd, wParam,
                                 lParam,
                                 WMCommandHandler);
    }

    case WM_DESTROY :
    {
        PostQuitMessage(0);
        return 0;
    }

    }

    return DefWindowProc (hWnd, message, wParam,
                          lParam);
}
```

Listing 5.16. PRNFILE.H header file.

```
/*
 * PRNFILE.H header file
 *
 */


#define IDM_OPEN    10
#define IDM_PRINT   20
#define IDM_EXIT    30
#define IDM_SETUP   40

#define IDD_FILENAME 99
```

Listing 5.17. PRNFILE.RC resource script.

```
/*
 * PRNFILE.RC resource script
 *
 */

#include "prnfile.h"

MAINMENU MENU
BEGIN
    POPUP "&File"
    BEGIN
        MENUITEM "&Specify Filename...", IDM_OPEN
        MENUITEM "Print...", IDM_PRINT
        MENUITEM "&Setup Printer...", IDM_SETUP
        MENUITEM SEPARATOR
        MENUITEM "E&xit", IDM_EXIT
    END

END

ABORTDLG DIALOG 20, 20, 140, 64
STYLE DS_MODALFRAME ¦ WS_CAPTION ¦ WS_SYSMENU
CAPTION "Print File"
BEGIN
    CONTROL "Cancel", IDCANCEL, "BUTTON", WS_GROUP,
54, 44, 32, 14
    CTEXT "Sending", -1, 1, 8, 139, 8
    CONTROL "", IDD_FILENAME, "STATIC", SS_CENTER ¦
```

continues

Listing 5.17. continued

```
WS_CHILD ¦ WS_VISIBLE ¦ WS_GROUP, 0, 18, 138, 8
      CTEXT "to print spooler.", -1, 0, 28, 139, 8
END
```

Listing 5.18. PRNFILE.DEF module definition file.

```
;
; PRNFILE.DEF module definition file
;

DESCRIPTION    'Print File'
NAME           PRNFILE
EXETYPE        WINDOWS
STUB           'WINSTUB.EXE'
HEAPSIZE       1024
STACKSIZE      8192
CODE           PRELOAD MOVEABLE DISCARDABLE
DATA           PRELOAD MOVEABLE MULTIPLE
```

Outputting a Bitmap to a Printer

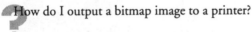

How do I output a bitmap image to a printer?

DESCRIPTION

Once a programmer has output text to the printer, the next thing he or she wants to do is display a bitmap on a printer. When bitmaps are loaded with the LoadBitmap function, Windows turns them into device-dependent bitmaps, intended for display on the screen. Therefore, if a programmer tries to output the image to a printer, it often comes out looking distorted because of the differences between the two output devices.

ANSWER

The bitmap must be loaded as a device-independent bitmap (DIB). This requires the resource to be loaded as a generic resource. You use the `LoadResource` function to load the bitmap as a device-independent image. This gives the program a pointer to the actual bits that make up the bitmap. You can then use the `CreateCompatibleDC` function and the `BitBlt` function to copy the bitmap from the compatible display context to the printer display context.

COMMENTS

The basic concepts of printing bitmaps is similar to printing text, which is covered elsewhere in this book (see the previous section in this chapter). Also, the concept of displaying a bitmap to the screen using `CreateCompatibleDC` and `BitBlt` is covered in other places in this book (see Chapter 4, "Graphics").

SEE ALSO

`CreateCompatibleDC` Windows API Function
`BitBlt` Windows API Function
`FindResource` Windows API Function
`LoadResource` Windows API Function

EXAMPLE CODE

The example program outputs a bitmap that has been stored as a resource to the printer. Listing 5.19 contains the PRNBMP.C source code; Listing 5.20 contains the PRNBMP.H header file; Listing 5.21 contains the PRNBMP.RC file; and Listing 5.22 contains the PRNBMP.DEF module definition file. You also need a bitmap with the name PRNBMP.BMP to compile this program.

Listing 5.19. PRNBMP.C source code.

```
// PRNBMP.C - Print a bitmap.  Uses print dialog
//            which is in Windows 3.1.
//
// Your Borland C++ Consultant by Paul J. Perry
//

#define STRICT

#include <windowsx.h>
```

continues

Listing 5.19. continued

```
#include <commdlg.h>
#include <stdlib.h>
#include <string.h>
#include <stdio.h>
#include <time.h>
#include "prnfile.h"


// Function Prototypes
LRESULT CALLBACK _export MainWndProc(HWND, UINT,
                                     WPARAM, LPARAM);
void WMCommandHandler(HWND, int, HWND, UINT);
BOOL CALLBACK _export AbortDlgProc(HWND, UINT, WPARAM,
                                   LPARAM);
BOOL CALLBACK _export AbortProc(HDC, int);
void PrintBitmapFile(HDC PrinterDC);


// Global Variables
char      FileName[256] = "\0";
BOOL      Abort;
HWND      hAbortDlgWnd;
HINSTANCE ghInstance;
PRINTDLG  pd;


/**********************************************/
#pragma argsused
int PASCAL WinMain(HINSTANCE hInstance, HINSTANCE
                   hPrevInstance, LPSTR lpCmdParam,
                   int nCmdShow)
{
    char      ProgName[] = "Print Bitmap";
    HWND      hWnd;
    MSG       msg;


    if (!hPrevInstance)
    {
        WNDCLASS      wndclass;

        wndclass.lpszClassName = ProgName;
        wndclass.lpfnWndProc   = (WNDPROC) MainWndProc;
        wndclass.cbClsExtra    = 0;
        wndclass.cbWndExtra    = 0;
        wndclass.hInstance     = hInstance;
        wndclass.hIcon         = LoadIcon(NULL,
```

```
IDI_APPLICATION);
    wndclass.hCursor        = LoadCursor(NULL,
                                IDC_ARROW);
    wndclass.hbrBackground = GetStockBrush(
                                WHITE_BRUSH);
    wndclass.lpszMenuName  = "MAINMENU";
    wndclass.style          = CS_VREDRAW |
                                CS_HREDRAW;

    if (!RegisterClass(&wndclass))
        exit(1);
}

ghInstance = hInstance;

hWnd = CreateWindow(ProgName, ProgName,
                    WS_OVERLAPPEDWINDOW,
                    CW_USEDEFAULT, CW_USEDEFAULT,
                    CW_USEDEFAULT, CW_USEDEFAULT,
                    NULL, NULL, hInstance, NULL);

ShowWindow(hWnd, nCmdShow);
UpdateWindow(hWnd);

while (GetMessage(&msg, NULL, 0, 0))
{
    TranslateMessage(&msg);
    DispatchMessage(&msg);
}

return msg.wParam;
}

/*********************************************/
#pragma argsused
BOOL CALLBACK _export AbortDlgProc(HWND hDlg, UINT
                                    message, WPARAM
                                    wParam, LPARAM
                                    lParam)
{
    if (message == WM_COMMAND)
    {
        Abort = TRUE;

        EndDialog(hDlg, wParam);
        return TRUE;
    }
```

continues

V

Listing 5.19. continued

```
    else if (message == WM_INITDIALOG)
    {
        SetFocus(hDlg);
        return TRUE;
    }

    return FALSE;

}


/*********************************************/
#pragma argsused
BOOL CALLBACK _export AbortProc(HDC hDC, int error)
{
    MSG msg;

    while (PeekMessage((LPMSG) &msg, NULL, NULL, NULL,
                       PM_REMOVE))
        if(!IsDialogMessage(hAbortDlgWnd, (LPMSG)&msg))
        {
            TranslateMessage((LPMSG)&msg);
            DispatchMessage((LPMSG)&msg);
        }

    return (!Abort); // Continue print job (in most
                                              cases)
}


/*********************************************/
#pragma argsused
void WMCommandHandler(HWND hWnd, int id, HWND hWndCtl,
                      UINT codeNotify)
{
    switch (id)
    {
        case IDM_PRINT :
        {
            // Set up the common Print dialog
            memset(&pd, 0, sizeof(PRINTDLG));

            pd.hwndOwner    = hWnd;
            pd.Flags        = PD_RETURNDC | \
                              PD_HIDEPRINTTOFILE | \
                              PD_NOPAGENUMS | \
```

```
                    PD_DISABLEPRINTTOFILE ¦ \
                    PD_NOSELECTION;

pd.lStructSize = sizeof(PRINTDLG);

// Call the Print Dialog box.  If it returns
//    a successful value, the file is printed
//    out.
if (PrintDlg(&pd) != NULL)
{
   DOCINFO DocInfo;
   char    buf[255];

   ABORTPROC lpAbortProc;
   DLGPROC   lpAbortDlgProc;

   // Create Abort procedure
   lpAbortProc = (ABORTPROC)MakeProcInstance(
                 (FARPROC)AbortProc,
                 ghInstance);
                 SetAbortProc(pd.hDC,
                 (ABORTPROC)lpAbortProc);

   // Create document name
   sprintf(buf, "Print File -- %s",
           FileName);

   // Fill out the DOCINFO structure members
   DocInfo.cbSize      = sizeof(DOCINFO);
   DocInfo.lpszDocName = buf;
   DocInfo.lpszOutput  = NULL;

   // Try to get access to the printer.  If
   // access is denied, then return;
   if (StartDoc(pd.hDC, &DocInfo) < 0)
   {
      // An error occured
      MessageBox(hWnd, "Unable to start print
                 job", NULL, MB_OK ¦
                 MB_ICONSTOP);
      FreeProcInstance((FARPROC)lpAbortProc);
      DeleteDC(pd.hDC);
      break;
   }

   Abort = FALSE;

   // Now, we are ready to display the Abort
   //    dialog box on the screen.
```

V

continues

Listing 5.19. continued

```
                lpAbortDlgProc = (DLGPROC)
                            MakeProcInstance(
                            (FARPROC)AbortDlgProc,
                            ghInstance);
            hAbortDlgWnd = CreateDialog(ghInstance,
                        "ABORTDLG", hWnd, (DLGPROC)
                        lpAbortDlgProc);
            ShowWindow(hAbortDlgWnd, SW_NORMAL);

            // Enable the cancel dialog box window
            UpdateWindow(hAbortDlgWnd);

            // Disable parent window.
            EnableWindow(hWnd, FALSE);

            // Go and actually print the file
            PrintBitmapFile(pd.hDC);

            // Remove abort dialog box and set focus
            //    back to the main window.
            EnableWindow(hWnd, TRUE);
            DestroyWindow(hAbortDlgWnd);


            // Cleanup
            FreeProcInstance((FARPROC)lpAbortProc);
            FreeProcInstance((FARPROC)lpAbortDlgProc);
            DeleteDC(pd.hDC);

        }

        break;
    }

    case IDM_SETUP :
    {
        memset(&pd, 0, sizeof(PRINTDLG));
        pd.hwndOwner   = hWnd;
        pd.nCopies     = -1;
        pd.Flags       = PD_PRINTSETUP;

        pd.lStructSize = sizeof(PRINTDLG);

        PrintDlg(&pd);
        DeleteDC(pd.hDC);

        break;
```

```
      }

      case IDM_EXIT :
      {
         SendMessage(hWnd, WM_CLOSE, 0, 0L);
         break;
      }

   }
}


/********************************************/
void PrintBitmapFile(HDC PrinterDC)
{
   HBITMAP  hBitmap;
   HGLOBAL  hRes;
   POINT    Size;

   // Load the bitmap resource ourselves
   hRes = LoadResource(ghInstance,
                       FindResource(ghInstance,
                            "PRNBITMAP",
                       RT_BITMAP));

   // If the resource exists...
   if (hRes)
   {
      int          Colors;
      LPBITMAPINFO bmi;
      HDC          hMemDC;
      HBITMAP      hOldBitmap;


      StartPage(PrinterDC);

      //Get bitmap information
      bmi = (LPBITMAPINFO)LockResource(hRes);

      // Find out the number of colors used
      if (bmi->bmiHeader.biClrUsed)
         Colors = (int)bmi->bmiHeader.biClrUsed;
      else
         Colors = 1 << (bmi->bmiHeader.biBitCount);

      // Save the size of the bitmap
      Size.x = (int)bmi->bmiHeader.biWidth;
```

V

continues

Listing 5.19. continued

```
        Size.y = (int)bmi->bmiHeader.biHeight;

        // Create a device-independent bitmap
        hBitmap = CreateDIBitmap(PrinterDC,
                        (LPBITMAPINFOHEADER)bmi,
                        CBM_INIT,
                        (((LPSTR)bmi)+
                        Colors*sizeof(RGBQUAD)),
                        bmi,
                        DIB_RGB_COLORS);

        hMemDC = CreateCompatibleDC(PrinterDC);
        hOldBitmap = SelectBitmap(hMemDC, hBitmap);

        BitBlt(PrinterDC, 0, 0, Size.x, Size.y, hMemDC,
               0, 0, SRCCOPY);

        SelectBitmap(hMemDC, hOldBitmap);

        // Cleanup
        DeleteDC(hMemDC);
        GlobalUnlock(hRes);
        FreeResource(hRes);
        DeleteBitmap(hBitmap);

        EndPage(PrinterDC);
        EndDoc(PrinterDC);

    }

}



/*********************************************/
LRESULT CALLBACK _export MainWndProc(HWND hWnd, UINT
                                        message, WPARAM
                                        wParam, LPARAM
                                        lParam)
{
    switch (message)
    {
        case WM_PAINT :
        {
            HDC         PaintDC;
            RECT        rect;
            PAINTSTRUCT ps;
```

```
            PaintDC = BeginPaint(hWnd, &ps);
            GetClientRect(hWnd, &rect);


            DrawText(PaintDC, "Bitmap Print Utility",
                    -1, &rect, DT_SINGLELINE ¦ DT_CENTER
                    ¦ DT_VCENTER);

            EndPaint(hWnd, &ps);
            return 0;
        }

        case WM_COMMAND :
        {
            return HANDLE_WM_COMMAND(hWnd, wParam,
                                    lParam,
                                    WMCommandHandler);
        }

        case WM_DESTROY :
        {
            PostQuitMessage(0);
            return 0;
        }

    }

    return DefWindowProc (hWnd, message, wParam,
                        lParam);
}
```

Listing 5.20. PRNBMP.H header file.

```
/*
 * PRNFILE.H header file
 *
 */


#define IDM_OPEN    10
#define IDM_PRINT   20
#define IDM_EXIT    30
#define IDM_SETUP   40

#define IDD_FILENAME 99
```

Listing 5.21. PRNBMP.RC resource script.

```
/*
 * PRNBMP.RC resource script
 *
 */

#include "prnbmp.h"

PRNBITMAP BITMAP "prnbmp.bmp"

MAINMENU MENU
BEGIN
     POPUP "&Bitmap"
     BEGIN
          MENUITEM "Print...", IDM_PRINT
          MENUITEM "&Setup Printer...", IDM_SETUP
          MENUITEM SEPARATOR
          MENUITEM "E&xit", IDM_EXIT
     END

END

ABORTDLG DIALOG 20, 20, 140, 64
STYLE DS_MODALFRAME ¦ WS_CAPTION ¦ WS_SYSMENU
CAPTION "Print Bitmap"
BEGIN
     CONTROL "Cancel", IDCANCEL, "BUTTON", WS_GROUP,
54, 44, 32, 14
     CTEXT "Sending", -1, 1, 8, 139, 8
     CONTROL "", IDD_FILENAME, "STATIC", SS_CENTER ¦
WS_CHILD ¦ WS_VISIBLE ¦ WS_GROUP, 0, 18, 138, 8
     CTEXT "to print spooler.", -1, 0, 28, 139, 8
END
```

Listing 5.22. PRNBMP.DEF module definition file.

```
;
; PRNBMP.DEF module definition file
;

DESCRIPTION     'Print Bitmap'
NAME            PRNBMP
EXETYPE         WINDOWS
STUB            'WINSTUB.EXE'
HEAPSIZE        1024
```

```
STACKSIZE    8192
CODE         PRELOAD MOVEABLE DISCARDABLE
DATA         PRELOAD MOVEABLE MULTIPLE
```

Monitoring System Events

How can I write a program that monitors system events similar to
WinSight?

DESCRIPTION

I have seen programs like WinSight (see Figure 5.7) that display all
the messages going through the system. There must be a way to
check system messages before they are processed by the system and
allow for some system message filtering to occur.

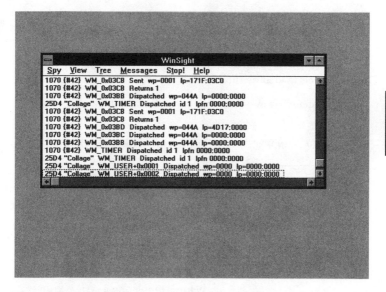

Figure 5.7. *WinSight monitoring system messages.*

ANSWER

The key to writing a program that intercepts messages from Windows before they are passed to an application is through something called a *Windows hook*. A Windows hook intercepts all messages and passes them through a filter function before sending them on to a final destination. Therefore, a program can take a look at all messages before they are processed. A filter function is merely a regular Windows callback function.

The `SetWindowsHookEx` function is used to install a hook function. The prototype looks like this:

```
HHOOK SetWindowsHookEx(int idHook, HOOKPROC hkprc,
                       HINSTANCE hinst, HTASK htask)
```

Where `idHook` is the type of hook to install, `hkprc` is the procedure-instance address of the filter function being installed; `hinst` is the handle of application instance; and `htask` is the task for which to install the hook. The function returns a handle to the Windows hook.

Filter functions are almost always required to be in a DLL (with one exception, the `WH_MSGFILTER`) because they need to be available even if an application is shut down. By being in the DLL, Windows has control over loading and unloading the DLL versus an application that gets loaded by the user.

There are many types of filter functions that can be installed, as follows:

`WH_CALLWNDPROC`	When this hook is installed, all messages sent with the `SendMessage` function will first be captured by the filter function.
`WH_CBT`	When this hook is installed, the filter function will be called before activating, creating, destroying, minimizing, maximizing, moving, or sizing a window. It will also be called before completing a system command, before removing a mouse or keyboard event from the system message queue, and before setting the input focus, or before

synchronizing with the system message queue. This type of hook is meant for computer-based training applications (CBT) in which a program can easily control the flow of another program.

WH_DEBUG — When this hook is installed, the system calls the filter function before calling any other filter functions installed. It allows a programmer to debug filter functions.

WH_GETMESSAGE — When this hook is installed, Windows calls the filter function every time a message is retrieved with a call to the `GetMessage` or `PeekMessage` function.

WH_HARDWARE — When this hook is installed, Windows calls the filter function whenever the application calls the `GetMessage` or `PeekMessage` functions and there is a hardware event other than a mouse or keyboard event to process.

WH_JOURNALPLAYBACK — When this hook is installed, Windows calls the filter function every time an event is requested from the Windows system queue. This works in combination with the `WH_JOURNALRECORD` hook. It allows applications like Windows Recorder to create system-wide keyboard macros.

WH_JOURNALRECORD — When this hook is installed, Windows calls the filter function every time an event is processed from the Windows system queue.

WH_KEYBOARD — When this hook is installed, Windows calls the filter function every time an application calls the `GetMessage` or `PeekMessage` function and a keyboard message is retrieved.

`WH_MOUSE`	When this hook is installed, Windows calls the filter function every time an application calls the `GetMessage` or `PeekMessage` function and mouse messages are retrieved.
`WH_MSGFILTER`	When this hook is installed, Windows calls the filter function every time a dialog box, message box, menu, or scroll bar belonging to the specified application that installed the hook is about to process a message. This is the only type of filter function that is not required to be located inside a DLL.
`WH_SHELL`	When this hook is installed, Windows calls the filter function with useful information about applications that are being opened and closed. It is meant for shell applications, such as Program Manager or Norton Desktop for Windows.
`WH_SYSMSGFILTER`	When this hook is installed, Windows calls the filter function every time a dialog box, message box, menu, or scroll bar is about to process a message.

The `fhook` is removed with a call to the `UnhookWindowsHookEx` function. All that is necessary is to pass a handle to the hook function that is to be removed, as follows:

```
UnHookWindowsHookEx(hHook);
```

The prototype for the filter function of each type of Windows hook is a little different. The best method to find the prototype for the function is to check the Borland C++ online Help system.

COMMENTS

The filter function must be exported and can be given any name. The manuals include the prototypes for the callback functions. Although default names have been given to the filter functions, any name can be assigned to the function. The only requirement is that it must have the same prototype as that specified in the documentation. The entries for the filter functions in the manual contain other valuable information about processing hook functions for each type of hook function.

SEE ALSO

CallWndProc Filter Function Prototype
CBTProc Filter Function Prototype
DebugProc Filter Function Prototype
GetMsgProc Filter Function Prototype
HardwareProc Filter Function Prototype
JournalPlaybackProc Filter Function Prototype
JournalRecordProc Filter Function Prototype
KeyboardProc Filter Function Prototype
MouseProc Filter Function Prototype
MessageProc Filter Function Prototype
ShellProc Filter Function Prototype
SysMsgProc Filter Function Prototype
SetWindowsHookEx Windows API Function
UnhookWindowsHookEx Windows API Function
CallNextHookEx Windows API Function

EXAMPLE CODE

The example program sets up a mouse hook that displays the color and the RGB value of the point under the cursor hot spot (see Figure 5.8). There are two parts to the example program: the main program and the DLL.

The main program is made up of four files: Listing 5.23 contains the HOOK.C source code; Listing 5.24 contains the HOOK.H header file; Listing 5.25 contains the HOOK.RC resource script; and Listing 5.26 contains the HOOK.DEF module definition file.

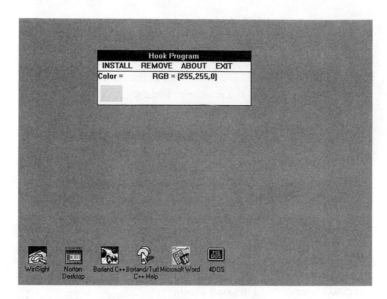

Figure 5.8. *HOOK program displays value of color under the mouse cursor.*

The dynamic link library is made up of two files: Listing 5.27 contains the HOOK.C source code, and Listing 5.28 contains the HOOK.DEF module definition file.

When compiling this program, you need to compile the DLL first. Then use the IMPLIB tool to create an import library, which must then be compiled in the project of the main program. Use the large memory model when compiling both of these modules.

Listing 5.23. HOOK.C main program source code.

```
// HOOK.C - Example hook program.
//
// Your Borland C++ Consultant by Paul J. Perry
//

#define STRICT

#include <windowsx.h>
#include <stdlib.h>
#include "hook.h"
```

```
// Function Prototypes
LRESULT CALLBACK _export MainWndProc(HWND, UINT,
                                     WPARAM, LPARAM);
void WMCommandHandler(HWND, int, HWND, UINT);

// Function inside the HOOK.DLL
BOOL FAR PASCAL _export InstallHookFunction(HWND, BOOL);


// Global Variables
HINSTANCE  hInstDLL;

/*******************************************/
#pragma argsused
int PASCAL WinMain(HINSTANCE hInstance, HINSTANCE
                   hPrevInstance,LPSTR lpCmdParam,
                   int nCmdShow)
{
    char        ProgName[] = "Hook Program";
    HWND        hWnd;
    MSG         msg;


    if (!hPrevInstance)
    {
        WNDCLASS    wndclass;

        wndclass.lpszClassName = ProgName;
        wndclass.lpfnWndProc   = (WNDPROC) MainWndProc;
        wndclass.cbClsExtra    = 0;
        wndclass.cbWndExtra    = 0;
        wndclass.hInstance     = hInstance;
        wndclass.hIcon         = LoadIcon(NULL,
                                   IDI_APPLICATION);
        wndclass.hCursor       = LoadCursor(NULL,
                                   IDC_ARROW);
        wndclass.hbrBackground = GetStockBrush
                                   (WHITE_BRUSH);
        wndclass.lpszMenuName  = "MAINMENU";
        wndclass.style         = CS_VREDRAW |
                                   sCS_HREDRAW;

        if (!RegisterClass(&wndclass))
            exit(1);
    }
```

continues

Listing 5.23. continued

```
hWnd = CreateWindow(ProgName, ProgName,
                    WS_OVERLAPPEDWINDOW &
                    !WS_MAXIMIZEBOX &
                    !WS_THICKFRAME,
                    CW_USEDEFAULT, CW_USEDEFAULT,
                    280, 100,
                    NULL, NULL, hInstance, NULL);


   ShowWindow(hWnd, nCmdShow);
   UpdateWindow(hWnd);

   while (GetMessage(&msg, NULL, 0, 0))
   {
      TranslateMessage(&msg);
      DispatchMessage(&msg);
   }

   return msg.wParam;
}

/*********************************************/
#pragma argsused
void WMCommandHandler(HWND hWnd, int id, HWND hWndCtl,
                      UINT codeNotify)
{
   switch (id)
   {
      case IDM_INSTALL :
      {
         InstallHookFunction(hWnd, TRUE);
         break;
      }

      case IDM_REMOVE :
      {

         InstallHookFunction(hWnd, FALSE);
         break;
      }


      case IDM_ABOUT :
      {
         MessageBox(
               hWnd, "This program creates a Windows "
               "hook which filters mouse messages "
               "before they are passed on to the "
```

```
                    "system.  In this case, it just "
                    "displays what color the mouse cursor"
                    "is positioned over\n\n"
                    "by Paul J. Perry",
                    "HOOK Demo", MB_OK);
          break;
        }


        case IDM_EXIT :
        {
            SendMessage(hWnd, WM_CLOSE, 0, 0L);
            break;
        }

    }
}


/**********************************************/
LRESULT CALLBACK _export MainWndProc(HWND hWnd, UINT
                                      message,WPARAM
                                      wParam, LPARAM
                                      lParam)
{
    switch (message)
    {
        case WM_PAINT :
        {
            HDC          PaintDC;
            PAINTSTRUCT ps;

            PaintDC = BeginPaint(hWnd, &ps);

            TextOut(PaintDC, 0, 0, "Color = ", 8);

            EndPaint(hWnd, &ps);
            return 0;
        }

        case WM_COMMAND :
        {
            return HANDLE_WM_COMMAND(hWnd, wParam,
                             lParam,WMCommandHandler);
```

continues

Listing 5.23. continued

```
    }

    case WM_DESTROY :
    {
        // Make sure hook function has
        //   been removed.
        InstallHookFunction(hWnd, FALSE);

        PostQuitMessage(0);
        return 0;
    }
  }

  return DefWindowProc (hWnd, message, wParam, lParam);
}
```

Listing 5.24. HOOK.H main program header file.

```
/*
 * HOOK.H header file
 *
 */

#define IDM_INSTALL 100
#define IDM_REMOVE  110
#define IDM_ABOUT   120
#define IDM_EXIT    130
```

Listing 5.25. HOOK.RC main program resource script.

```
/*
 * HOOK.RC resource script
 *
 */

#include "hook.h"

MAINMENU MENU
```

```
BEGIN
     MENUITEM "INSTALL", IDM_INSTALL
     MENUITEM "REMOVE", IDM_REMOVE
     MENUITEM "ABOUT", IDM_ABOUT
     MENUITEM "EXIT", IDM_EXIT
END
```

Listing 5.26. HOOK.DEF main program module definition file.

```
;
; HOOK.DEF module definition file
;

DESCRIPTION      'Hook Application'
NAME             HOOK
EXETYPE          WINDOWS
STUB             'WINSTUB.EXE'
HEAPSIZE         1024
STACKSIZE        8192
CODE             PRELOAD MOVEABLE DISCARDABLE
DATA             PRELOAD MOVEABLE MULTIPLE
```

Listing 5.27. HOOKDLL.C dynamic link library source code.

```
// HOOKDLL.C - Example hook dynamic link library
//
// Your Borland C++ Consultant by Paul J. Perry
//

#define STRICT

#include <windowsx.h>
#include <stdio.h>
#include <string.h>


// Function Prototypes
int FAR PASCAL LibMain(HINSTANCE, WORD, WORD, LPSTR);
int FAR PASCAL _export WEP(int);
LRESULT CALLBACK _export MouseProc(int, WPARAM, LPARAM);
BOOL FAR PASCAL _export InstallHookFunction(HWND, BOOL);
```

continues

Listing 5.27. continued

```
// Global Variable
HINSTANCE ghInstance;
HHOOK     hHook;
HWND      hOutWnd;

/*********************************************/
#pragma argsused
 int FAR PASCAL LibMain(HINSTANCE hInstance, WORD
                         wDataSeg,WORD wHeapSize, LPSTR
                         lpszCmdLine)
{
   if (wHeapSize > 0)
      UnlockData(0);

   ghInstance = hInstance;

   return 1;

}


/*********************************************/
#pragma argsused
int FAR PASCAL _export WEP(int nShutDownFlag)
{
   return 1;

}

/*********************************************/
BOOL FAR PASCAL _export InstallHookFunction(HWND hWnd,
                                     BOOL Install)
{
   if (Install)
   {
       static FARPROC lpHookFunc;

       lpHookFunc = GetProcAddress(ghInstance,
                           "MouseProc");

       if (lpHookFunc)
       hHook = SetWindowsHookEx(WH_MOUSE, (HOOKPROC)
                           lpHookFunc,ghInstance,
                           NULL);
       hOutWnd = hWnd;
       return TRUE;
```

```
    }
    else
    {
       UnhookWindowsHookEx(hHook);
       return TRUE;
    }

}


/*********************************************/
#pragma argsused
LRESULT CALLBACK _export MouseProc(int code, WPARAM
                                    wParam,LPARAM lParam)
{
    COLORREF  Color;
    RECT      rect;
    HDC       hDC, hWinDC;
    HBRUSH    hBrush;
    BYTE      R, G, B;
    char      buff[50];
    MOUSEHOOKSTRUCT FAR *mhs;

    if (code < 0)
        return CallNextHookEx(hHook, code, wParam, lParam);

    mhs = (MOUSEHOOKSTRUCT FAR *)lParam;

    hDC = CreateDC("DISPLAY", NULL, NULL, NULL);

    Color = GetPixel(hDC, mhs->pt.x, mhs->pt.y);

    hBrush = CreateSolidBrush(Color);

    SetRect(&rect, 5, 25, 45, 55);

    R = GetRValue(Color);
    G = GetGValue(Color);
    B = GetBValue(Color);

    // Add extra spaces so the line gets
    //   repainted  correctly.
    sprintf(buff, "RGB = (%d,%d,%d)              ", R, G, B);

    hWinDC = GetDC(hOutWnd);
    FillRect(hWinDC, &rect, hBrush );

    TextOut(hWinDC, 100, 0, buff, strlen(buff));
```

continues

Listing 5.27. continued

```
// Cleanup
DeleteDC(hDC);
ReleaseDC(hOutWnd, hWinDC);
DeleteBrush(hBrush);

return 0;

}
```

Listing 5.28. HOOKDLL.DEF dynamic link library module definition file.

```
;
; HOOKDLL.DEF module definition file
;

DESCRIPTION      'Hook DLL'
LIBRARY          HOOKDLL
EXETYPE          WINDOWS
STUB             'WINSTUB.EXE'
HEAPSIZE         0
CODE             MOVEABLE DISCARDABLE
DATA             PRELOAD MOVEABLE SINGLE
```

 # Changing the Font in an Edit Control

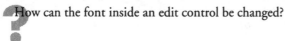 How can the font inside an edit control be changed?

DESCRIPTION

Sometimes it is nice to change the default fonts used by Windows inside controls. With the method described here, the font inside any standard control can be changed.

ANSWER

To change the font used for a control, retrieve the handle to the window of the control, and use the `SendMessage` function to send the `WM_SETFONT` windows message. The `wParam` must contain a handle to the font, and the `lParam` should be passed the value `TRUE` in order for the control to be updated immediately.

COMMENTS

The `WM_SETFONT` message can be used not only with edit controls, but also with all the standard Windows controls including static text, buttons, listboxes, checkboxes, and radio buttons.

 WARNING Remember to delete the font that was passed to the control when the program is done with it. The font is not deleted automatically by the control. Also, the program should not delete the font until the control is finished using it.

SEE ALSO

`SendMessage` Windows API Function
`WM_GETFONT` Windows Message
`WM_SETFONT` Windows Message

EXAMPLE CODE

The program creates an edit control the full size of the client area of the main window, thereby emulating an editor (see Figure 5.9). The user can choose which font to display text in by choosing the Font item from the main menu and choosing the font from the Choose Font common dialog box.

Listing 5.29 contains the EDITCTL.C source code; Listing 5.30 contains the EDITCTL.RC resource script; and Listing 5.31 contains the EDITCTL.DEF module definition file.

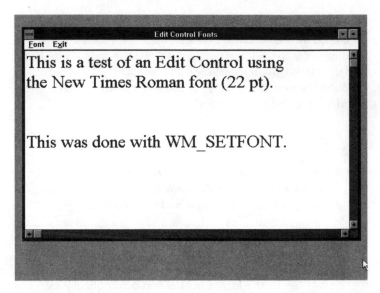

Figure 5.9. *EDITCTL demonstration program.*

Listing 5.29. EDITCTL.C source code.

```
// EDITCTL.C - Modifying the font used within an
//             edit control.
//
// Your Borland C++ Consultant by Paul J. Perry
//

#define STRICT
#define IDM_FONT 100
#define IDM_EXIT 110


#include <windowsx.h>
#include <commdlg.h>
#include <stdlib.h>
#include <string.h>


// Function Prototypes
LRESULT CALLBACK _export MainWndProc(HWND, UINT,
                                     WPARAM, LPARAM);
void WMCommandHandler(HWND, int, HWND, UINT);
```

```
// Global Variable
HWND     hEditWnd;
LOGFONT  CurrentFont;
HFONT    hFont = NULL;


/*******************************************/
#pragma argsused
int PASCAL WinMain(HINSTANCE hInstance, HINSTANCE
                hPrevInstance,LPSTR lpCmdParam, int
                nCmdShow)
{
    char         ProgName[] = "Edit Control Fonts";
    HWND         hWnd;
    MSG          msg;


    if (!hPrevInstance)
    {
        WNDCLASS     wndclass;

        wndclass.lpszClassName = ProgName;
        wndclass.lpfnWndProc   = (WNDPROC) MainWndProc;
        wndclass.cbClsExtra    = 0;
        wndclass.cbWndExtra    = 0;
        wndclass.hInstance     = hInstance;
        wndclass.hIcon         = LoadIcon(NULL,
                                   IDI_APPLICATION);
        wndclass.hCursor       = LoadCursor(NULL,
                                   IDC_ARROW);
        wndclass.hbrBackground = GetStockBrush
                                   (WHITE_BRUSH);
        wndclass.lpszMenuName  = "MAINMENU";
        wndclass.style         = CS_VREDRAW | CS_HREDRAW;

        if (!RegisterClass(&wndclass))
            exit(1);
    }

    hWnd = CreateWindow(ProgName, ProgName,
                    WS_OVERLAPPEDWINDOW,
                    CW_USEDEFAULT, CW_USEDEFAULT,
                    CW_USEDEFAULT, CW_USEDEFAULT,
                NULL, NULL, hInstance, NULL);

    // Create edit window.  It starts out being
    //   invisible, because the coordinates are
    //   all set to zero.
```

continues

Listing 5.29. continued

```
    hEditWnd = CreateWindow("EDIT", NULL, WS_CHILD |
                            WS_VISIBLE | WS_HSCROLL |
                            WS_VSCROLL | WS_BORDER |
                            ES_MULTILINE | ES_LEFT |
                            ES_AUTOHSCROLL |
                            ES_AUTOVSCROLL,
                            0, 0, 0, 0, hWnd, (HMENU)1,
                            hInstance, NULL);

    ShowWindow(hWnd, nCmdShow);
    UpdateWindow(hWnd);

    while (GetMessage(&msg, NULL, 0, 0))
    {
       TranslateMessage(&msg);
       DispatchMessage(&msg);
    }
    return msg.wParam;
}

/*********************************************/
#pragma argsused
void WMCommandHandler(HWND hWnd, int id, HWND hWndCtl,
                      UINT codeNotify)
{

    switch (id)
    {
       case IDM_FONT :
       {
          CHOOSEFONT ChooseFnt;

          // Set up data structure for font common
             dialog
          memset(&ChooseFnt, 0, sizeof(CHOOSEFONT));

          ChooseFnt.hwndOwner   = hWnd;
          ChooseFnt.lpLogFont   = &CurrentFont;
          ChooseFnt.Flags       = CF_FORCEFONTEXIST | \
                                  CF_SCREENFONTS;
          ChooseFnt.nFontType   = SCREEN_FONTTYPE;
          ChooseFnt.lStructSize = sizeof(CHOOSEFONT);

          // User entered a valid font, so the program
          //    first deletes a font (if one has
                                        already)
```

```
                //    been created.  It then creates a new
                //    font and sends it as the wParam for the
                //    WM_SETFONT message to the edit control.
                if (ChooseFont(&ChooseFnt))
                {
                   if (hFont)
                      DeleteFont(hFont);

                   hFont = CreateFontIndirect(&CurrentFont);
                   SendMessage(hEditWnd, WM_SETFONT,
                               (WPARAM)hFont, TRUE);

                }

                InvalidateRect(hWnd, NULL, TRUE);

                break;
             }

             case IDM_EXIT :
             {
                SendMessage(hWnd, WM_CLOSE, 0, 0L);
                break;
             }

          }

}


/*********************************************/
LRESULT CALLBACK _export MainWndProc(HWND hWnd, UINT
                                     message,WPARAM
                                     wParam, LPARAM
                                     lParam)
{
   switch (message)
   {
      case WM_SIZE :
      {
         // If the main window is moved, make sure
         //    the edit control always stays within
         //    its borders.
         MoveWindow(hEditWnd, 0, 0, LOWORD(lParam),
                    HIWORD(lParam), TRUE);
         return 0;
      }
```

continues

Listing 5.29. continued

```
case WM_SETFOCUS :
{
    // Set focus to the edit control window.
    SetFocus(hEditWnd);
    return 0;
}

case WM_COMMAND :
{
    return HANDLE_WM_COMMAND(hWnd, wParam,
                            lParam,WMCommandHandler);
}

case WM_DESTROY :
{
    // Make sure that all fonts are
    //   deleted before leaving.
    if (hFont)
        DeleteFont(hFont);

    PostQuitMessage(0);
    return 0;
}
}

return DefWindowProc (hWnd, message, wParam, lParam);

}
```

Listing 5.30. EDITCTL.RC resource script.

```
/*
 * EDITCTL.RC resource script
 *
 */

MAINMENU MENU
BEGIN
    MENUITEM "&Font", 100
    MENUITEM "E&xit", 110
END
```

Listing 5.31. EDITCTL.DEF module definition file.

```
;
; EDITCTL.DEF module definition file
;

DESCRIPTION    'Edit Control Fonts'
NAME           EDITCTL
EXETYPE        WINDOWS
STUB           'WINSTUB.EXE'
HEAPSIZE       1024
STACKSIZE      8192
CODE           PRELOAD MOVEABLE DISCARDABLE
DATA           PRELOAD MOVEABLE MULTIPLE
```

Resizeable Windows

How do I create a program with a horizontal sizing bar that allows the user to change the relative size of two child windows?

DESCRIPTION

The WinSight utility, which comes with Borland C++, has a main window that is divided into several panes, or sections, as in Figure 5.10. The user can resize the panes with the mouse by clicking on the sizing bar, dragging the cursor, and letting go of the mouse button. This effect increases the size of one window and decreases the size of the other window.

ANSWER

Each pane inside the main window is a child window (WS_CHILD style). It is easy to create the child windows and place them within the main client window. The tricky part is allowing the user to resize these panes with the mouse.

The trick is to create a small window (the sizing window) that is only several pixels high which is stuck in-between the two panes. The window class for this window is given a cursor that lets the user know the window is to be resized. Then, the program must trap the WM_LBUTTONDOWN, WM_MOUSEMOVE, and WM_LBUTTONUP messages.

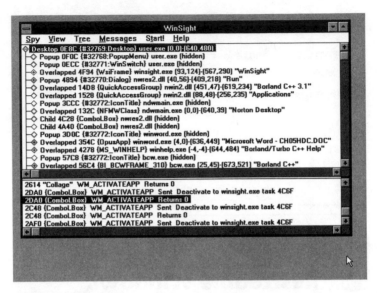

Figure 5.10. *WinSight program with sizing bar.*

The program must get a handle to the display context for the display, thereby allowing the program to display a sizing bar that moves as the mouse cursor is moved. By using the R2_NOT raster operation (ROP) code when displaying the sizing line, the line that is drawn actually inverts the image that was already there. Therefore, if two lines are drawn, one over the other, it is as if the line were never drawn.

After the user lets go of the mouse, the panes (as well as the sizing window) must be moved using the SetWindowPos function. It is also important to resize the child windows whenever the main window is resized by the user.

COMMENTS

This technique is useful for any application that uses multiple panes within a main window to display segregated information. Some programs also use a sizing bar for windows that are split vertically.

SEE ALSO

SetWindowPos Windows API Function
WM_LBUTTONDOWN Windows Message
WM_LBUTTONUP Windows Message
WM_MOUSEMOVE Windows Message

EXAMPLE CODE

The example program creates two window panes that can be resized with the mouse by clicking on the sizing bar, moving the mouse, and letting go of the mouse button (see Figure 5.11). Listing 5.32 contains the SPLIT.C source code; Listing 5.33 contains the SPLIT.RC resource script; and Listing 5.34 contains the SPLIT.DEF module definition file. The program also requires the SPLIT.CUR (see Figure 5.12) cursor resource file in order to be compiled.

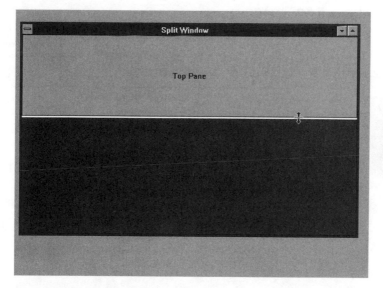

Figure 5.11. *SPLIT.EXE program in action.*

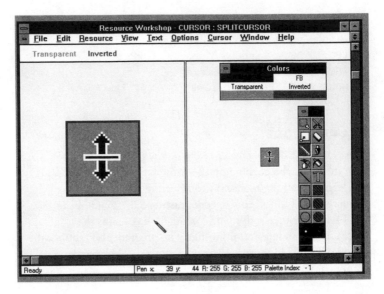

Figure 5.12. *SPLIT.CUR cursor resource.*

Listing 5.32. SPLIT.C source code.

```
// SPLIT.C - Example program shows how to create
//           a window that is split into two panes
//           that can be resized with the mouse.
//
// Your Borland C++ Consultant by Paul J. Perry
//

#define STRICT

#define SPLITSIZE 3
#define STEP      10

#include <windowsx.h>
#include <stdlib.h>

// Function Prototypes
LRESULT CALLBACK _export MainWndProc(HWND, UINT,
                                   WPARAM, LPARAM);
LRESULT CALLBACK _export TopWndProc(HWND, UINT,
                                   WPARAM, LPARAM);
LRESULT CALLBACK _export BottomWndProc(HWND, UINT,
                                   WPARAM,
                                   LPARAM);
```

```
LRESULT CALLBACK _export SizerWndProc(HWND, UINT,
                                      WPARAM, LPARAM);


// Global Variables
HWND  hMainWnd, hTopWnd, hBottomWnd, hSizerWnd;
POINT SplitPt;

/*********************************************/
#pragma argsused
int PASCAL WinMain(HINSTANCE hInstance, HINSTANCE
                   hPrevInstance,LPSTR lpCmdParam, int
                   nCmdShow)
{
    char         ProgName[] = "Split Window";
    MSG          msg;


    if (!hPrevInstance)
    {
        WNDCLASS    wndclass;

        // Main Window class
        wndclass.lpszClassName = ProgName;
        wndclass.lpfnWndProc   = (WNDPROC) MainWndProc;
        wndclass.cbClsExtra    = 0;
        wndclass.cbWndExtra    = 0;
        wndclass.hInstance     = hInstance;
        wndclass.hIcon         = LoadIcon(NULL,
                                      IDI_APPLICATION);
        wndclass.hCursor       = LoadCursor(NULL,
                                      IDC_ARROW);
        wndclass.hbrBackground = GetStockBrush
                                      (WHITE_BRUSH);
        wndclass.lpszMenuName  = NULL;
        wndclass.style         = CS_VREDRAW ¦ CS_HREDRAW;

        if (!RegisterClass(&wndclass))
            exit(1);


        wndclass.lpszClassName = "TOP";
        wndclass.lpfnWndProc   = (WNDPROC) TopWndProc;
        wndclass.hInstance     = hInstance;
        wndclass.hIcon         = NULL;
        wndclass.hCursor       = LoadCursor(NULL,
                                      IDC_ARROW);
        wndclass.hbrBackground = GetStockBrush
                                      (LTGRAY_BRUSH);
```

continues

Listing 5.32. continued

```
    wndclass.lpszMenuName  = NULL;
    wndclass.style         = CS_VREDRAW ¦ CS_HREDRAW;

    if (!RegisterClass(&wndclass))
        exit(1);


    wndclass.lpszClassName = "BOTTOM";
    wndclass.lpfnWndProc   = (WNDPROC)
                             BottomWndProc;
    wndclass.hInstance     = hInstance;
    wndclass.hIcon         = NULL;
    wndclass.hCursor       = LoadCursor(NULL,
                             IDC_ARROW);
    wndclass.hbrBackground = GetStockBrush
                             (DKGRAY_BRUSH);
    wndclass.lpszMenuName  = NULL;
    wndclass.style         = CS_VREDRAW ¦ CS_HREDRAW;

    if (!RegisterClass(&wndclass))
        exit(1);


    wndclass.lpszClassName = "SIZER";
    wndclass.lpfnWndProc   = (WNDPROC) SizerWndProc;
    wndclass.hInstance     = hInstance;
    s
    wndclass.lpszMenuName  = NULL;
    wndclass.style         = CS_VREDRAW ¦ CS_HREDRAW;

    if (!RegisterClass(&wndclass))
        exit(1);

}

hMainWnd = CreateWindow(ProgName, ProgName,
                WS_OVERLAPPEDWINDOW,
                CW_USEDEFAULT, CW_USEDEFAULT,
                CW_USEDEFAULT, CW_USEDEFAULT,
                NULL, NULL, hInstance, NULL);

hTopWnd = CreateWindow("TOP", NULL,
                WS_CHILD ¦ WS_BORDER ¦
                WS_VISIBLE,
                0, 0, 0, 0, hMainWnd, NULL,
                hInstance, NULL);
```

```
    hBottomWnd = CreateWindow("BOTTOM", NULL,
                              WS_CHILD | WS_BORDER |
                              WS_VISIBLE,
                              0, 0, 0, 0, hMainWnd, NULL,
                              hInstance, NULL);

    hSizerWnd = CreateWindow("SIZER", NULL,
                             WS_CHILD | WS_VISIBLE,
                             0, 0, 0, 0, hMainWnd, NULL,
                             hInstance, NULL);


    ShowWindow(hMainWnd, nCmdShow);
    UpdateWindow(hMainWnd);

    while (GetMessage(&msg, NULL, 0, 0))
    {
        TranslateMessage(&msg);
        DispatchMessage(&msg);
    }
    return msg.wParam;
}

/*********************************************/
LRESULT CALLBACK _export MainWndProc(HWND hWnd, UINT
                                      message,WPARAM
                                      wParam, LPARAM
                                      lParam)
{
    switch (message)
    {
        case WM_CREATE :
        {
            RECT rect;

            // Set the initial size of the top and
            //    bottom window to be half of
            //    the main window.
            GetClientRect(hWnd, &rect);
            SplitPt.x = rect.right;
            SplitPt.y = rect.bottom/2;

            return 0;
        }

        case WM_SIZE :
        {
            RECT rect;
```

continues

Listing 5.32. continued

```
            GetClientRect(hMainWnd, &rect);

            SplitPt.x = LOWORD(lParam);

            // Move child windows if main window is
               resized
            //    by the user.
            MoveWindow(hTopWnd, 0, 0, SplitPt.x,
                SplitPt.y, TRUE);
            MoveWindow(hBottomWnd, 0,
                SplitPt.y+SPLITSIZE,
                LOWORD(lParam), rect.bottom - SplitPt.y-
                SPLITSIZE, TRUE);
            MoveWindow(hSizerWnd, 0, SplitPt.y,
                SplitPt.x, SPLITSIZE, TRUE);

            return 0;
         }

      case WM_DESTROY :
         {
            PostQuitMessage(0);
            return 0;
         }

   }

   return DefWindowProc (hWnd, message, wParam, lParam);
}


/*********************************************/
LRESULT CALLBACK _export TopWndProc(HWND hWnd, UINT
                                    message,WPARAM
                                    wParam, LPARAM
                                    lParam)
{
   switch (message)
   {
      case WM_PAINT :
         {
            HDC        PaintDC;
            RECT       rect;
            PAINTSTRUCT ps;

            PaintDC = BeginPaint(hWnd, &ps);
            GetClientRect(hWnd, &rect);
```

```
            SetBkMode(PaintDC, TRANSPARENT);
            DrawText(PaintDC, "Top Pane",
                        -1, &rect, DT_SINGLELINE ¦ DT_CENTER
                                    ¦ DT_VCENTER);

            EndPaint(hWnd, &ps);
            return 0;
        }

        case WM_DESTROY :
        {
            PostQuitMessage(0);
            return 0;
        }
    }

    return DefWindowProc (hWnd, message, wParam, lParam);
}

/*******************************************/
LRESULT CALLBACK _export BottomWndProc(HWND hWnd, UINT
                                        message,WPARAM
                                        wParam, LPARAM
                                        lParam)
{
    switch (message)
    {
        case WM_PAINT :
        {
            HDC         PaintDC;
            RECT        rect;
            PAINTSTRUCT ps;

            PaintDC = BeginPaint(hWnd, &ps);
            GetClientRect(hWnd, &rect);

            SetBkMode(PaintDC, TRANSPARENT);
            DrawText(PaintDC, "Bottom Pane",
                        -1, &rect, DT_SINGLELINE ¦ DT_CENTER
                                    ¦ DT_VCENTER);

            EndPaint(hWnd, &ps);
            return 0;
        }

        case WM_DESTROY :
        {
            PostQuitMessage(0);
```

continues

Listing 5.32. SPLIT.C source code.

```
            return 0;
        }
    }

    return DefWindowProc (hWnd, message, wParam, lParam);
}

/**********************************************/
LRESULT CALLBACK _export SizerWndProc(HWND hWnd, UINT
                                      message,WPARAM
                                      wParam, LPARAM
                                      lParam)
{
    static int    Moving;
    static POINT lt, rb;    // left-top and right-bottom
                            //        coordinates

    switch (message)
    {
        case WM_LBUTTONDOWN :
        {
            RECT    SizeRect, rect;

            // Set flag so that program knows user is
            //    resizing Window
            Moving = TRUE;

            // Force all mouse messages to come to this
            //    WindProc
            SetCapture(hSizerWnd);

            // Set current location of size marker
            GetClientRect(hSizerWnd, &SizeRect);
            lt.x = SizeRect.left+2;
            lt.y = SizeRect.top;
            ClientToScreen(hSizerWnd, &lt);
            rb.x = SizeRect.right-2;
            rb.y = SizeRect.top;
            ClientToScreen(hSizerWnd, &rb);
            return 0;
        }

        case WM_MOUSEMOVE :
        {
            if (Moving)
```

```
{
   POINT  pt;
   RECT   rect;
   int    x;
   HDC    hDC;
   HPEN   hPen, hOldPen;

   hDC = CreateDC("DISPLAY", NULL, NULL, NULL);

   hPen = CreatePen(PS_SOLID, SPLITSIZE,
                    RGB(0,0,0));
   hOldPen = SelectPen(hDC, hPen);
   SetROP2(hDC, R2_NOT);

   // Convert Current cursor position to
      screen coordinates
   pt.x = LOWORD(lParam);
   pt.y = HIWORD(lParam);
   ClientToScreen(hSizerWnd, &pt);

   GetWindowRect(hMainWnd, &rect);
   rect.top = rect.top +
            GetSystemMetrics(SM_CYCAPTION)
            + GetSystemMetrics(SM_CYFRAME);
   rect.bottom = rect.bottom -
               GetSystemMetrics(SM_CYFRAME);

   if ( ( rect.bottom-20 > rb.y) &&
         (rect.top+20 < rb.y) )
   {
      MoveTo(hDC, lt.x, lt.y);
      LineTo(hDC, rb.x, rb.y);

      MoveTo(hDC, lt.x, lt.y);
      LineTo(hDC, rb.x, rb.y);
   }

   lt.y = pt.y;
   rb.y = pt.y;

   // Cleanup
   SelectPen(hDC, hOldPen);
   DeletePen(hPen);
   DeleteDC(hDC);
}

return 0;
}
```

continues

Listing 5.32. continued

```
case WM_LBUTTONUP :
{
   RECT  rect;

   Moving = FALSE;

   ReleaseCapture();

   GetWindowRect(hSizerWnd, &rect);
   rect.top = rect.top + GetSystemMetrics(
              SM_CYCAPTION) +
              GetSystemMetrics(SM_CYFRAME);
   rect.bottom = rect.bottom -
              GetSystemMetrics(SM_CYFRAME);

   SplitPt.x = rb.x;
   SplitPt.y = rb.y;
   ScreenToClient(hMainWnd, &SplitPt);

   // Move Windows
   SetWindowPos(hTopWnd, NULL, rect.left,
              rect.top, SplitPt.x, SplitPt.y,
              SWP_SHOWWINDOW | SWP_NOZORDER);
   SetWindowPos(hBottomWnd, NULL, rect.left,
              SplitPt.y+SPLITSIZE, rect.right,
              rect.bottom, SWP_SHOWWINDOW |
              SWP_NOZORDER);
   SetWindowPos(hSizerWnd, NULL, rect.left,
              SplitPt.y, SplitPt.x,
              SplitPt.x+SPLITSIZE,
              SWP_SHOWWINDOW | SWP_NOZORDER);


   GetClientRect(hMainWnd, &rect);

   // Send WM_SIZE to main Window
   if (IsZoomed(hMainWnd))
      SendMessage(hMainWnd, WM_SIZE,
              SIZE_MAXIMIZED,
              MAKELONG(rect.right,
              rect.bottom));
   else
      SendMessage(hMainWnd, WM_SIZE,
              SIZE_RESTORED,
              MAKELONG(rect.right,rect.bottom));
```

```
            ClientToScreen(hMainWnd,&SplitPt);

            return 0;
        }

        case WM_DESTROY :
        {
            PostQuitMessage(0);
            return 0;
        }
    }

    return DefWindowProc (hWnd, message, wParam, lParam);
}
```

Listing 5.33. SPLIT.RC resource script.

```
/*
 * SPLIT.RC resource script
 *
 */

SPLITCURSOR CURSOR "split.cur"
```

Listing 5.34. SPLIT.DEF module definition file.

```
;
; SPLIT.DEF module definition file
;

DESCRIPTION     'Split Window Processing '
NAME            SPLIT
EXETYPE         WINDOWS
STUB            'WINSTUB.EXE'
HEAPSIZE        1024
STACKSIZE       8192
CODE            PRELOAD MOVEABLE DISCARDABLE
DATA            PRELOAD MOVEABLE MULTIPLE
```

V

Rubberband Drawing

How are rubberband drawing techniques implemented in a
Windows application?

DESCRIPTION

Rubberband drawing refers to a technique used in paint programs
to allow the user to draw graphical objects. The user clicks and
drags the mouse inside a window to draw the shape. As the mouse
is dragged across the screen, a rubberband outline of the shape
appears, showing the size and location of the shape. When the user
releases the mouse button, the object is painted on the screen. This
effect is useful for any program that needs to define an area within a
window.

ANSWER

The key to creating rubberbanding effects is to trap the
WM_LBUTTONDOWN, WM_MOUSEMOVE, and WM_LBUTTONUP messages.
The program retrieves the mouse coordinates within the window
from the WM_LBUTTONDOWN message, sets the raster operation to
R2_NOT, and draws the image.

Within the WM_MOUSEMOVE message, the program makes sure that
the user is indeed in the middle of a rubberband operation (by
checking the value of a flag which was previously set by the
WM_LBUTTONDOWN message). The shape is then drawn a second time
using the previous mouse coordinates (thereby negating the drawing
effects because of the R2_NOT raster operation). The shape is then
displayed with the new mouse coordinates.

Finally, in the WM_LBUTTONUP message processing, the program
draws the shape with the same R2_NOT raster operation with the
points retrieved while processing the last WM_MOUSEMOVE message.
It then sets the raster operation to R2_BLACK and draws the final
shape.

Notice that this technique violates one of the laws of windows programming. That is, it does not release a display context between message processing. The display context is created within the WM_LBUTTONDOWN message and not deleted until the WM_LBUTTONUP message. You should not normally do this because of the nature of these messages: they are always called in conjunction with each other. Consequently, only one call to GetDC and ReleaseDC are necessary for each rubberband operation.

COMMENTS

Not only can this rubberband method be used with shapes, such as lines, circles, and rectangles, it can also be used in a resource editor that allows the user to place Windows controls, such as buttons, listboxes, and checkboxes.

SEE ALSO

ReleaseCapture Window API Function
SetCapture Window API Function
SetCursor Window API Function
SetROP2 Window API Function
WM_LBUTTONDOWN Windows Message
WM_LBUTTONUP Windows Message
WM_MOUSEMOVE Windows Message

EXAMPLE CODE

The example program, RUBBER.EXE (see Figure 5.13), lets the user select which shape to draw from a menu. It then allows the user to draw the shape within the window using rubberband drawing techniques.

The program saves all shapes within a linked list; therefore, when the program screen is invalidated, the screen image is correctly updated. Listing 5.35 contains the RUBBER.C source code; Listing 5.36 contains the RUBBER.H header file; Listing 5.37 contains the RUBBER.RC resource script; and Listing 5.38 contains the RUBBER.DEF module definition file.

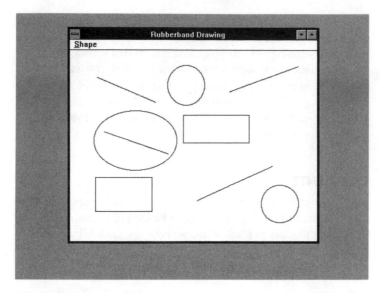

Figure 5.13. *Program demonstrating rubberband drawing techniques.*

Listing 5.35. RUBBER.C source code.

```
// RUBBER.C - Example of rubberband drawing
//               techniques.
//
// Your Borland C++ Consultant by Paul J. Perry
//

#define STRICT

#include <windowsx.h>
#include <stdlib.h>
#include "rubber.h"

// Function Prototypes
LRESULT CALLBACK _export MainWndProc(HWND, UINT,
                                     WPARAM, LPARAM);
void WMCommandHandler(HWND, int, HWND, UINT);
void DrawShape(HDC hDC, int Shape, RECT rect);


// Structure Definition
struct shape
{
```

```
    RECT rect;
    int Shape;
    struct shape *next;
} SHAPE;


// Global Variables
int X1, Y1, X2, Y2, CurrentShape, ButtonDown;
struct shape *first = NULL;
struct shape *current;


/*********************************************/
#pragma argsused
int PASCAL WinMain(HINSTANCE hInstance, HINSTANCE
                   hPrevInstance, LPSTR lpCmdParam,
                   int nCmdShow)
{
    char        ProgName[] = "Rubberband Drawing";
    HWND        hWnd;
    MSG         msg;


    if (!hPrevInstance)
    {
        WNDCLASS    wndclass;

        wndclass.lpszClassName = ProgName;
        wndclass.lpfnWndProc   = (WNDPROC) MainWndProc;
        wndclass.cbClsExtra    = 0;
        wndclass.cbWndExtra    = 0;
        wndclass.hInstance     = hInstance;
        wndclass.hIcon         = LoadIcon(NULL,
                                   IDI_APPLICATION);
        wndclass.hCursor       = LoadCursor(NULL,
                                   IDC_ARROW);
        wndclass.hbrBackground = GetStockBrush
                                   (WHITE_BRUSH);
        wndclass.lpszMenuName  = "MAINMENU";
        wndclass.style         = CS_VREDRAW | CS_HREDRAW;

        if (!RegisterClass(&wndclass))
            exit(1);
    }

    hWnd = CreateWindow(ProgName, ProgName,
                        WS_OVERLAPPEDWINDOW,
                        CW_USEDEFAULT, CW_USEDEFAULT,
```

continues

Listing 5.35. continued

```
                        CW_USEDEFAULT, CW_USEDEFAULT,
                        NULL, NULL, hInstance, NULL);

    ShowWindow(hWnd, nCmdShow);
    UpdateWindow(hWnd);

    while (GetMessage(&msg, NULL, 0, 0))
    {
        TranslateMessage(&msg);
        DispatchMessage(&msg);
    }
    return msg.wParam;
}


/***********************************************/
#pragma argsused
void WMCommandHandler(HWND hWnd, int id, HWND hWndCtl,
                      UINT codeNotify)
{
    HMENU hMenu;

    hMenu = GetMenu(hWnd);
    CheckMenuItem(hMenu, CurrentShape, MF_UNCHECKED);

    switch (id)
    {
        case IDM_LINE :
        {
            CurrentShape = IDM_LINE;
            CheckMenuItem(hMenu, IDM_LINE, MF_CHECKED);
            break;
        }

        case IDM_CIRCLE :
        {
            CurrentShape = IDM_CIRCLE;
            CheckMenuItem(hMenu, IDM_CIRCLE, MF_CHECKED);
            break;
        }

        case IDM_RECTANGLE :
        {
            CurrentShape = IDM_RECTANGLE;
            CheckMenuItem(hMenu, IDM_RECTANGLE, MF_CHECKED);
            break;
        }
```

```
         case IDM_EXIT :
         {
            SendMessage(hWnd, WM_CLOSE, 0, 0L);
            break;
         }

      }
   }

/**********************************************/
void DrawShape(HDC hDC, int Shape, RECT rect)
{
   if (Shape == IDM_LINE)
   {
      MoveTo(hDC, rect.left, rect.top);
      LineTo(hDC, rect.right, rect.bottom);
   }
   else if(Shape == IDM_CIRCLE)
      Ellipse(hDC, rect.left, rect.top, rect.right,
              rect.bottom);
   else
      Rectangle(hDC, rect.left, rect.top, rect.right,
                rect.bottom);
}


/**********************************************/
LRESULT CALLBACK _export MainWndProc(HWND hWnd, UINT
                                     message, WPARAM
                                     wParam, LPARAM
                                     lParam)
{
   static HDC hDC;

   switch (message)
   {
      case WM_CREATE :
      {
         HMENU hMenu;

         CurrentShape = IDM_LINE;

         hMenu = GetMenu(hWnd);
         CheckMenuItem(hMenu, IDM_LINE, MF_CHECKED);
         return 0;
      }

      case WM_PAINT :
```

continues

Listing 5.35. continued

```
{
    HDC         PaintDC;
    RECT        rect;
    PAINTSTRUCT ps;

    PaintDC = BeginPaint(hWnd, &ps);
    GetClientRect(hWnd, &rect);

    SelectBrush(hDC, GetStockObject
                (HOLLOW_BRUSH));

    current = first;

    // Walk through the linked list.
    while (current != NULL)
    {
        DrawShape(PaintDC, current->Shape,
                current->rect);
        current = current->next;
    }

    EndPaint(hWnd, &ps);
    return 0;
}

case WM_LBUTTONDOWN :
{
    RECT rect;

    hDC = GetDC(hWnd);
    SelectBrush(hDC, GetStockObject(
                HOLLOW_BRUSH));
    SetROP2(hDC, R2_NOT);

    X1 = LOWORD(lParam);
    Y1 = HIWORD(lParam);

    X2 = X1;
    Y2 = Y1;

    SetRect(&rect, X1, Y1, X2, Y2);
    DrawShape(hDC, CurrentShape, rect);

    ButtonDown = TRUE;
    SetCursor(LoadCursor(NULL, IDC_CROSS));
    SetCapture(hWnd);
```

```
      return 0;
   }

   case WM_MOUSEMOVE :
   {
      if (ButtonDown)
      {
         RECT rect;

         SetRect(&rect, X1, Y1, X2, Y2);
         DrawShape(hDC, CurrentShape, rect);

         X2 = LOWORD(lParam);
         Y2 = HIWORD(lParam);

         SetRect(&rect, X1, Y1, X2, Y2);
         DrawShape(hDC, CurrentShape, rect);
      }

      return 0;
   }

   case WM_LBUTTONUP :
   {
      struct shape *temp;
      RECT rect;

      SetRect(&rect, X1, Y1, X2, Y2);
      DrawShape(hDC, CurrentShape, rect);
      ButtonDown = FALSE;

      SetROP2(hDC, R2_BLACK);
      DrawShape(hDC, CurrentShape, rect);

      SetCursor(LoadCursor(NULL, IDC_ARROW));

      ReleaseDC(hWnd, hDC);
      ReleaseCapture();

      // Add item to linked list
      temp = first;
      first = (struct shape*)
              malloc(sizeof(SHAPE));
      first->rect.left   = X1;
      first->rect.top    = Y1;
      first->rect.right  = X2;
      first->rect.bottom = Y2;
      first->Shape = CurrentShape;
      first->next = temp;
```

continues

Listing 5.35. continued

```
            return 0;
        }

        case WM_COMMAND :
        {
            return HANDLE_WM_COMMAND(hWnd, wParam,
                                     lParam,
                                     WMCommandHandler);
        }

        case WM_DESTROY :
        {
            struct shape *temp;

            // Release memory which was
            //    used for the linked list.
            current = first;
            while (current != NULL)
            {
                temp = current->next;
                free(current);
                current = temp;
            }

            PostQuitMessage(0);
            return 0;
        }

    }

    return DefWindowProc (hWnd, message, wParam, lParam);
}
```

Listing 5.36. RUBBER.H header file.

```
/*
 * RUBBER.H header file
 *
 */

#define IDM_LINE      100
#define IDM_RECTANGLE 110
#define IDM_CIRCLE    120
#define IDM_EXIT      130
```

Listing 5.37. RUBBER.RC resource script.

```
/*
 * RUBBER.RC resource script
 *
 */

#include "rubber.h"

MAINMENU MENU
BEGIN
     POPUP "&Shape"
     BEGIN
          MENUITEM "&Line", IDM_LINE
          MENUITEM "&Rectangle", IDM_RECTANGLE
          MENUITEM "&Circle", IDM_CIRCLE
          MENUITEM SEPARATOR
          MENUITEM "E&xit", IDM_EXIT
     END

END
```

Listing 5.38. RUBBER.DEF module definition file.

```
;
; RUBBER.DEF module definition file
;

DESCRIPTION     'Demo of rubberband drawing '
NAME            RUBBER
EXETYPE         WINDOWS
STUB            'WINSTUB.EXE'
HEAPSIZE        1024
STACKSIZE       8192
CODE            PRELOAD MOVEABLE DISCARDABLE
DATA            PRELOAD MOVEABLE MULTIPLE
```

V

In This Chapter

This chapter is different from the other chapters in this book. It is intended as a reference to additional resources for the serious Windows programmer. This book alone can not provide all the answers to your Windows programming questions. The subject of programming for Windows is much more complex than what can be covered in any single book. This is evidenced by the great quantity of information currently available to the programmer. Some of it is good, some is not.

Invariably, I am asked the question, "Can you recommend a good book?" or "What is a good technical journal you could recommend?" By taking a look through this chapter, you will be able to answer these questions yourself. I want to point you to the most valuable information possible.

Even More Help

This chapter is short and to the point. The following topics are covered:

- Third party programming libraries that will help you with your productivity by providing extended functions, custom controls, and dialog boxes.

- A look at a Windows editor that can make creating your programs easier.

- A fabulous tool for creating Windows Help files.

- Additional books you may find valuable.

- Technical journals and magazines that will bring new answers to questions on a regular basis.

By the way, I am not associated with any of the manufacturers or products mentioned in this chapter. The comments and recommendations found in this chapter are my own and obviously don't necessarily reflect the feelings of all programmers. If you are interested in any of the products mentioned here, you should contact the company and request more information before doing anything else.

Programming Libraries

Programming libraries are not new to Windows. They have been available as long as compilers have been around. Programming libraries provide extra functions for specialized situations. For example, you might find database libraries or graphics libraries that provide high-level functions that cover a specific area of programming.

Because Windows provides the facility of dynamic linking through DLLs, programming libraries have taken on a new meaning. By being packaged as a dynamic link library, your program can take advantage of the functions in the library by merely using an import library and header file. Because the DLL is a separate file, it only increases the size of your executable by a small fraction.

The two programming libraries mentioned here are ones I have used and have found to be very good.

Control Palette

Blaise Computing, Inc.
819 Bancroft Way
Berkeley, CA 94710
510/540-5441
FAX: 510/540-1938

Cost: About $170

Control Palette is a collection of custom controls, Windows elements like status lines and ToolBars, and a new dialog class for building unique user interfaces. All the functions are packaged inside a dynamic link library, so using them is easy. Furthermore (and something that is unique for programming libraries), the full commented source code is included.

Some of the custom controls include new radio buttons and checkboxes that combine color with a selected state. Default bitmaps are included to create fancy pushbuttons with large colored fonts. You can give your application a new look by using this library.

Control Palette/NC

Blaise Computing, Inc.
819 Bancroft Way
Berkeley, CA 94710
510/540-5441
FAX: 510/540-1938

Cost: About $170

The NC in this product stands for nonclient, and this version of Control Palette works either in conjunction with the regular Control Palette or separately. It allows you to customize the nonclient area of a window. This includes borders, title bars, system menu boxes, and minimize and maximize buttons. Anyone who has looked at the default window procedure knows this is just a matter of responding to the WM_NCPAINT message. Although it sounds easy, it takes a lot of work. The code provided with this library makes it very easy to add a new visual appeal to your application.

Again, the capabilities of this package are in a dynamic link library, and full source code is included. I highly recommend this package to any programmer who wants to put a unique interface on an application that runs in an otherwise generic environment.

A Window Editor

An editor is to a programmer what a hammer is to a carpenter. It is one of your tools of the trade. Every programmer has a tried and trusted editor. Some prefer Brief. Others prefer Quick Edit. Yet others love the Integrated Development Environment that comes with the compiler.

With the advent of Windows, new Windows-based editors were bound to become available. Well, your dreams have been answered!

Codewright

Premia Software
1075 MW Murray Blvd., Suite 268
Portland, OR 97229
503/641-6000
FAX: 503/641-6001

Cost: About $250

Codewright is advertised as one of the fastest editors on the market. Although I haven't done any tests, I think this is true. The speed at which this editor scrolls text is amazing. It is much faster than anything I have used in Windows, and might even equal the speed of a text-based editor.

It provides several command sets, including CUA, Brief, and VI. If that is not enough, it is fully customizable. You customize it by writing your own DLLs that can call any of the 400 functions in the Codewrite API. Best of all, instead of having to write macros in some unique macro-language, you can write them in C. Although I personally don't use this editor, many programmers have reported that they really like this product.

Easy Help Files

If you work as a consultant or work at a small shop, you will probably end up creating your own Help (.HLP) files at one point or another. It seems that creating Help files is always the most rushed part of a project. The reason being that the product is already finished (or in beta testing) and the online help must be added as soon as possible.

Well, creating HLP files for the Windows Help engine is not the easiest task. Especially if you are in a rush. By using add-in tools, you can make the task of creating Help files much easier.

RoboHelp

Blue Sky Software Corporation
7486 La Jolla Blvd., Suite 3
La Jolla, CA 92037
800/677-4946 or 619/459-6365
FAX: 619/459-6366

Cost: About $450

RoboHelp is a Windows Help authoring tool that makes creating Help files easy. It integrates itself into Microsoft Word for Windows. The product is actually a series of Word for Windows templates, macros, and add-in DLLs that guide the user through the steps of creating Help files.

In fact, this tool makes creating Help files so easy, it is not necessary to be a programmer to create Help files. RoboHelp generates the necessary Windows Help file source code, takes care of running the Help compiler, and allows you to test the Help system by running WinHelp with your newly created Help file.

Books

The following is a partial list of other books you may be interested in obtaining for additional information about programming Windows. Although this is not any type of endorsement for these books, these are ones I have found helpful.

Programming Windows 3.1, by Charles Petzold. Microsoft Press.

This was the first book written about programming for Windows. It is considered by many to be the "bible" of Windows programming. Although it does not cover the ObjectWindows library or specifically the Borland tools, all Windows programmers should have this book.

Undocumented Windows, by Andrew Schulman, David Maxey, and Matt Pietrek. Addison-Wesley Publishing Company.

This informative book discusses the Windows functions that Microsoft uses but does not make available to other developers.

VI

It includes a disk containing tools for finding these undocumented functions. Although all the information is not the most useful, it is an invaluable book for getting an idea about how Windows works internally.

Windows 3.1: A Developer's Guide, by Jeffrey M. Richter. M&T Books.

A great book to have when you want to learn about some of the more advanced elements of programming for Windows. Topics include installation programs, setting up printers, special dialog box techniques, and many other goodies. It even shows how to create drag-and-drop programs where your program can be the one from which a file is dragged. As you create more advanced programs, you will probably want to read this book.

The Waite Group's Windows API Bible, by James L. Conger. Waite Group Press.

Includes 30 chapters (and over 1,000 pages) that describe every Windows 3.0 API function available. Although the book does not cover Windows 3.1-specific information, this is a good book to have. I may be biased toward this book (because I did a technical edit for it), but what I like the most about this book is that for every API function, the author provides a short code example demonstrating exactly how the function is used.

Windows Programmer's Guide to OLE/DDE, by Jeffrey Clark. SAMS Publishing.

A great book that focuses entirely on dynamic data exchange using message-based DDE and the dynamic data exchange management library (DDEML), as well as object linking and embedding (OLE). Although somewhat technical, this is a good book to have if you are working with any type of inter-application communication. The first half of the book covers DDE and DDEML. The second half covers OLE. Although the book does not use Borland language tools, most of the examples can be recompiled with only minor modifications, and the Windows API function calls will all be the same.

Windows Programmer's Guide to ObjectWindows Library, by Namir Shammas. SAMS Publishing.

If you want to program exclusively with the ObjectWindows Library, this is the book you will want to read. It covers the ObjectWindows library extensively. You learn about the classes that come with OWL and how to use them. Many example programs are included with this book.

Windows Programmer's Guide to Serial Communications, by Timothy S. Monk. SAMS Publishing.

If you need to write a program that uses the serial port, you won't want to miss this book. It has extensive coverage of the Windows API functions for accessing the serial port. It then goes into a discussion of creating a dynamic link library that makes accessing the serial ports easier. Finally, it adds functions to allow XMODEM file transfer. A full reference to the serial communications functions is included.

Windows API Guides, Volumes 1-4, by Microsoft Press.

These four books document every function, message, and file format that Microsoft makes available to developers. Although these books are rather expensive, they contain valuable information and are required material for the serious Windows developer. As a note, most of the information in these books is the same information available in the online Help system of Borland C++.

Magazines

Trade journals provide some of the most up-to-date information available for programmers. A subscription to any one (or all) of these publications will ensure a constant source of new information about the industry. If you are interested in subscribing to any of these publications, I recommend going to a good technical bookstore and buying an issue. From that, you can get information on subscribing.

Microsoft Systems Journal
P.O. Box 5662
Boulder, CO 80322-6622

Cost: About $35 for 12 issues (1 year)

Although the name suggests that this is a Microsoft Publication, it is not. *MSJ* is a monthly magazine that usually provides three main articles that go into depth about a specific topic. Advertising is kept to a minimum, and there are regular columns on Windows, DOS, and C++ programming.

> *PC Magazine*
> P.O. Box 51524
> Boulder, CO 80321-1524
>
> Cost: About $30 for 22 issues (1 year)

Although *PC Magazine* is more of a user's magazine (versus a programmer's magazine), there are several good columns on Windows programming by industry experts. It is also a good magazine to use to keep an eye out for new product announcements and new developments in technology.

> *PC Techniques*
> 7721 E. Gray Road Ste. 204
> Scottsdale, AZ 85260-9747
>
> Cost: About $22 for 6 issues (1 year)

PC Techniques is the proverbial hacker's magazine. It contains all kinds of good information for programmers, and it covers everything from assembly language to Visual BASIC. Although it is not Windows specific, lately the number of Windows articles versus DOS articles has definitely increased. What I especially like about this magazine is that when you read it, the editors sound as if they are talking to you, rather than at you. It is almost like having a friend at your side coaching you with your programming projects.

> *Windows/DOS Developers Journal*
> 1601 W. 23rd St., Suite 200
> Lawrence, KS 66046-9950
>
> Cost: About $30 for 12 issues (1 year)

Another magazine that is moving more toward Windows programming instead of DOS programming, *WDDJ*, is an excellent source of information for more complex Windows programming topics.

A recent issue had articles on creating a listbox that could hold more than 64K of data, accessing custom control dialog box interfaces, and subclassing with C++. A regular Windows question-and-answer column is in itself well worth the cost of the magazine.

> *Windows Tech Journal*
> P.O. Box 70087
> Eugene, OR 97401-9943

> Cost: About $30 for 12 issues (1 year)

Although this magazine calls itself a technical journal, it is probably the least technical of the ones presented. Articles usually have cutesy titles (such as "Grinding Out C++ Code" or "The Wide World Of Databases"); however, this magazine does present some good information for the Windows programmer. On the positive side, *Windows Tech Journal* only covers Windows programming and does not touch on DOS programming (unless necessary to describe something about Windows).

Another Resource

> *Microsoft Developer Network*
> P. O. Box 51812
> Boulder, CO 80322-1812
> 800/759-5474

> Cost: About $200 for a year subscription

If you don't have a CD-ROM drive yet, this product may make it time to get one. The Microsoft Developer Network (besides giving discounts on Microsoft Press books and providing a bimonthly newsletter) includes a CD-ROM that is issued quarterly. It contains many megabytes of information you can search for information on that most pressing problem.

The CD-ROM contains over 15 volumes of information including the full text of the Windows API guides, Petzold's Programming Windows, special knowledgebase articles, and much, much more. It also contains the text of back issues of *Microsoft Systems Journal* (*MSJ*).

VI

Although none of the Borland programming tools are mentioned specifically, most of the information can be applied to programming with Borland C++. This product is one of the greatest single sources of information for programming Windows you will find today.

Epilogue

I sincerely hope this book has helped improve your Windows programming experience. Although I cannot provide technical support, if you have any comments or suggestions for this book, feel free to leave me a comment. My personal CompuServe ID is 71530, 3701. I look forward to hearing from you.

I N D E X

M